# Secured Transactions

Carolina Academic Press

*Context and Practice Series*

Michael Hunter Schwartz
*Series Editor*

**Administrative Law**
Richard Henry Seamon

**Advanced Torts**
Alex B. Long and Meredith J. Duncan

**Civil Procedure for All States**
Benjamin V. Madison, III

**Constitutional Law**
David Schwartz and Lori Ringhand

**A Context and Practice Global Case File:**
**An Intersex Athlete's Constitutional Challenge,**
**Hastings v. USATF, IAAF, and IOC**
Olivia M. Farrar

**Contracts**
Michael Hunter Schwartz and Denise Riebe

**Current Issues in Constitutional Litigation**
Sarah E. Ricks, with contributions by Evelyn M. Tenenbaum

**Employment Discrimination**
Second Edition
Susan Grover, Sandra F. Sperino, and Jarod S. Gonzalez

**Energy Law**
Joshua P. Fershee

**Evidence**
Pavel Wonsowicz

**International Business Transactions**
Amy Deen Westbrook

**International Women's Rights, Equality, and Justice**
Christine M. Venter

**The Lawyer's Practice**
Kris Franklin

**Professional Responsibility**
Barbara Glesner Fines

**Sales**
Edith R. Warkentine

**Secured Transactions**
Edith R. Warkentine and Jerome A. Grossman

**Torts**
Paula J. Manning

**Workers' Compensation Law**
Michael C. Duff

**Your Brain and Law School**
Marybeth Herald

# Secured Transactions

## A Context and Practice Casebook

**Edith R. Warkentine**
WESTERN STATE COLLEGE OF LAW

**Jerome A. Grossman**
GRESHAM SAVAGE NOLAN & TILDEN

Carolina Academic Press
Durham, North Carolina

ISBN 978-1-61163-488-4
LCCN 2014951782

Carolina Academic Press
700 Kent Street
Durham, NC 27701
Telephone (919) 489-7486
Fax (919) 493-5668
www.cap-press.com

Printed in the United States of America
2020 Printing

To my husband, Erich, and our two wonderful children, Evan and Ellen. Your love and support make it all worthwhile! — E.R.W.

I would not be in a position to have participated in this project at all had my wife of 41 years, Mary O'Brien Grossman, when I first approached her back in 1977 with the proposal that I go to law school, put the kibosh on the idea. Instead, she allowed me to quit my job, sell our house, and move the family to Berkeley. Since then, in all ways, she has encouraged me to do the work that I enjoy. I cannot thank Mary enough. — J.A.G.

# Contents

# Table of Principal Cases

# Series Editor's Preface

Welcome to a new type of casebook. Designed by leading experts in law school teaching and learning, Context and Practice casebooks assist law professors and their students to work together to learn, minimize stress, and prepare for the rigors and joys of practicing law. **Student learning and preparation for law practice are the guiding ethics of these books**.

Why would we depart from the tried and true? Why have we abandoned the legal education model by which we were trained? Because legal education can and must improve.

In Spring 2007, the Carnegie Foundation published *Educating Lawyers: Preparation for the Practice of Law* and the Clinical Legal Education Association published *Best Practices for Legal Education*. Both works reflect in-depth efforts to assess the effectiveness of modern legal education, and both conclude that legal education, as presently practiced, falls quite short of what it can and should be. Both works criticize law professors' rigid adherence to a single teaching technique, the inadequacies of law school assessment mechanisms, and the dearth of law school instruction aimed at teaching law practice skills and inculcating professional values. Finally, the authors of both books express concern that legal education may be harming law students. Recent studies show that law students, in comparison to all other graduate students, have the highest levels of depression, anxiety and substance abuse.

**The problems with traditional law school instruction begin with the textbooks law teachers use.** Law professors cannot implement *Educating Lawyers* and *Best Practices* using texts designed for the traditional model of legal education. Moreover, even though our understanding of how people learn has grown exponentially in the past 100 years, no law school text to date even purports to have been designed with educational research in mind.

The Context and Practice Series is an effort to offer a genuine alternative. Grounded in learning theory and instructional design and written with *Educating Lawyers* and *Best Practices* in mind, Context and Practice casebooks make it easy for law professors to change.

I welcome reactions, criticisms, and suggestions; my e-mail address is mhschwartz@ualr.edu. Knowing the author(s) of these books, I know they, too, would appreciate your input; we share a common commitment to student learning. In fact, students, if your professor cares enough about your learning to have adopted this book, I bet s/he would welcome your input, too!

Michael Hunter Schwartz, Series Designer and Editor
Consultant, Institute for Law Teaching and Learning
Dean and Professor of Law, William H. Bowen School of Law,
University of Arkansas at Little Rock

# Preface

This student-centered book draws on a wide variety of teaching materials that Professor Warkentine developed over a twenty-plus-year teaching career plus "real world" problems drawn from Mr. Grossman's thirty years of experience as an expert secured transactions practitioner. Professor Warkentine is indebted to generations of law students who challenged her to find effective ways to introduce difficult and often obtuse material. Our three primary objectives are:

- To help law students further develop analytical skills, with a particular emphasis on statutory interpretation;
- To provide students with an opportunity to master the substantive law of Article 9 of the Uniform Commercial Code; and
- To expose students to how the doctrine learned in this class translates into an exciting and intellectually challenging legal career.

## Book Organization and Coverage

This book begins with a quick overview of the entire UCC. Because statutory analysis is at the core of the course, the book then discusses how to read and apply a statute. Following is an overview of UCC Article 9 and the law of secured transactions in general, including the role of attorneys in secured transactions. Doctrine is then introduced in the order that students should follow when analyzing a secured transactions problem. After all of the doctrinal material has been covered, the final book chapter presents a series of problems that will help students to review and "put it all together."

After the three introductory chapters, each chapter follows the same organizational approach. Beginning in Chapter 4, each chapter begins with an Article 9 Graphic Organizer, depicting the overall coverage of Article 9. The organizer is highlighted to identify the subject studied in that chapter, and to help you remember where that subject fits in the "big picture." Following the Graphic Organizer is a Chapter Problem, which helps put the chapter material into context. Next is a list of the code sections to be studied in that chapter. Each chapter includes descriptive text, one or two cases or excerpts from cases, and several smaller exercises that draw on the material studied in that chapter and require students to select and apply the applicable code sections to solve the problems. At the end of the chapter is a list of additional resources, including ALR annotations, law review articles, and cases. None of these additional resources are required reading. These are sources for those students who always come up after class and request some additional reading. If you are not one of those students, you can easily be successful in this course without ever consulting any of the cited material.

Professor Douglas Whaley, a renowned professor and himself the author of seven textbooks on contracts and commercial law, suggested that when writing a textbook, the author follow this basic guideline: "Give the students enough understanding that they know the basics and can avoid malpractice by looking up the subtleties when they arise later in life. If you teach too many details, the students end up overloaded and top heavy so that the basics elude them."[1] We have followed that guideline in this book; as a result, not every section of Article 9 is discussed, nor is there an exercise or problem illustrating every legal issue raised in Article 9. However, the book teaches you all of the tools you will need successfully to attack an Article 9 problem.

# Appendices

Because one of our goals is to introduce students to the practical aspects of a secured transactions practice, we have included in the Appendices a variety of forms that might be used in a typical secured transaction. These forms are not intended to be used as models, and are certainly not "forms" to be followed; rather, they are presented for their educational value; they provide a starting point for discussion and illustrate specific problems confronting the practicing lawyer.

# How to Use This Book

This book is deceptively short. The "star" of the book is the text of the Uniform Commercial Code, and its Official Comments. You must purchase and use a complete version of the text of the Code and the Comments. You will need to spend a significant amount of time reading the statute and the Official Comments. For emphasis, we have included excerpts of text and comments in the book.

This book does include cases, but only a limited number of them, and the cases that we include have not been heavily edited. We have, however, omitted many footnotes. When footnotes are included we have placed them in brackets [ ] within the text. The purpose of including cases in this format is to prepare you to read cases as lawyers read cases—unedited—and to prepare you to use the cases as lawyers use cases—to solve problems.

To get the most out of this book, read the Chapter Problem as you begin each new chapter. You will not be prepared to analyze the problem fully until you have completed the entire chapter, but reviewing the Chapter Problem initially will help to provide context for the material you will be studying. Next, read each of the code sections indicated for that chapter, along with the Official Comments. Read difficult code sections aloud. Deconstruct each section. Do not skip this step! Students who are successful in Code courses all emphasize that they spent a lot of time reading the statute and the Official Comments. In addition, be sure that you have your Code open and that you refer to it frequently as you read the text that explains each code section.

After you have completed the assigned reading, including the Code, you are ready to read and prepare your answers to the chapter exercises. We purposely do not indicate what code sections you will have to consult to work through the exercises—learning how to find the appropriate code section is an essential part of what this course is about. In

---

1. Douglas J. Whaley, *Commentary: Teaching Law: Thoughts on Retirement*, 68 Ohio St. L. J. 1387, 1400 (2007).

class, be prepared to discuss how you selected the applicable code sections and how you applied them to reach a conclusion. Work on the shorter exercises first. When you think you have mastered the material in the chapter, return to the Chapter Problem and try to write out a complete analysis.

This book uses visual aids extensively to help students picture how the individual code sections fit together to reach a conclusion. Students who do not customarily use visual aids such as those contained in this book find them to be extremely helpful. Many students who customarily prepare their own flowcharts continue to prepare their own material, but they tell us that they nevertheless use the figures in the book to help them refine their own work. **All students should always keep in mind that the original sources, the statute and the Official Comments, are the primary authority on which they should rely for analysis.** Everything else can be used, if helpful, but never to the exclusion of the statute itself.

*Edith R. Warkentine*
*Jerome A. Grossman*

July, 2014

# Acknowledgments

This student-centered book is my second in the Carolina Academic Press Context and Practice series. Students who took my Secured Transactions class after taking my Sales class (where I used my CAP Sales book) urged me to write my own book. I was reluctant to do so, because Article 9 and Secured Transactions practice have changed significantly since I was last in practice. However, Jerry Grossman, a distinguished practitioner whom I met in the context of work for the California State Bar, was kind enough to agree to be my co-author for this book. I think it is particularly appropriate for a practitioner to co-author a text for the Context and Practice series. As a result of our collaboration, we have created a text that is truly unique among other available texts. The perspective of most of the questions is that of a transactional lawyer preparing for client meetings, interviews and negotiations. So I must first thank Jerry for agreeing to do this with me and for his terrific contributions.

Next, I thank the "early readers" of the text: my husband, Erich, and my colleague, Professor Elizabeth N. Jones, the director of our school's Criminal Law Practice Center and herself an expert in criminal law and procedure. When I wrote the Sales book I learned that willing readers without a legal background or without a legal background in the substantive area in which I write, can make important contributions to the readability of the text. If they can understand the text, it will be accessible to our students as well. I think law professors sometimes assume that law students have background that we would not assume a lay person has. Accordingly, by having a lay person and a non-expert read the book, we were forced to explain context in a user-friendly way. My husband, who has served as my "reasonable man" since I went to law school, has always scrutinized my work to be sure it was accessible to students, and his contribution this time was invaluable. Professor Jones, who has more than enough on her plate, and could easily have refused to help due to time constraints, nevertheless was generous with her time; she read critically and gave excellent input on a timely basis. I can't thank her enough!

As I learned in the past, it "takes a village" for me to write a book! I want to thank my secured transactions students, Western State College of Law Class of 2013, who urged me to write this book, and particularly the five students who served as my research assistants in the early stages: Kyle Adamson, Joseph Chaparo, Steven Giammichele, Amanda Huff, Alex Nguyen, and Michael Valentine. I also want to thank all of the students in my Spring 2014 Secured Transactions class, who were the "beta site" for this book.

I am again indebted to Professor Sidney DeLong, Seattle University School of Law, who graciously shared with me the materials he created and uses in his own classes. I have always thought his discussion of how to analyze a statute is one of the best I've seen, and he has been kind enough to permit me to adapt and use that discussion in Chapter 2 of this book.

Finally, words cannot express my appreciation of Jacqueline Alvarino, who went above and beyond, doing meticulous work in typing and editing the manuscript. Her thoughtfulness and attention to detail while maintaining a wonderful attitude were remarkable. This book simply would not have happened without her.

*Edith R. Warkentine*, July, 2014

———————

My major professional thanks, of course, must go to Professor Edith Warkentine, who invited me to participate in this project, who wrote the initial draft of every chapter and cheerfully accepted my kibitzing, who taught the course and took that opportunity to vet the material, and who ensured that we timely produced a completed manuscript. I also echo her thanks to everyone who assisted with the production of this text.

I acknowledge, too, the many mentors who shaped my career, making it possible for me to enter the field of secured transactions, for which I have been temperamentally well-suited: Professor Peter Winship, the visiting professor from Southern Methodist University who first introduced me to the UCC; Paul J. Mundie, my initial partner assignment and mentor at Heller Ehrman, who encouraged me to remain in the Corporate Department and fostered my interest in commercial finance; David A. Rosinus, with whom I worked closely for almost the entire 14 years that I was with Heller Ehrman, who actively supported my desire to focus my practice on commercial finance and whose rigorous approach to legal analysis demanded that I "show my work"—to map out the analytical steps that I took to move from statement of an issue to resolution (one of the pedagogical tools espoused by this text); Steven O. Weise (a name familiar to everyone whose practice involves secured transactions), with whom I had the good fortune to cross paths, not only as a colleague at Heller Ehrman, but also as a participant in various bar projects, and who has allowed me to importune him whenever I've had a question I wanted to bounce off someone who has seen it all; Michael T. Andrew, former partner and counsel at Luce Forward Hamilton & Scripps (now merged into McKenna Long & Aldridge), another proponent of rigorous analysis and willing consultant; Harry C. Sigman, permanent member of the State Bar Business Law Section's Commercial Transactions (nee "UCC") Committee (among many other things), who has periodically reached out to keep me involved in matters affecting the UCC, as enacted in California.

*Jerome A. Grossman,* July, 2014

# Secured Transactions

# Chapter 1

# The Uniform Commercial Code ("UCC")

## 1. Uniform Commercial Code Overview

The focus of this course is UCC Article 9. However, before we start on Article 9, you must first be introduced to the entire UCC.[1] Most law students taking this course will be somewhat familiar with the UCC because they studied portions of Article 2 in their Contracts classes. Therefore, this chapter presents only a quick overview of the UCC. It next emphasizes important parts of Article 1, which you will need to learn and use, and then introduces Article 9.

*Figure 1-1* on the next page gives you a quick glimpse at the basic coverage of the UCC. What else do you need to know? Does the title accurately describe the statute? Critics suggest that it does not: no state has adopted the UCC verbatim, and there are conflicting judicial interpretations of certain code provisions. Hence, it is not truly "uniform." Moreover, the UCC does not apply solely to "commercial" transactions. A common student misconception is that the UCC applies only to transactions involving "merchants,"[2] but, except for specific provisions of the UCC, it applies equally to transactions when one or both of the parties are not merchants. Hence, it is not truly "commercial." Indeed, it is not really a "code" in the civil law sense of the meaning of the term.[3] However, it is one of the most successful of the uniform laws to be promulgated by its sponsors, the Uniform Law Commission (ULC)[4], and the American Law Institute

---

1. Unless otherwise stated in this book, all references to sections are to UCC sections. The UCC is sometimes referred to as "the Code." Specific code sections are either referenced by number alone, by "section number," or by "UCC number."

2. Throughout this book, you will find words in quotation marks when significant terms are introduced for the first time. These words and phrases will become important additions to your legal vocabulary.

3. Grant Gilmore, one of its drafters, stated: "The Uniform Commercial Code, so-called, is not that sort of Code—even in theory.... We shall do better to think of it as a big statute—or a collection of statutes bound together in the same book—which goes as far as it goes but no further. It assumes the continuing existence of a large body of pre-Code and non-Code law on which it rests for support, which it displaces to the least possible extent, and without which it could not survive." Grant Gilmore, *Article 9: What it does for the past*, 26 LA.L. REV. 285, 285-86 (1966).

4. The ULC was formerly known as the National Conference of Commissioners on Uniform State Laws. Its website states: "[It] has worked for the uniformity of state laws since 1892. It is a non-profit unincorporated association, comprised of state commissions on uniform laws from each state, the District of Columbia, the Commonwealth of Puerto Rico, and the U.S. Virgin Islands. Each jurisdiction determines the method of appointment and the number of commissioners actually appointed. Most jurisdictions provide for their commission by statute." http://www.uniformlaws.org/Narrative.aspx?title=About%20the%20ULC (last visited June 29, 2014).

## Figure 1-1: Uniform Commercial Code Overview

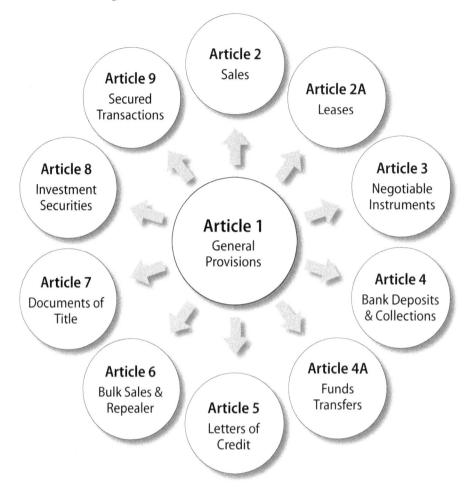

(ALI).[5] The UCC has been enacted into law, with some variation, in every state in the United States, in the District of Columbia, and in many United States territories.

As *Figure 1-1* illustrates, the UCC addresses almost every aspect of a typical commercial transaction. UCC Article 1 is applicable to all of the other UCC articles. It contains basic definitions and some of the most important concepts students need to learn and use whenever they solve a UCC problem. Article 2, Sales, contains the rules applicable to contract formation, performance, breach, and remedies when a transaction involves the sale of goods. Article 2A provides similar rules to govern leases of goods. Articles 3, 4, 4A and 5 concern methods of payment. Article 6 governs bulk sales,[6] and Article 7 deals with the shipment and storage of goods. Article 8 governs certain transactions involving

---

5. According to its website, the American Law Institute is "the leading independent organization in the United States producing scholarly work to clarify, modernize, and otherwise improve the law." http://www.ali.org/index.cfm?fuseaction=about.overview (last visited June 29, 2014).

6. Bulk sales are defined in §6-102(c). The UCC sponsors recommend the repeal of this Article, and a majority of states have followed that recommendation.

investment securities, and Article 9 addresses personal property secured financing.[7] Articles 10 and 11 contain transition provisions, which determine what version of the UCC applies to a transaction, based on the date of the transaction and the effective dates of different versions of the Code. A "typical" commercial transaction may involve legal concepts drawn from all or most of the articles of the UCC, or from just two or three of them. For example, a sale of goods implicates Article 1 and Article 2. Since goods must be paid for, any of Articles 3, 4, 5 or 9 may be involved as well, depending on the type of payment called for in the transaction. On the other hand, a straightforward secured loan transaction might involve only Articles 1 and 9.

Because the UCC is a statute, students should always begin their analysis of a legal problem by reviewing the applicable part(s) of the statute. Therefore, they should always have a copy of the UCC, with its Official Comments, on hand.[8] Students will find it helpful to put index tabs in their copy of the UCC, so that they quickly can move from article to article and so that they quickly can find important definitions. Before you read the rest of this chapter, look at your copy of the UCC. Start with the table of contents, which lists every article by title. Note how Code sections are constructed. Each article in the UCC is divided into parts, which are further divided into sections. The sections are sometimes divided into subsections. The UCC sections consist of four-digit numbers, representing the article, part and section number. Thus, in *Figure 1-2*, the Code section is in Article 9, part 1, section 02. You will refer to that section as section 9-102 ("nine-one-oh-two" or—in states that don't follow the hyphenation convention of the uniform version— "ninety-one-oh-two.")

### Figure 1-2: Construction of a UCC Code Section

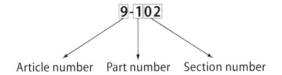

Article number    Part number    Section number

---

### Exercise 1-1: Tabbing the Code

To assist you in navigating through the Code, purchase some tabs and put tabs on the pages to let you rapidly find: (1) the table of contents of Article 1; (2) the table of contents of Article 9; (3) section 1-201, definitions in Article 1; (4) each of the parts of Article 9; and (5) section 9-102, definitions of Article 9. As you work through this course, you may wish to add additional tabs, but too many tabs may actually be more confusing. Don't overdo it!

---

7. Article 8's coverage appears to be a departure from the UCC's otherwise consistent coverage, mirroring "standard" commercial transactions; however, it is frequently used in connection with Article 9 financing.

8. For convenience, most law professors teach from the uniform version of the UCC, rather than the version enacted in a particular state. Of course, practitioners must consult the version of the Code that is the law of their state.

# 2. Article 1

Next, look at the table of contents to Article 1, which appears at the beginning of that article. It provides a convenient outline of Article 1's contents. Note the scope of Article 1. Section 1-102 states, "This article applies to a transaction to the extent that it is governed by another article of the Uniform Commercial Code." Section 1-102 therefore tells you that when you analyze a problem within the scope of Article 9, you need to incorporate the applicable general provisions of Article 1 into your analysis. As you work on Article 9 problems, you will often need to refer to certain sections in Article 1, especially 1-103 (rules of construction; UCC purposes and policies), 1-201 (general definitions and principles of interpretation),[9] 1-202 (notice; knowledge), 1-205 (reasonable time; seasonableness), 1-301 (choice of law), 1-302 (variation by agreement), 1-303 (course of performance, course of dealing and usage of trade), 1-304 (good faith) and 1-305 (remedies to be liberally administered).

The concepts of course of performance, course of dealing and usage of trade are so important throughout the Secured Transactions course that we introduce them now. The basic notion is that when parties have been performing a specific contract in a particular way (**course of performance**), it makes sense that their performance reflects their understanding of the contract. Accordingly, if a dispute arises over a specific term and the parties have previously acted in a way that sheds light on the meaning of that term, their course of performance is important to explain what the parties intended that specific term to mean. For example, if an installment contract provides for payment "within five days" of an event and the parties have always made and accepted payment within five **business** days of that event, their **course of performance** shows that they must have meant that five business days, rather than five calendar days, would be used to calculate the time for payment. Similarly, if parties had several contracts in the past for the same goods as are the subject of a new contract, and each of the past contracts contained a particular term, if the parties leave that term out of the new contract, it is likely that they both intended the same term to apply, but "took it for granted" because of their past history. Thus, their past **course of dealing** is probative to understand their current contract. Finally, where the contract parties both have experience in a particular trade, and in that trade a term has a particular meaning, or most contracts contain a particular term, it is very possible that they assumed that that term would be part of their contract, even if they did not express it. Therefore, the **usage of trade** can shed light on the parties' intention with respect to their current contract. *Figure 1-3* suggests an easy way to remember what each of these terms represents.

### Figure1-3:  Understanding Course of Performance,
### Course of Dealing, Usage of Trade

Course of Performance  ———————▶  Same parties: same contract

Course of Dealing  ———————▶  Same parties: different contract

Usage of Trade  ———————▶  Different parties: different contract

---

9. Many of the definitions pertinent to Article 9—including even the definition of "security interest"—are found in § 1-201.

**Exercise 1-2: Course of Performance, Course of Dealing, Usage of Trade**

Read the Code's definition of "agreement" and "contract" in section 1-201. What is the relationship between "agreement" and "contract," on the one hand, and course of performance, course of dealing, and usage of trade, on the other hand?

# 3. The Official Comments

Each Code section is followed by an Official Comment. The drafters wrote the Official Comments to clarify or expand on the statutory text. On occasion, you will see an Official Comment that seems to contradict the statute. Be careful! Remember that although the Comments are sometimes easier to read than the statutory text, they are not part of the statutory text. When state legislatures enact the Code, they do not enact the Official Comments as law. Accordingly, the Official Comments are not law, and do not have the force of legislative history. Technically, if a Comment conflicts with the text of the Code, the Code controls. Nevertheless, even if the Comments are neither statutes nor legislative history, they are very persuasive authority, and the vast majority of courts, commentators, and lawyers consider the Comments of virtually equal status with the Code, citing the Comments liberally to construe the Code's meaning.

**Exercise 1-3: The Official Comments**

Skim the Official Comments to sections 1-201, 1-301, and 9-101. You will find that collectively they contain all of the types of information that you can typically expect to find in the Official Comments. List at least eight types of information you can generally expect to find in the Official Comments.

# 4. UCC Amendments

The UCC has been amended several times since its promulgation. A major revision of Article 9 was completed in 1998; a set of minor revisions was adopted by the Code sponsors in 2010, and has been adopted in almost every state. Article 1 was revised in 2001, and the revised version has now been adopted in more than half of the states.[10] All references in this book are to the 2010 version of Article 9 and the 2001 version of Article 1. When you read cases, you should keep in mind that the cases may be citing to different versions of Article 1 and Article 9.

---

10. As of June 29, 2014, Revised Article 1 was in effect in thirty-nine states. http://ucclaw.blogspot .com/2010/05/coming-soon-to-ucc-article-1.html (last visited June 29, 2014).

# 5.  Relationship of UCC to Other Laws

As you study the UCC, you will encounter many familiar concepts. You have studied some of these concepts in your Contracts, Torts, or Property classes. The UCC supersedes some of these areas of common law. However, in many other instances, common law supplements the UCC, and you will find that this course is a helpful review of many common law concepts. Section 1-103 makes the key statement of the relationship between the UCC and common law; it provides both that (1) the UCC may displace other bodies of law (in other words, if there is a conflict between the UCC and common law, the UCC prevails); and (2) unless displaced by particular provisions of the UCC, the principles of law and equity **supplement** the Code.

You will need to refer back to section 1-103 constantly, when Article 9 does not spell out a legal rule necessary for your analysis, so that you can supplement Article 9 with common law rules.

This chapter was designed to lay a foundation for the remainder of the course. Now, you are almost ready to begin an intensive study of UCC Article 9. Before going directly to the substantive law, however, Chapter 2 is designed to prepare you for learning from statutes.

# Chapter 2

# Statutory Analysis[1]

This course is based on a statute. Chapter 2, therefore, teaches how to analyze a statute and apply it to solve a legal problem. Not only is this an important skill for you to learn for this course, but it is also a critically important skill for lawyers in practice. You may have already been introduced to the skill of statutory analysis in other law school classes. If so, some of the material in this chapter will appear to be somewhat basic. However, many students have not yet had an opportunity to focus on reading and applying statutes. This chapter provides all students the opportunity to gain, or to refine their existing, statutory analysis skills.

This chapter uses UCC Article 9 as an exemplar statute to teach the process of statutory analysis. This analytical approach will accelerate your ability to read and understand Article 9.

# 1. The Anatomy of a Modern Statute

New law students learn that most appellate opinions contain the same parts in more or less the same order: facts, procedural history, issue, etc. Students look for these parts when they read cases and organize their case briefs around them.

Similarly, most modern statutes and regulations exhibit a uniform structure. Like cases, statutes contain basically the same parts in basically the same order. Using the parts, students can "brief" or "deconstruct" a statute just as they brief a case. Occasionally, a statute may lack one of these parts, but you can usually find the function of the "missing" part being fulfilled by other parts. These parts usually appear in the order shown in *Figure 2-1*.

### Figure 2-1:  Parts of a Modern Statute

**Purpose:** Why was the statute enacted? This part states the legislators' purpose in enacting the statute and is intended as an aid to interpretation and application. It may include legislative findings about the problems the statute was intended to solve. A statute that is the result of political compromise may assert several inconsistent purposes.

---

1. This chapter is based on materials authored by Professor Sidney DeLong, Seattle University School of Law. Reproduced with permission.

Some statutes omit a purpose provision, necessitating recourse to legislative history. Others simply recite whatever legislative purpose is necessary to the statute's constitutionality.

**Scope:** a.k.a. "Applicability." What kinds of events or persons does the statute apply to? Some statutes omit the scope provision, leaving the scope to be deduced from the next three parts.

**Exclusions:** What things that would otherwise be within the scope of the statute are excluded from its coverage? Exclusions often reflect either the existence of conflicting regulations or the political victory of some special interest. Sometimes exclusions are combined with the scope section and sometimes they are hidden in, or inferable from, the definitions.

**Definitions:** What do the words of the statute mean? Defined words are the terms of art the statute uses. The more modern the statute, the more terms it will define. A defined term is like an algebraic sign whose definition should be plugged into the statutory formula wherever the defined term appears. The more modern the statute, the more technical and less intuitive the definitions will be and the more you will have to be careful to keep them in mind in applying the statute. (Developing dexterity in this part of the analysis will also assist transactional attorneys in their day-to-day practice generally, since almost all agreements used to document transactions incorporate the use of defined terms to some degree.)

**Operative Provisions:** What does the statute do? Operative provisions serve as the motor that drives the statute. They usually take one of three main forms: (1) They prohibit or require certain acts: "Thou shalt not kill"; "All contracts by minors are voidable"; (2) They state requirements: "A lender must file a financing statement to perfect a security interest"; (3) They state the consequences of the action or omission: "Any lender who omits to state the rate shall forfeit its claim to interest." You can think of the operative provisions as containing the elements of the rule that, if satisfied, lead to a legal consequence.

**Consequences:** What happens if the statute is complied with or violated? The consequences include private remedies for violating the statute, public penalties for violation, and the legal effect of the actions and omissions that the operative provisions address.

Although *Figure 2-1* describes the parts you may expect to find in a modern statute, not every statute has exactly one of each of these parts. For example, as noted above, there may be no specific "scope" provision. There may be multiple sections that state rules. Sometimes the same section that states a rule also states the consequences for following (or not following) the stated rule; sometimes the consequences are stated separately.

Furthermore, most statutes contain other, less important, parts: The **title** names the statute. The **effective date** tells when the statute goes into effect and what events it applies to. **Repealer provisions** eliminate inconsistent legislation. **Transition provisions** explain how to transition from a prior law to the current statute. Some statutes contain explicit instructions on how to interpret or construe them. A **severability** clause preserves the rest of the statute if part of it is declared to be **invalid**. Remedies may be made subject to

**statutes of limitations**. Certain courts may be given **subject matter jurisdiction** of enforcement actions arising out of the statute.

---

### Exercise 2-1: Identifying the Parts of a Statute

This exercise is designed to help you apply what you have learned about a statute to an actual statute that you will be referring to repeatedly throughout this course.

Read UCC Article 1. How many of the parts of a statute listed in *Figure 2-1* can you find? Try to complete the following chart, to show which section or sections of Article 1 correspond to the identified parts of a statute.

| Part of Statute | Article 1 Section Number |
|---|---|
| Purpose | |
| Scope | |
| Exclusions | |
| Definitions | |
| Operative Provisions | |
| Consequences | |

# 2. Types of Statutes: Rules v. Standards

As you work with statutes, keep in mind the difference between statutory "rules" and statutory "standards."[2] Statutory rules attempt to describe with precision the type of permitted or prohibited activity. Statutory standards, on the other hand, are more vague. Each has its own advantages and disadvantages. Rules give greater certainty and predictability, but have little flexibility and are often arbitrary. Standards are more flexible, but give less certainty. People are encouraged to behave "right up to the edge" of a rule; *e.g.*, if a statute permits driving up to 55 mph, they will drive at 54.5 mph. Standards may have more deterrent power "at the edge" precisely because they are more vague; *e.g.*, if a statute provides for driving at a rate of speed "reasonable under the circumstances," drivers may drive more slowly in appropriate weather conditions than if a rule applied.

*Figure 2-2* gives examples of common statutory rules and standards with which you may already be familiar, and adds some examples of each taken from UCC Article 9.

---

2. This important distinction was explained in Duncan Kennedy, *Form and Substance in Private Law Adjudication*, 89 Harv. L. Rev. 1685 (1976).

**Figure 2-2:  Table of Examples of Rules and Standards**

| Goal | Rule | Standard |
|------|------|----------|
| Regulate driving behavior. | All motor vehicles traveling on a class two highway must not exceed 50 miles per hour. | All motor vehicles traveling on a class two highway must travel at a reasonable rate of speed in light of road conditions. |
| Impose requirements attendant to a foreclosure sale of collateral. | Specified persons must be given prior notice of dispositions of collateral. (UCC Section 9-611). | Every aspect of a disposition of collateral, including the method, manner, time, place, and other terms, must be *commercially reasonable* (UCC Section 9-610(b); emphasis added). |
| Provide a consumer debtor with an explanation of calculation of surplus or deficiency to be accounted for after a foreclosure sale. | In a consumer goods transaction in which the debtor is entitled to a surplus … the secured party shall: (1) send an explanation to the debtor … (B) *within 14 days after receipt of a request* (UCC Section 9-616(b); emphasis added). | |

The UCC is replete with the most common legal standard, reasonableness. Sometimes it appears three or four times in the same sentence. The problem is the lack of predictability that this standard creates.

# 3.  Types of Statutory Disputes

The six general types of disputes that involve statutes are shown in *Figure 2-3*.

**Figure 2-3:  General Types of Statutory Disputes**

1. Disputes about the **facts:** *e.g.,* what happened?
2. Disputes over the **validity** of the statute: *e.g.,* is it constitutional? Was it implicitly repealed? Is it pre-empted by federal law?
3. Disputes over the **choice of law** to be applied to the dispute: *e.g.,* does California's tort law apply to a plane crash in Oregon?

4. Disputes about **classifying** real world events in the terms used by the statute: *e.g.*, is a mobile home a "motor vehicle"? Was the defendant's reliance "reasonable"?

5. Disputes about statutory **interpretation**: *e.g.*, does sub-section (b) create an exception to the general rule in part II? Are these requirements to be read in the disjunctive or the conjunctive?

6. Disputes about whether a court should recognize a **non-statutory exception** to the literal application of a valid statute; *e.g.*, should a murderer be permitted to inherit from the estate of his victim under the inheritance statutes? Should the court recognize an equitable defense to liability under the Sherman Act?

The types of statutory disputes described in *Figure 2-3* are not conceptually watertight. For example, most disputes about classification can be re-cast as disputes about interpretation, and vice versa. And an argument about an exception to the statute might be recast as one about classification or interpretation. But most arguments still seem to take one of these forms, and some disputes will involve more than one of the forms.

The different parts of a statute come into play in the typical statutory dispute. Thus, in deciding what the meaning of a term is in a classification dispute, you can often get guidance from the purpose clause or the definitions. To decide whether to create an exception to the statute, you might be able to make arguments from the purpose clause or the exclusions.

# 4. Statutory Analysis, General

Statutory analysis can be divided into the basic steps shown in *Figure 2-4*.

### Figure 2-4: Basic Steps of Statutory Analysis

**Step 1: Scope.** Determine whether the statute applies to the problem at hand. Most statutes contain provisions that define their applicability.

**Step 2: Deconstruct the statute.** The process of deconstructing a statute is the same as the process of identifying the elements of any rule of law. Every law student develops his/her own way of effectually deconstructing a rule (*i.e.*, breaking it down to its constituent elements). We suggest that you always read a statute **aloud** and use punctuation as a key to help identify the parts or elements of the statutory rule.

**Step 3: Define terms.** Many statutes contain definitions of key terms. The definitions of some terms may refer to other defined terms. The definitions may conflict with ordinary usage; indeed, in some statutes the definitions may change from part to part. (Compare, for example, the definition of "instrument" in UCC section 3-104 to the definition of that term in UCC section 9-102.) Some key terms may not be defined at all. Definitions should be treated like any other rule statements. Statutory legal analysis should quote and apply definitions to the facts of the issue to reach a conclusion.

**Step 4: Apply the statute to your facts.** Once you have broken the rule down to its constituent elements (Step 2), simply discuss each element in order.

**Step 5: Linking up.** Generally, when students have previously performed a legal analysis of a common law problem, they have worked with only one legal rule and, maybe, an exception to it. But many statutes will require reference to more than one section. Several provisions may apply to the analysis of one problem, and students will need to go through Step 4 for several different sections. They will then have to link one provision to another to another until they construct a logical chain leading to their conclusion.

**Step 6: Consult secondary sources.** Just as in any legal analysis, secondary sources may be extremely helpful in statutory analysis.

# 5. Statutory Analysis Under the UCC

## 5.1 Types of Disputes

Disputes under the UCC can be of any of the six types suggested in *Figure 2-3*. Disputes over **validity** can occur when the Code, as state law, is pre-empted by federal legislation, or when a party challenges the constitutionality of Code provisions, such as those relating to self-help repossession.[3]

Most Code disputes are of the four other types: **factual, classification, interpretation,** and **exceptions.** In real-life litigation, factual disputes often predominate: If you can prove what happened, you win. Most problems presented in law school eliminate factual disputes by requiring that you assume an agreed-upon statement of facts. Thus, the primary issues you will encounter in this course are the three remaining types.

To successfully analyze a UCC problem, you must be able to read statutory language closely and carefully in light of terms of art defined in the statute. Discovery of the appropriate language in the statute, and identification of—and application of the statute to—appropriate facts, lead to a solution. This analytical process resembles the common law reasoning that you learned in your Legal Writing course and in doctrinal courses, such as Contracts. That reasoning will be informed, in this course, by the special policies of the UCC, which will become apparent from the Official Comments, case law and legislative history.

---

3. For the most part, choice of law disputes have been eliminated because the UCC is in effect in all states, but some local variations still exist. For example, the California version of Article 9 applies to the creation and perfection of security interests in insurance policies as original collateral, while the officially-promulgated version of the UCC (at §9-109(d)(8)) expressly excludes such security interests from the scope of Article 9. The Code permits the parties to select applicable law, within certain limits. *See* UCC §1-105.

## 5.2 UCC Statutory Analysis

UCC statutory analysis follows the basic steps outlined in *Figure 2-4*. The following discussion emphasizes particular provisions of the UCC that assist in analysis, and gives an example using UCC section 9-109.

### Step 1: Scope.

Article 9's scope is defined in section 9-109, which contains both inclusionary and exclusionary provisions.

### Step 2: Deconstruct the statute.

You may find it helpful, whenever you want to apply the UCC to solve a legal problem, to first identify the applicable code section(s) and begin to read **aloud**, pausing at every punctuation mark and coordinating conjunction.[4] This is the first step in "deconstructing" the statute — that is, breaking it down into understandable parts. After you deconstruct the statute, you can then begin to apply the statute to the facts of your problem. Take, for example, UCC section 9-109(a)(1):

> Except as otherwise provided in subsections (c) and (d), this article applies to: (1) a transaction, regardless of its form, that creates a security interest in personal property or fixtures by contract....

As you can see when you compare the preceding simple statute to all of section 9-109, you will not be able to solve a legal problem by reference to section 9-109(a)(1) in isolation. Section 9-109(a)(1) defines *one* type of transaction (out of six) to which Article 9 applies. Moreover, subsequent subsections define exclusions and limitations. Nevertheless, even the short rule contained in section 9-109(a)(1) contains several very different ideas. Let's break it down, to focus on the different ideas:

- The prefatory clause, "Except as otherwise provided in subsections (c) and (d)," alerts the reader that any conclusion reached after application of this rule is subject to revision. For now, let's translate it to mean: "After you go through all the work of applying this provision of the statute to reach a determination, you will have to continue on to apply subsections (c) and (d) to see if you have to change your mind because of the provisions of those subsections."

- The provision that follows the first comma and continues until the next comma ("regardless of its form") is a phrase that modifies the word "transaction." The purpose of this phrase is to emphasize that the applicability of Article 9 is a matter of substance over form. (A transaction that the parties call a "lease," for example, may actually be a "secured loan.") We will explore the different forms of transactions to which Article 9 applies in Chapter 4.

- The remainder of the subsection is the positive rule of the statute — **the operative provision**: "this Article applies to (1) a transaction, regardless of its form, that creates a security interest in personal property or fixtures by contract." That is the statement of one type of transaction that is within the scope of Article 9. (The fact that it is subsection (a)(1) indicates that it is not a complete list of all types

---

4. The coordinating conjunctions are: and, but, or, yet, for, nor and so.

of transactions that are within that scope; the other included transactions are listed in subsections (a)(2) through (a)(6).)

### Step 3: Define Terms.

Like other statutes, the UCC has its own terms of art. Words may have meanings that differ from common usage, and some frequently used terms, such as "transaction," or "reasonable," are not defined—they mean whatever you can persuade a court that they mean. It is not possible to tell whether a word in Article 9 is a defined term just by looking at it. (When in doubt, of course, look for a definition, starting with Article 1, section 1-201 (the general definitions), and section 9-102 (the definitions and index of definitions specific to Article 9). You must also take into account the UCC purposes and policies.[5]

In addition, each Code section is followed by an **Official Comment** that also can be helpful. Many **Official Comments** include examples and cross-references to different parts of the UCC. If you do not find the necessary definition within the statute, you also can use common law precedent, and even everyday dictionary definitions, to help you understand the statute.[6]

As you work with the UCC, you will become more familiar with its terms of art and you will learn which terms are defined and which are not. You also will learn the definitions of frequently used words. In practice, you will need to consult treatises and case law to determine the meaning of undefined terms.

### Step 4: Apply the statute to your facts.

After you have deconstructed the statute, you are ready to apply it to your legal problem. Take each separate part and try to identify the facts that are affected by that part. Again, read the statute aloud. This time, stop at each separate part that has been listed above and try to "fit" the applicable facts into that part. It is possible that this approach will not always work, especially if one of the elements requires extended analysis. But your initial read-through can settle the clear points, and you can reserve the difficult ones for later. We refer to this process as **thinking aloud**; an example of a problem, and a possible think-aloud approach to its analysis, follow:

#### Facts

In real life litigation, factual disputes usually predominate. In this course, as in most other law school courses, you will receive a narrative statement of "the facts," and you must decide how to apply the statute to the given facts.

Victoria Vendor sold a collection of furniture to Barbie Businessowner for $25,000. Barbie added the furniture to her inventory of furniture she sells to the public. To evidence the sale, Victoria and Barbie signed a written agreement called a conditional sales contract that stated, among other things, that Victoria retained title to the goods until receipt of payment in full. After making several payments, but before Victoria was paid in full, Barbie stopped making the payments called for under the agreement. What are Victoria Vendor's rights with respect to (1) the furniture that Barbie has already sold to members of the public; (2) the furniture Victoria sold to Barbie that is still in Barbie's possession; and (3) Victoria's claim for the unpaid balance of the $25,000 sales price?

---

5. UCC § 1-103(a).
6. UCC § 1-103(b).

### The Call of the Question

Before you begin to analyze the problem, be sure you understand the question you are being asked to address. Here, you must analyze Victoria Vendor's rights upon Barbie's default.

### The Problem

To determine Victoria's rights, Victoria's lawyer first must (1) determine whether the problem involves issues that are governed by Article 9; and (2) then, if it does, recognize that different parts of Article 9 may be relevant to answering the questions posed—part 3 (perfection and priority), for example, with respect to question 1, and part 6 (default) with respect to questions 2 and 3. If Article 9 does not apply, Victoria's lawyer must research and apply some other law that governs Victoria's rights. Making that determination (*i.e.*, whether Article 9 applies) requires the lawyer to read and apply Article 9's scope provision, section 9-109. Using the above deconstruction of the statute, Victoria's lawyer must apply the elements of the statute to the relevant facts.

The think-aloud approach involves plugging relevant facts into the deconstructed statute. Based on the statement of facts, a lawyer might do the initial read-through of the statute somewhat as follows, with the words of the statute in bold, and the mental processes in bullets.

### Think Aloud

**Except as otherwise provided in subsections (c) and (d) . . .**

- I'll have to remember to read and apply those subsections after I finish this analysis before I reach any final conclusion . . .

 **. . . [,] this article applies to: (1) a transaction, regardless of form . . .**

- This is one of the elements needed to decide that Article 9 applies to my client's situation–what does it mean?

- I've looked everywhere in Article 1 and Article 9, and there does not appear to be a statutory definition of the word "transaction." I will have to see if a common dictionary definition is available, or if there are any cases on point.

- Here, based on the facts given, I think there is a "transaction," because the loose definition of "transaction" seems to be some sort of business deal or exchange, and here there is an exchange of goods for money (or a promise to pay money).

 **. . . that creates a security interest in personal property or fixtures by contract;**

- This is the other element. I could break it into two elements: (1) a security interest in (a) personal property, or (b) fixtures; and (2) arising out of a contract. My facts aren't real complicated here, so I can combine the two.

- We are told that there is a legal contract that the parties called a "conditional sales contract," so, whatever the agreement accomplishes, it does it "by contract." Therefore, the question is whether the agreement creates a security interest in personal property or fixtures.

- For this analysis, I need to define both "security interest" and "personal property"—and "fixtures." I find the term "fixtures" defined in section 9-102. I don't find a definition of "personal property," but I remember from my Property class that personal property refers to everything that can be owned that is not real property—I will see if I can do a decent analysis of the problem using that definition, or whether I need to do more research. I know the furniture is not fixtures, because there are no facts about affixation to real property. So, I can conclude for now that the furniture is personal property.

So the final question is whether this "conditional sales contract" creates a security interest. Section 1-201(36) defines a "security interest" as "an interest in personal property ... which secures payment or performance of an obligation...." It also specifically states, "retention or reservation of title by a seller of goods ... is limited in effect to a reservation of a 'security interest.'" Since that is what the parties have done here—delivered goods to the buyer while the seller purported to "retain title" until paid in full—I can conclude that the agreement creates a security interest in personal property.

· As indicated above, the other relevant subsections in section 9-109 would have to be consulted before reaching a final conclusion.

### Step 5: Linking Up.

The UCC is an integrated code. Its parts are not freestanding, but have meaning only in relation to each other. You will usually have to work through Step 4 for several different Code sections to resolve an issue arising under the Code. Then, you will have to link one provision to another to another until you construct a logical chain that leads to your conclusion. If you fail to link the necessary steps up, you invite confusion and error. At a minimum, you will have to refer to definitional sections along with operative sections. (Notice that in this simple problem, we needed to look at several other Code sections, including 1-201 and 9-102.)

### Step 6: Consult secondary sources.

One treatise is uniformly recognized as authoritative on issues involving the Code: James J. White and Robert S. Summers, *The Uniform Commercial Code.*[7] It is clearly written, occasionally entertaining, and highly recommended. Courts often cite it and most commercial lawyers use it. Many practitioners would not think of concluding an analysis of a UCC problem without checking that treatise. This is not to say that White and Summers' analysis is always above reproach; they even disagree with each other on a number of issues. But even when you disagree with their analysis, you must be prepared to respond to it, because you can be sure that your opponent and the judge will have consulted it. Another major source for understanding Article 9 is Grant Gilmore's two-volume treatise, *Security Interests in Personal Property* (1965). Although the treatise is now somewhat dated, and Article 9 has been revised since it was written, it still contains valuable explanations of complex doctrine. Other helpful sources are identified at the end of this chapter.[8]

## 5.3  Conclusion: Statutory Analysis and the UCC

The preceding brief survey demonstrates that statutory analysis is simply another branch of legal reasoning and analysis that all law students strive to master during their

---

7. James J. White & Robert S. Summers, THE UNIFORM COMMERCIAL CODE (6th ed.) [hereinafter "White & Summers"].

8. See Additional Resources, at the end of this chapter.

law school careers. The main difference is the relatively easy accessibility of the "black letter law" in statutes. With practice, as demonstrated in *Figure 2-4*, students can learn to deconstruct statutes into elements and apply the elements to the relevant facts. The UCC is a good statute to use as the basis for improving your statutory analysis skills.

Legal analysis of a problem involving the possible creation of a security interest in personal property—and even some problems involving the sale of personal property—should always begin with a determination of whether the statute is applicable. Thereafter, students should identify the individual Code sections that are relevant to an analysis of the problem at hand, and demonstrate how those sections link up. In some cases, there may be a dispute other than the interpretation of a particular section, or even a question regarding its applicability. Such disputes can often be resolved by reference to the Code's underlying purposes and policies and the Official Comments, as well as case law and commentaries by learned academics and practitioners.

Finally, in some situations, none of the Code provisions discloses any obvious rule that would apply to your facts. If the issue in questions falls within such a gap, you should first say so, then proceed to try to fill the gap from other sources of law. Supplemental principles of law and equity apply under section 1-103.

---

## Exercise 2-2: Think-Aloud Statutory Analysis

Now that you have read about how to deconstruct a statute using the think-aloud approach, and have seen an example based on section 9-109, this exercise gives you an opportunity to try it yourself. Using the set of facts provided below, and sections 1-102, 9-102, and 9-109 (and other sections you decide you need to use), prepare a written response to the problem presented. (The "call of the question," and "the problem" portions of the analysis are provided for you.)

Your response should be in the think-aloud format illustrated above.

**Facts**

Frank Furniture Seller is engaged in the retail sale of furniture. Moneybags Lender is in the business of financing furniture dealers such as Frank. Frank and Moneybags enter into an agreement for the financing of Frank's accounts receivable.[9] The agreement provides, among other things, that

> [f]rom time to time, Frank shall sell to Moneybags accounts receivable. Such sales shall be with full recourse against Frank.[10] Moneybags may, in its sole discretion, refuse to purchase any account. The amount paid by Moneybags to Frank for each account shall be the unpaid face amount of the account less a fifteen percent discount plus another ten percent of the unpaid face amount as a reserve against bad debts."

In addition, Frank is required to repurchase any account sold to Moneybags that remains in default for more than 60 days.

Under the agreement, Frank transferred over 600 accounts to Moneybags. Frank claims that Moneybags has collected more money than the sum of what

---

9. Accounts receivable, very broadly, are monies due a business from its customers for goods sold or services rendered.

10. Basically, in the context of the agreement, a "with recourse" sale means that if the account debtor fails to pay when due, Moneybags can make a claim against Frank for the amount due.

Frank received from Moneybags plus the 15% discount, and that Frank is entitled to the surplus. Frank consults you to see if he has any claim against Moneybags for the excess amounts collected by Moneybags. You have read the agreement, and it is silent as to the matter.

### The Call of the Question

Before you begin to analyze the problem, be sure you understand the question you are being asked to address. Here, the ultimate questions — whether there *are* any "surplus" funds with respect to the accounts receivable assigned to Moneybags, and, if so, who is entitled to them — may depend upon whether there is a true sale or a secured transaction, and, therefore, on what impact Article 9 of the UCC has on the transaction. Therefore, the first question you need to address is the applicability of Article 9 of the UCC.

### The Problem

To determine whether Frank can successfully assert a claim to the surplus money collected by Moneybags, Alpha's lawyer first must decide if Article 9 of the UCC governs the problem. If Article 9 does not apply, Alpha's lawyer must research and apply some other law that governs the analysis of the parties' transaction. That determination requires the lawyer to read and apply Article 9's scope provision, section 9-109.

Use what you have learned about deconstructing the statute, and apply the elements of the statute to the relevant facts. Discuss the "scope" issue *only*.

### Think Aloud

(Students should write out a response.)

---

# Additional Resources

Barkley Clark & Barbara Clark, Clarks' the Law of Secured Transactions Under the Uniform Commercial Code (A.S. Pratt 3d ed. 2010).

Linda H. Edwards, Legal Writing Process, Analysis and Organization, 128-31 (Aspen Publishers 5th ed. 2010).

Kent Greenawalt, Legislation: Statutory Interpretation: 20 Questions (Foundation Press 1999).

William D. Hawkland, Uniform Commercial Code Series (1982).

Karl N. Llewellyn, *Remarks on the Theory of Appellate Decision and Rules or Canons about How Statutes are to be Construed*, 3 Vand. L. Rev. 395 (1950).

Thomas M. Quinn, Quinn's Uniform Commercial Code Commentary & Law Digest (Warren, Gorham & Lamont 2d ed. 1991).

Finally, for a quick way to find UCC cases, use the digest for the Uniform Commercial Code Reporting Service.

# Chapter 3

# Introduction to Personal Property Secured Transactions

## Chapter Problem[1]

You have passed the Bar, had letterhead and business cards printed, paid for your City Business License, received your federal and state tax identification numbers, and purchased errors and omissions insurance. Your mother's friend, Betty, has a son, Ben, who has built a fairly successful business, manufacturing and distributing cardboard boxes. Ben wants to meet with you to discuss his desire for legal representation, and, specifically, his financing needs.

In particular, Ben wants to discuss with you his options for getting more money to continue to conduct his business. He has consulted his banker, and he is aware that there are a variety of options that may be available to him for obtaining financing and additional operating capital. His banker has told him that possible options include credit card debt, unsecured credit, secured credit (secured by either real or personal property), and leasing. (Ben has already considered and rejected the possibility of raising capital through other means, such as venture capital.)

Prepare an outline of your upcoming interview with Ben. You will need to include both questions you need to ask and information you will need to convey to Ben. For example, first you might explain to Ben the difference between secured and unsecured financing, giving examples of each. Then you would explain to him how the sources of funding he has identified fit into each category. Finally, you might ask questions designed to see what kind of financing would likely be available to him and would best suit his needs.

---

1. At the beginning of each chapter, you will find a chapter problem, like this one, designed to help you understand the context of the material you will be studying. Read the problem before you begin to read the rest of the chapter. See if you can predict how you would answer the questions raised. First, develop a hypothesis that you will test as you work your way through the chapter. Then, as you read the chapter, keep the problem in mind and look for hints on how to go about solving it. By the end of the chapter, you will be able to fully analyze the problem.

# 1. The Context of Personal Property Secured Transactions

Before we begin to study Article 9 in depth, this chapter presents an overview of the context in which Article 9 operates: the realm of personal property secured transactions and the role of lawyers in personal property secured transactions.

The majority of transactions involving Article 9 are transactions that include obligations that arise out of loans or out of sales in which the seller provides financing by selling to the buyer on credit. To understand secured transactions, you must understand why people enter into these types of transactions. The primary reason is risk-mitigation. In the ordinary course, I can lend money to someone, or sell something to someone on credit, and hope that I will be repaid. If I am not repaid, my legal recourse is to file a lawsuit and try to get a judgment. I will have to prove the existence of the obligation to prevail in the lawsuit. If I prevail, I receive a money judgment—a piece of paper that says "A [the "someone" I have contracted with] must pay B [me] on the complaint the sum of $."[2] To actually get paid, I (now known as the "judgment creditor") must then use legal process to try to identify property of A that can be seized and sold, also with the aid of judicial process. If A is experiencing financial difficulties, I may be only one of a throng of A's creditors who are trying to get judgments against A and seize A's assets.

In contrast, if I lend money (or sell on credit) to A in a secured transaction, I know at the beginning of the deal that there are specific assets of A that will be available if A fails to pay when payment is due. Those assets are generally referred to as "collateral." In some instances, which we will study, a secured lender can use "self-help" and sell the collateral in satisfaction of its debt (remitting any surplus to the borrower). More often, however, even a secured lender must resort to legal process to realize on its collateral, but such a lender will nevertheless be significantly advantaged over general creditors, who do not have specific assets upon which to rely.

## Asset-Based Lending: An Introduction to Personal Property Secured Financing

Not all law students are familiar with commercial lending practices. Although this class focuses on personal property secured transactions, it is helpful to understand lending practices in general. Doing so will help you appreciate the differences between unsecured and secured lending and the reasons why borrowers and lenders agree to different types of loans. First, we introduce two common types of loan structures: short-term loans and lines of credit. Then, we discuss forms of secured lending.

## Short-Term Loans

When a borrower needs money on a short-term basis, the borrower may be able to get money in the form of a short-term loan. Such loans are usually for less than one year;

---

2. California Judicial Council Form JUD-100 (2002), available at http://www.courts.ca.gov/documents/jud100.pdf (last visited July 10, 2013).

they have a specific maturity date and call for repayment in full at maturity. Loans are disbursed in one lump sum at the beginning of the term of the loan. Depending on the creditworthiness of the borrower, the loan may be completely unsecured.

## Lines of Credit

A line of credit is a lender's agreement to lend up to a specified maximum amount of money. Disbursements may be revolving or non-revolving (*i.e.*, the borrower may pay down the principal, and later reborrow amounts repaid). The loan may be secured or unsecured. The borrower may be required to reduce the outstanding balance to zero periodically (quarterly, semi-annually or annually) as a condition to the renewal of the line of credit.

## Secured Loans

Many students are already somewhat familiar with loan transactions involving real property collateral. The basic Property course usually introduces residential loan transactions, and the mortgage or deed of trust that is recorded in real property records to evidence a lender's lien. However, in our experience, most students are not as familiar with loan transactions involving personal property collateral. Lawyers who practice in this area generally refer to the area as "asset-based lending," and the "assets" they refer to are personal property. Following is a brief overview of the primary different types of asset-based lending, to give you some context for understanding the situations in which the Article 9 rules apply.

## Equipment and Fixture Financing

One of the simplest types of asset-based lending is an equipment loan: a seller or a lender takes a security interest in the equipment of a business to secure the repayment of a loan. Such a loan is often a "purchase-money" loan—that is, the seller extends credit or the lender lends money to enable the borrower to buy the piece of equipment that is then the security for the repayment of the loan. An equipment loan will typically be for a specified term and the principal of the loan amortized over that period of time, so that when all of the payments on the loan have been made, the loan will have been paid in full.

## Accounts Receivable Loans

Another type of loan is based on a business's accounts receivable. In the Code, accounts receivable are referred to simply as "accounts," a term that includes rights to payment that have not yet been earned by performance. Those terms are used interchangeably in this text. Such a loan is often a "line of credit." That means that the lender agrees to lend up to a specified amount of money, over a specified term, and the borrower can "draw" on the line of credit from time to time: the outstanding balance of the loan will "revolve." In other words, the balance will rise and fall as the borrower borrows, repays and re-borrows money, based on the value of the collateral (the outstanding accounts receivable). Principal reductions will be required if the value of the collateral drops. Such loans are used for rapidly growing or immature companies that need credit to continue expanding. An important distinction between such loans and equipment loans is that in an equipment loan the collateral is usually specified at the beginning of the term of the loan and remains the same throughout the term of the loan. In contrast, accounts receivable change — accounts are generated as new sales are made, giving rise to new accounts. Accordingly, in loans based on accounts receivable, the concepts of "after acquired property" (accounts that are generated after the first day of the loan) and "future advances" (new loan advances made as the loan "revolves") are very important. Read section 9-204. The lender's lien is known as a "floating lien," because the collateral that is encumbered constantly changes, and the lien "floats" to cover the new collateral. In accounts receivable financing, the lender will monitor the creation and collection of accounts.

Historically, lenders who financed accounts receivable were known as "factors," and the lending practice was called "factoring." Factoring agreements generally reflected an outright sale by a business to its factor of accounts receivable. By purchasing the accounts the factor essentially took the credit risk of nonpayment. Accordingly, it made the decision as to which accounts it would purchase, and the purchase was at a steep discount. Sales might be with or without recourse to the seller of the accounts. In other cases, instead of buying accounts, the lender takes a security interest in the accounts, and the borrower pays the lender as it receives payments from its account debtors.

In either case, the lender determines which accounts are "eligible" to serve as collateral. Eligibility will include consideration of a variety of things, such as whether the account debtor is related to the borrower, whether the accounts are "concentrated" too heavily (such as whether 25% or more of all accounts are due from one account debtor), and whether accounts are "late" (in that they have been outstanding for more than a stated number of days), and will limit eligibility to accounts that have been earned by performance.

## Inventory Loans

Inventory loans are similar to loans based on accounts in many respects. One of the major similarities is that inventory, like accounts, will turn over. Since inventory is sold in the ordinary course of business, an inventory lender must understand that its security interest in the goods will be cut off at the time of sale.

The proceeds of inventory sales are usually accounts — hence, the lender will typically take as collateral for a specific loan both inventory and accounts receivable. The lender must have a floating lien to maintain a security interest in its collateral, and the lender will typically make advances against a revolving line of credit. One major difference between receivables lending and inventory lending is that inventory may be financed on a "purchase money" basis. To encourage lenders (and sellers) to extend credit to enable a business to acquire new inventory, Article 9 recognizes the concept of a "purchase-money" loan and gives "super" priority to purchase-money loans in certain situations.

One specific type of inventory financing, used when individual units are large enough or expensive enough to justify financing on an individual unit basis rather than a bulk basis, is known as "floor planning." An example of floor planning is in the motor vehicle industry, where the car manufacturer finances the dealer's acquisition of cars under a floor planning arrangement. As each individual unit is sold, the proceeds of the sale are used to pay off the floor planner's loan against that individual car, and the individual car is released as collateral. Floor planning is reserved for use where the debtor is holding the financed goods for resale.

# Securitization

Securitization is the name of a complex financial practice in one variety of which a lender itself creates a group of assets, consisting of loans that it has made (or originated), generally evidenced by promissory notes or chattel paper, and sells them (in a variety of ways) to enable the issuance of securities to investors. Certificates representing an interest in a pool of residential mortgages, for example, would commonly be known as "mortgage-backed securities." Securitizations are used with a variety of debt instruments, including residential mortgages, commercial mortgages, automobile loans and credit card obligations. As you will see in Chapter 4, the sale of promissory notes is an example of a transaction that is within the scope of Article 9. Thus, the sophisticated lawyers who structure securitizations must be experts in secured transactions, in addition to securities laws and other applicable laws.

# Agricultural Financing

Agricultural financing, financing businesses engaged in farming or raising livestock, is a highly specialized area of secured lending that raises issues beyond the scope of this introductory course. Federal law (*e.g.*, the Perishable Agricultural Commodities Act, 7 U.S.C. §§ 499a-499t, and the Packers and Stockyards Act of 1921, 7 U.S.C. §§ 181-229b) provide special protections (giving in effect, super-priority liens) to businesses that sell perishable agricultural products or livestock to dealers or processors. You must be aware of those protections, and familiar with their operation, if you are to protect adequately the interests of a client providing credit to the beneficiaries of such laws, or to those who buy from, or provide services to, those beneficiaries.

# Consumer Loans

As you learned in Chapter 1, a transaction may be governed by the UCC even though it involves non-merchants. Hence, secured transactions involving consumers are commercial transactions governed by the Code. Most of the rules you will study in this text apply equally to consumer and non-consumer transactions; however, particularly in connection with default rules, there are some special rules that apply only to consumer transactions. Furthermore, many states have additional consumer protections embodied in non-UCC laws, which can affect the operation of Article 9 rules where the debtor is a consumer. Additional limitations are found in the Federal Trade Commission (FTC) Fair Credit Practices Rule in 16 CFR Part 444.2. In any transaction involving a consumer borrower, you should be sure to investigate possibly applicable state and federal laws to supplement the provisions of Article 9.

# 2. The Lawyer's Role in Personal Property Secured Transactions

Although every generation of law students has grown up with some television series version of what lawyers do, very few of those television series depict a personal property secured transaction. (The reality television show "Operation Repo" is one of the rare exceptions.) The absence of these television programs is understandable; the typical personal property secured transaction practice undoubtedly would make boring television. However, many talented lawyers agree that, as a practice area, personal property secured transactions cannot be beat! Most lawyers in this area are transactional lawyers — that is to say, they spend the majority of their time working on deals, working with other lawyers and clients, writing and negotiating specialized contracts, and negotiating "workouts" for failed transactions. Some lawyers represent primarily borrowers, finding themselves called upon from time to time to assist in a loan transaction. A borrower's lawyer can explain complex loan documents to her client and, possibly, negotiate or at least suggest changes. Many smaller lenders prepare "boilerplate" documents and are neither prepared nor willing to negotiate any changes. Even in that case, however, a borrower's lawyer can, at a minimum, work with her client to ensure that the borrower will be able comply with the requirements of the loan documents and that the loan documents accurately reflect the client's understanding of the business deal. In more complex transactions, the borrower's lawyer may get more involved in negotiating changes to the loan documents; and, in some transactions, the borrower's lawyer will be required to write an "opinion letter," addressed to the lender, that opines as to various aspects of the transaction, such as her client's authority to enter into the loan and to incur its obligations under the loan documents and the enforceability of the loan documents. In a secured transaction, the borrower's lawyer may be asked to opine as to the creation and perfection of the security interests granted to the lender.[3]

Other secured transactions lawyers represent secured lenders. They are also typically transactional lawyers, and they spend much of their time structuring loan transactions and writing and negotiating loan documents. Because many smaller lenders use standard form documents for their transactions, lenders' lawyers may write such documents for document providers, such as Harland Financial Solutions (provider of LaserPro loan documents); for industry groups, such as the Commercial Finance Association, or for corporate law departments and institutional lenders, such as GE Capital. Lenders' lawyers will also become involved in default situations, advising the lender throughout the collection process.

Another group of lawyers who are often involved in aspects of secured transactions are lawyers who specialize in insolvency law and practice in the federal bankruptcy arena. As you will learn in this book, bankruptcy is sometimes referred to as the "acid test" of a security interest. If a borrower files for relief under the Federal Bankruptcy Code, there are a variety of attacks that can be made on the validity or perfection of a security interest.

---

3. "Perfection" is the UCC term of art for taking steps to give notice to third parties of the lender's claim on the borrower's property and to obtain priority for the lender's interest in that property over the rights of a "lien creditor" with respect to that property. The requisite steps vary depending on the type of collateral, and even the type of loan, involved. Perfection is one of the most important aspects of a secured transaction practice, because proper perfection can protect a secured party against most competing claims to the same collateral.

If the security interest holds up against all these attacks, the lender's lawyer has done a good job. Lawyers who represent debtors and bankruptcy trustees will try to defeat a security interest so that more assets are available for the bankruptcy estate.[4]

# 3.  Article 9 Overview

Although collateral may be either real property or personal property, this course focuses on personal property secured transactions. The law that governs such transactions is contained in UCC Article 9. Before we study the "trees" (the individual sections and official comments) in Article 9, this chapter takes a quick look at the entire "forest" (an overview of the contents of Article 9). It is easier to understand the individual Code sections by first looking at the entire forest. Also, this section introduces some key concepts that you will continue to encounter as you work with Article 9.

Although Article 9 addresses comprehensively virtually all of the issues that may arise between a borrower and a personal property secured lender, students may find it helpful to think of Article 9 as telling two stories. The first story has two characters: a borrower and a lender. The story tells how a lender makes a loan secured by personal property collateral. The plot—the sequence of events that makes up the story, begins with (1) understanding what transactions are within the scope of Article 9; and then looks at (2) how a security interest is created (attachment and enforceability). Sometimes that is the entire story! The borrower pays the loan when it is due, and the lender releases the collateral. In other situations, however, the plot continues, and the borrower defaults. Then, we must examine (3) the lender's rights upon the borrower's default (remedies); and (4) the borrower's rights if the lender fails to properly pursue its remedies after default.

In the "real world," the second story dominates the stage. The second story has a multitude of potential characters. In addition to the borrower and the lender, there may be additional lenders, sellers, buyers, providers of services, and even bankruptcy trustees. In the second story, the plot is all about conflicting claims to the same collateral, known as priority disputes. The setting for exploring the many possible priority disputes is often a bankruptcy court.

The second story is more complex. Initially it follows the same plot. Then it explodes right after the lender obtains a security interest in the borrower's collateral. In anticipation of possible conflicting third party claims, the lender must take appropriate action to "perfect" its security interest.

Not every secured transaction requires telling the second story. However, experienced lawyers know that when they help structure loan transactions, they need to consider the second story, which means they must pay close attention to properly perfecting the lender's security interest. For example, (1) the borrower might contract with more than one lender, and grant each a security interest in the same collateral; (2) the borrower might sell the collateral to a third party and fail to pay the proceeds of the sale over to the lender; or (3) the borrower might experience significant financial difficulties and file for relief under the Federal Bankruptcy Code. Even where there are no competing secured parties, a borrower can use the bankruptcy process to avoid a lender's security interest, placing

---

4. We will study the acid test of bankruptcy in Chapter 11.

its claim on a par with the claims of unsecured trade creditors. Practitioners sometimes call this thought process considering "the parade of horribles." To properly represent a lender client, attorneys must be sure that the lender's position is protected, to the extent possible under the law, regardless of whether any of the "horribles" occurs.

In this book, we will first consider the first story, starring the borrower and the lender. Next, we will move to the second story and study how to perfect a security interest; and then we will consider the priority disputes that can arise between a lender and a variety of third parties who may assert conflicting claims to the same collateral. You will continue to use the "first story" approach until you determine that a security interest has been created. Then you will follow the "second story" approach. This "two story" approach to secured transactions will give you an opportunity to learn the basics first, and then move on to the more complex world of perfection and priority disputes.[5] In this way, you can learn the basics without being overwhelmed, and your understanding of the basics will be reinforced as we add more complex topics. You will see from the cases that are included in the text that most of the legal issues involved in both the first and second story are told in the context of a priority dispute, often in a bankruptcy court. However, this book tries to present the first story in as simple a manner as possible. Therefore, we will move relatively quickly through the material that precedes perfection and priority disputes. At that point, we will study complex and sophisticated problems that draw on everything you will have learned.

Some students prefer a "narrative" overview in the form of a list of the questions that cover all of the material. *Figure 3-1* is a list of the questions we will address, with an indication of where this book discusses those questions. You can use this series of questions as your basic outline for analyzing an Article 9 problem. Other students find it helpful to have a visual overview of the material before the in-depth study begins. *Figure 3-2* offers such a broad overview. Notice how the chart is divided into the two stories described above.

## Figure 3-1:  Question/Checklist Approach to Article 9

- Is the transaction within the **Scope** of Article 9? (*Chapter 4*)
- Characterize the **Collateral.** (*Chapter 5*)
- Has a security interest been **Created**? (*Chapter 5*)
- Has the security interest been **Perfected**? (*Chapters 7 and 8*)
- Are there any **Priority Disputes** with third parties asserting conflicting claims to the same collateral? (*Chapters 8, 9, 10 and 11*)
- Is the Debtor in **Default**? (*Chapter 6*)
- What are the Secured Party's **Remedies** after the Debtor's default? (*Chapter 6*)

---

5. It is important for students to understand that, even though we are taking this two-story approach for pedagogical purposes, in practice it is vital to perfect a security interest at creation, since the borrower's decisions about whether (and how) to default (as opposed to paying off the loan without default, so that, ostensibly, only parts (1) and (2) of the story come into play) may depend upon whether the security interest has been perfected. (And even if the borrower pays the loan back without default, lack of perfection can haunt the lender if the borrower declares bankruptcy within 90 days and the payment is not otherwise exempt from recovery as a preferential transfer.)

**Figure 3-2:  Article 9 Graphic Organizer**

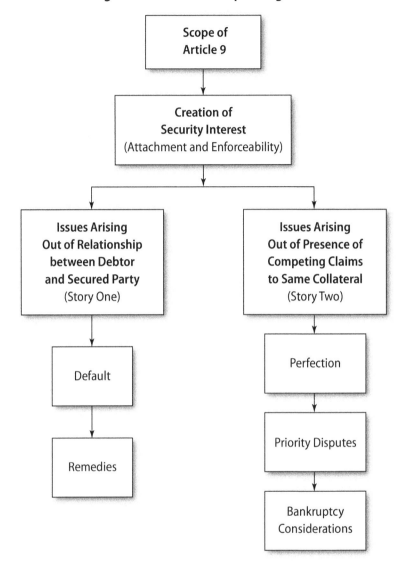

## Exercise 3-1:  Article 9 Overview

*Figure 3-1* suggests a checklist approach to Article 9, and indicates where this book addresses each topic. Keeping in mind the "two story" approach of *Figure 3-2*, complete the following table to indicate what Part of Article 9 addresses each topic.

### Story One: Secured Party and Debtor

| Topic | Article 9, Part _____ |
|---|---|
| Is the transaction within the **Scope** of Article 9? | |
| **Characterize** the Collateral. | |
| Has a security interest been **Created**? (Attachment and Enforceability) | |
| Is the Debtor in **Default**? | |
| What are the Secured Party's **Remedies** after the Debtor's default? | |

### Story Two: Secured Party and Third Party Disputes

| Topic | Article 9, Part _____ |
|---|---|
| Is the transaction within the **Scope** of Article 9? | |
| **Characterize** the Collateral. | |
| Has a security interest been **Created**? (Attachment and Enforceability) | |
| Has the security interest been **Perfected**? | |
| Are there any **Priority Disputes** with third parties asserting conflicting claims to the same collateral? (Including disputes with a trustee in bankruptcy.) | |

# Additional Resources

For a useful practice guide that provides both analysis of the Code as well as sample forms drawn from real life, check out Howard Ruda, Asset Based Financing: A Transactional Guide (Matthew Bender, 1985).

# Chapter 4

# The Scope of Article 9

Figure 4-1:  Article Graphic Organizer

```
                    ┌─────────────────┐
                    │    Scope of     │
                    │    Article 9    │
                    └────────┬────────┘
                             │
                    ┌────────▼────────────┐
                    │    Creation of      │
                    │  Security Interest  │
                    │(Attachment and      │
                    │  Enforceability)    │
                    └────────┬────────────┘
              ┌──────────────┴──────────────┐
    ┌─────────▼──────────┐       ┌──────────▼─────────┐
    │   Issues Arising   │       │   Issues Arising   │
    │ Out of Relationship│       │  Out of Presence of│
    │   between Debtor    │       │  Competing Claims  │
    │  and Secured Party  │       │  to Same Collateral│
    └─────────┬──────────┘       └──────────┬─────────┘
              │                             │
        ┌─────▼─────┐                 ┌─────▼──────┐
        │  Default  │                 │ Perfection │
        └─────┬─────┘                 └─────┬──────┘
              │                             │
        ┌─────▼─────┐                 ┌─────▼──────────┐
        │ Remedies  │                 │ Priority Disputes│
        └───────────┘                 └─────┬──────────┘
                                            │
                                      ┌─────▼──────────┐
                                      │   Bankruptcy   │
                                      │ Considerations │
                                      └────────────────┘
```

## Chapter Problem

---

**INTRA-OFFICE MEMORANDUM**

**Date:**       September 13
**To:**         Ann Associate
**From:**       Ima Partner
**Subject:**    AllNationsCredit (ANC)

We represent AllNationsCredit (ANC) in connection with a dispute arising out of a transaction between ANC and BigBuyer (BIG) that arose in connection with BIG's acquisition of nearly $10 million of commercial telecommunications transmission equipment ("Equipment"). To finance the purchase of the Equipment, BIG entered into a written agreement entitled "lease" with ANC ("Agreement"). In broad terms, the Agreement provided that ANC would first purchase approximately $9.8 million worth of the Equipment, as assignee of BIG's interest in the purchase agreement governing its Equipment acquisition, and then lease the Equipment to BIG for use in BIG's fiber optic telecommunications system.

In its relevant articles, the Agreement provided that the Basic Term of the lease would run for 84 months. BIG would pay monthly rental payments of $122,895.89 for the first forty-one months, $147,687.63 for months forty-two through fifty-two, and $150,169.31 for the remaining months of the Basic Term, not including applicable sales taxes (for which BIG was responsible). The Agreement thus contemplated that over the Basic Term of the lease, BIG would pay approximately $11.5 million in rental payments. Upon expiration of the Basic Term after 84 months, the Agreement provided that BIG could either: (1) renew the lease for an additional 12-month term at a monthly rent of $135,518.09, for a total payment of $1,638,217.08 over that additional term ("Basic Term Renewal Option"); or (2) purchase the Equipment for a purchase price equal to the greater of the fair-market value of the Equipment and 15% of the total acquisition cost of the Equipment ("Basic Term Purchase Option"). The Agreement further stated that in the absence of written notice from BIG expressing its intention to exercise the Basic Term Purchase Option, BIG would be presumed to have exercised the Renewal Option. If BIG exercised, or was deemed to have exercised, the Renewal Option, the Agreement provided that BIG could, at the end of the 12-month Renewal Term, either: (1) purchase the equipment for fair-market value ("Renewal Term Purchase Option"); or (2) return the equipment to ANC and end the contractual relationship ("Renewal Term Return Option").

BIG contends that the Agreement is not a true lease, as the Agreement defines itself, but rather a disguised security arrangement. I understand that if BIG is correct, Article 9 of the UCC will govern this dispute. Therefore, to determine what body of law governs the analysis of this dispute, I need you to determine whether BIG is correct.

---

# Code Sections[1]

1-201(b)(35), 1-203, 9-102(a)(2), 9-102(a)(5), 9-102(a)(11), 9-102(a)(20), 9-102(a)(61), 9-102(a)(65), 9-109, 9-110

# 1.  The Importance of Analyzing Scope

To analyze a legal problem, the first thing a lawyer should do is determine the body of law that provides the appropriate rules for the analysis. It is a rare client who walks into a lawyer's office and says, "Hello, I have an Article 9 problem!" Accordingly, our study of Article 9 begins by studying the scope of Article 9: *i.e.*, when does Article 9 govern the legal analysis of a specific problem? As you learned in Chapter 2, many statutes contain a "scope" section that helps a lawyer determine whether the statutes apply to the problem at hand. UCC Article 9 is no exception. Section 9-109 is Article 9's basic scope section. As *Figure 4-2* on the next page illustrates, section 9-109 divides transactions into (1) those that are specifically governed by Article 9; (2) those that are specifically excluded from the scope of Article 9; and (3) those to which Article 9 applies only to a limited extent. In Chapter 2, you saw a simple think-aloud application of section 9-109; a full "scope" analysis requires students to "link up" a number of other code sections. Students must also study the code sections referenced above.

# 2.  The Basic Scope Rule

When Article 9 was first written, it represented a dramatic change in the law governing personal property security. Before the enactment of Article 9, a wide range of state laws governed voluntary liens on personal property, and each type of security device had a different name and a different mechanism for creation and enforcement of those liens.[2] In place of that body of law, Article 9 created a comprehensive scheme for regulating security interests in personal property and fixtures. Section 9-109 both defines the types of transactions that are within Article 9's scope and identifies transactions that are outside of that scope. Legal analysis should dispose of scope and exclusions in one or two sentences unless an issue is presented. If the issue is presented, it deserves full analysis. Section 9-109 breaks the scope analysis into three parts: included transactions,

---

1. Commencing with this chapter, in all of the remaining chapters of this book you will find a list of code sections immediately after the Chapter Problem. This list is intended to identify the most important sections that you need to consult as you solve the problems in a particular chapter. Students should read all of the identified code sections, (even when the list is quite long) and the official comments to those code sections, before proceeding to work through the remaining material in the chapter. A more complete list of both the primary and secondary code sections pertaining to the major topics in Article 9 is contained in Appendix I, An Abbreviated Roadmap to Article 9.

2. Like the Official Comments to the 2010 text of Article 9, this text dwells very little on the pre-UCC state of the law. However, because the older terms still crop up from time to time, students may want to familiarize themselves with the major types of pre-Code security devices. A glossary of these terms is included in Appendix E.

## Figure 4-2:  Section 9-109 Deconstructed

| Applicable | (Exclusions) Not Applicable | Limited Applicability |
|---|---|---|
| • Security Interests<br>• Sale of<br>  • Accounts<br>  • Chattel paper<br>  • Promissory Notes<br>• Consignments<br>• Agricultural Liens<br>• Secured Obligations | • Liens<br>  • Landlord<br>  • Statutory<br>• Sale of<br>  • Accounts, chattel paper, payment intangibles, or promissory notes<br>    • If their sale is part of a sale of the business out of which they arose<br>• Assignment of<br>  • Accounts, chattel paper, payment intangibles, or promissory notes<br>    • If assigned to an assignee for the purpose of collection only<br>    • If only a single account, payment intangible or promissory note was assigned to an assignee for full or partial satisfaction of a preexisting debt<br>• Claims<br>  • For wages, salary, or other compensation<br>  • Arising out of tort, other than commercial tort<br>  • Health insurance<br>• A Right<br>  • To payment under a contract if assigned to an assignee that is also obligated to perform under the contract<br>  • Represented by a judgment, other than a judgment taken on a right to payment that was collateral<br>• Deposit accounts<br>  • If the assignment was in a consumer transaction<br>• Creation or transfers of interests in real property | • *Does not apply* to the extent that<br>  • Federal law preempts<br>  • State statute expressly governs<br>  • Statute of another state or foreign nation expressly governs<br>• *Applies with respect to*<br>  • Priority<br>    • Statutory Lien<br>  • Proceeds & Priority in Proceeds<br>    • Health insurance claims<br>    • Assignment of tort claims<br>    • Deposit accounts in a consumer transaction<br>• Real property provisions regarding<br>  • § 9-203 & § 9-308 Liens<br>  • § 9-334 Fixtures<br>  • Part 5 Fixture Filings<br>  • § 9-604 Security Agreements |

excluded transactions, and transactions to which Article 9 applies to only a limited extent. This Chapter introduces the primary included transactions, as well as the exclusions that are most frequently at issue. It does not illustrate every single provision of section 9-109.

## 2.1 Included Transactions

Section 9-109(a) identifies included transactions. The general rule is that Article 9 applies to "a transaction, regardless of its form, that creates a security interest in personal property or fixtures by contract." In other words, Article 9 applies when someone has granted a consensual lien to another.[3] In addition, section 9-109(a) lists five other transactions that are within the scope of Article 9: (1) agricultural liens; (2) sales of accounts, chattel paper, payment intangibles or promissory notes; (3) consignments; (4) security interests arising under other certain sections of Article 2 and 2A; and (5) security interests arising under specified sections of Articles 4 and 5. *Figure 4-3* is a graphic depiction of section 9-109(a).

The starting point for identifying an included transaction is determining whether the transaction involves a security interest in personal property. Section 1-201(b)(35) defines

### Figure 4-3: Included Transactions

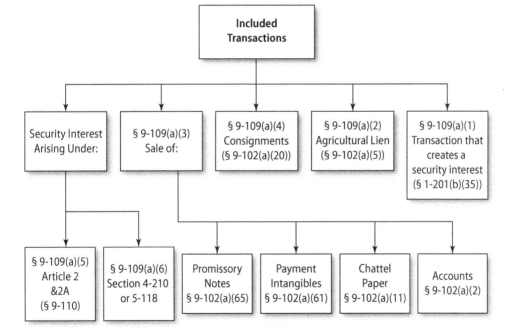

---

3. Consensual liens are different from statutory liens, which are creations of legislation, and other involuntary liens, such as judgment liens, which arise after a creditor receives a judgment in court and follows appropriate procedures to place a lien on the judgment debtor's property. Because consensual liens are voluntary liens, they will have priority in certain situations, and general debtor protections, such as homestead laws, will not affect them.

a security interest as "an interest in personal property or fixtures that secures payment or performance of an obligation." Accordingly, students must look to the substance of a transaction, rather than its form, and determine if it involves personal property collateral to secure the repayment of an obligation. If so, Article 9 will apply. The majority of transactions within the scope of Article 9 will be consensual liens such as these.

As indicated above, Article 9 also encompasses a variety of transactions that do not involve consensual liens. Specifically, Article 9 applies to some security interests that arise by operation of law under other state laws and under other articles of the UCC. Not all of the general rules we study in Chapter 5 on creating security interests apply to such liens; however, other Article 9 rules such as rules on perfection and priority may apply. We will consider these rules in later chapters of this book.

---

### Exercise 4-1:  Applying Section 9-109(a)

Determine whether the following transactions are governed by Article 9 of the Uniform Commercial Code:

1. D, a dentist, borrows $10,000 from C. To induce C to make the loan, D agrees that her dental equipment will be collateral for the loan (*i.e.*, if D defaults on her obligation to repay the loan, C may take possession of the equipment, sell it, and use the proceeds of the sale to repay the loan).

2. Same as transaction 1, except that the collateral is D's house in Port Washington.

3. D would like to buy a new dental chair, but does not have the ability to pay the $4,800 purchase price in cash. S, the seller of the dental chair, agrees to allow D to pay the $4,800 in 12 monthly installments of $400 each, on the condition that S retain title to the chair (*i.e.*, S will not deliver a bill of sale transferring the chair to D) until the full $4,800 is paid. D takes possession of the chair.

4. D is owed $50,000 by her patients for dental work that has already been performed. She borrows $40,000 from F. As part of the transaction, it is agreed that the loan will be secured by the money owed D by her patients.

5. Same as transaction 4, except that D sells her rights to be paid by her patients for the work already performed to F for $40,000.

6. D rents a car from H for five days at a rate of $39.95 per day.

7. D leases a car from P. Pursuant to the terms of the contract, D will pay P $500 per month for 48 months. At the end of the 48-month period, D becomes the owner of the car.

8. Same as transaction 7, except that D has an option to purchase the car from P for $25 at the end of the 48-month lease term.

9. Same as transaction 7, except D has the right to terminate the lease at any time.

10. D leases a car from P. Pursuant to the terms of the contract, D will pay P $500 per month for 48 months. At the end of the 48-month period, the contract provides that D may (i) buy the car from P for its fair market value as determined by an appraisal; (ii) return the car; or (iii) enter into a second 48-month lease of the car (for $350 per month), at the conclusion of which D automatically becomes the owner of the car.

11. D sells her entire dental practice to Z. Among the assets sold by D are her claims against patients for dental work that has been performed but not paid for.

---

In certain circumstances, Article 9 applies to transactions that are structured as outright sales. Specifically, sales of accounts and chattel paper have been included in the scope of Article 9 since its inception (and sales of payment intangibles and promissory notes since the 2000 revision of Article 9 became effective) due to their similar use in the world of finance. One business owner might finance her needs for operating capital by borrowing money from a lender, secured by an assignment of her accounts receivable. Another business owner might sell her receivables outright as a source of cash. To protect a lender from an unscrupulous owner who might try to use the same receivables as a source of cash, Article 9 requires compliance with Article 9 rules in both cases.

Another transaction that does not immediately appear to involve a classic security interest is a consignment. Article 9 specifically provides that certain types of consignments are now subject to Article 9 rules. In a consignment, the owner of goods (the consignor) delivers physical possession of the goods to another party (the consignee) who holds them for sale to third parties. When the consignee sells the goods, he remits the proceeds (less an agreed upon amount) to the consignor. If the goods are not sold, the consignee can return them to the consignor without liability. Consignments have always created a problem, in that creditors of the consignee may view the consignor's goods as the consignee's property. By subjecting consignments to Article 9 rules, the Code allows the same perfection and priority rules to govern these transactions.

---

## Exercise 4-2: Consignments

Read section 9-102(a)(20). Explain why a consignment might mislead a consignee's creditors about the extent of the consignee's assets. Develop a checklist to determine whether or not a transaction is a consignment subject to Article 9.

---

One of the persistent scope problems students and lawyers face is distinguishing between a transaction that is properly characterized as a sale of goods with a security interest created by the seller's retention of title, and therefore governed by Article 9, and a transaction that is a "true lease," and therefore governed by Article 2A. Section 1-203 provides some bright-line tests for making this determination; nevertheless, even if a lease is not clearly a security agreement under those tests, courts must still evaluate all the facts and circumstances of a particular transaction to determine if the putative lessor has retained a meaningful reversionary interest in the goods.

---

## Exercise 4-3: *In the Matter of Marhoefer Packing Company, Inc.*

Read the following decision of the Seventh Circuit Court of Appeals. As discussed in Chapter 3, this decision arose out of an appeal from a bankruptcy court proceeding, where the trustee in bankruptcy challenged a creditor's claim to certain equipment. The creditor claimed that it had leased the equipment to the debtor and was therefore entitled to its return. The trustee claimed that the "lease" was in fact a disguised sale with a retained security interest (*i.e.*, a secured transaction), and that the lessor had failed to take the necessary action to protect its security interest in the event of bankruptcy. The case has been edited to highlight the scope issue. Note that the case was decided under an earlier version of the Code. Compare revised section 1-203 to former section 1-201(37), which is set forth in the body of the opinion. As you read the case, consider the following questions:

1. According to the court, what are the criteria for determining whether a transaction is a "true lease" or a sale with a security device? How do these criteria differ under the revised Code?

2. How important is the presence or absence of an option to purchase to that determination?

3. What "other facts" should be taken into account to make that determination?

4. Do you think the decision in this case would change if revised section 1-203 were applied to these facts?

---

# In the Matter of Marhoefer Packing Company, Inc., Bankrupt, Appeal of Robert Reiser & Company, Inc., Creditor

## 674 F.2d 1139 (7th Cir. 1982)

Before PELL, SPRECHER and WOOD, Circuit Judges.

PELL, Circuit Judge.

This appeal involves a dispute between the trustee of the bankrupt Marhoefer Packing Company, Inc., ("Marhoefer") and Robert Reiser & Company, Inc., ("Reiser") over certain equipment held by Marhoefer at the time of bankruptcy. The issue presented is whether the written agreement between Marhoefer and Reiser covering the equipment is a true lease..., or whether it is actually a lease intended as security ...

I

In December of 1976, Marhoefer Packing Co., Inc., of Muncie, Indiana, entered into negotiations with Reiser, a Massachusetts based corporation engaged in the business of selling and leasing food processing equipment, for the acquisition of one or possibly two Vemag Model 3007-1 Continuous Sausage Stuffers. Reiser informed Marhoefer that the units could be acquired by outright purchase, conditional sale contract or lease. Marhoefer ultimately acquired two sausage stuffers from Reiser. It purchased one under a conditional sale contract. Pursuant to the contract, Reiser retained a security interest in the machine, which it subsequently perfected by filing a financing statement with the Indiana Secretary of State. Title to that stuffer is not here in dispute. The other stuffer was delivered to Marhoefer under a written "Lease Agreement."

The Lease Agreement provided for monthly payments of $665.00 over a term of 48 months. The last nine months payments, totaling $5,985.00, were payable upon execution of the lease. If at the end of the lease term the machine was to be returned, it was to be shipped prepaid to Boston or similar destination "in the same condition as when received, reasonable wear and tear resulting from proper use alone excepted, and fully crated."

In a letter accompanying the lease, Reiser added two option provisions to the agreement. The first provided that at the end of the four-year term, Marhoefer could purchase the stuffer for $9,968.00. In the alternative, it could elect to renew the lease for an additional four years at an annual rate of $2,990.00, payable in advance. At the conclusion of the second four-year term, Marhoefer would be allowed to purchase the stuffer for one dollar.

Following a trial on this issue, the bankruptcy court concluded that the agreement between Marhoefer and Reiser was in fact a true lease.... The trustee appealed to the district court, which reversed on the ground that the bankruptcy court had erred as a matter of law in finding the agreement to be a true lease. We now reverse the judgment of the district court.

## II

The dispute in this case centers on section 1-201(37) of the Uniform Commercial Code, I.C. 26-1-1-201. [Section 1-201(37) of the Uniform Commercial Code states: "'Security interest' means an interest in personal property or fixtures which secures payment or performance of an obligation.... Unless a lease or consignment is intended as security, reservation of title thereunder is not a 'security interest' but a consignment is in any event subject to the provisions on consignment sales. Whether a lease is intended as security is to be determined by the facts of each case; however, (a) the inclusion of an option, to purchase does not of itself make the lease one intended for security, and (b) an agreement that upon compliance with the terms of the lease the lessee shall become or has the option to become the owner of the property for no additional consideration or for a nominal consideration does make the lease one intended for security.] In applying this section, the bankruptcy court concluded that "the presence of the option to renew the lease for an additional four years and to acquire the Vemag Stuffer at the conclusion of the second four-year term by the payment of One Dollar ($1.00) did not, in and of itself, make the lease one intended for security."

The district court disagreed. It held that the presence of an option to purchase the stuffer for one dollar gave rise to a conclusive presumption under clause (b) of section 1-201(37) that the lease was intended as security. Although it acknowledged that the option to purchase the stuffer for only one dollar would not have come into play unless Marhoefer chose to renew the lease for an additional four-year term, the district court concluded that this fact did not require a different result. "It would be anomalous," said the court, "to rule that the lease was a genuine lease for four years after its creation but was one intended for security eight years after its creation."

Reiser, relying on Peter F. Coogan's detailed analysis of section 1-201(37), Coogan, Hogan & Vagts, Secured Transactions Under the Uniform Commercial Code, ch. 4A, (1981) (hereinafter "Secured Transactions Under UCC"), argues that the district court erred in construing clause (b) of that section as creating a conclusive presumption that a lease is intended as security where the lease contains an option for the lessee to become the owner of the leased property for no additional consideration or for only nominal consideration. It contends that by interpreting clause (b) in this way, the district court totally ignored the first part of that sentence which states that "(w)hether a lease is intended as security is to be determined by the facts of each case." Reiser claims that because the totality of facts surrounding the transaction indicate that the lease was not intended as security, notwithstanding the presence of the option to purchase the stuffer for one dollar, the district court erred in reversing the bankruptcy court's determination.

We agree that the district court erred in concluding that because the Lease Agreement contained an option for Marhoefer to purchase the Vemag stuffer at the end of a second four-year term, it was conclusively presumed to be a lease intended as security. However, in our view, the district court's error lies not in its reading of clause (b) of section 1-201(37) as giving rise to such a presumption, but rather in its conclusion that clause (b) applies under the facts of this case.

(1) The primary issue to be decided in determining whether a lease is "intended as security" is whether it is in effect a conditional sale in which the "lessor" retains an interest in the "leased" goods as security for the purchase price. 1C Secured Transactions Under UCC § 29A.05(1)(C), p. 2939. By defining the term "security interest" to include a lease intended as security, the drafters of the Code intended such disguised security interests to be governed by the same rules that apply to other security interests. See UCC, Art. 9. In this respect, section 1-201(37) represents the drafter's refusal to recognize form over substance.

(2) Clearly, where a lease is structured so that the lessee is contractually bound to pay rent over a set period of time at the conclusion of which he automatically or for only nominal consideration becomes the owner of the leased goods, the transaction is in substance a conditional sale and should be treated as such. It is to this type of lease that clause (b) properly applies. Here, however, Marhoefer was under no contractual obligation to pay rent until such time as the option to purchase the Vemag stuffer for one dollar was to arise. In fact, in order to acquire that option, Marhoefer would have had to exercise its earlier option to renew the lease for a second four-year term and pay Reiser an additional $11,960 in "rent." In effect, Marhoefer was given a right to terminate the agreement after the first four years and cease making payments without that option ever becoming operative.

Despite this fact, the district court concluded as a matter of law that the lease was intended as security. It held that, under clause (b) of section 1-201(37), a lease containing an option for the lessee to purchase the leased goods for nominal consideration is conclusively presumed to be one intended as security. This presumption applies, the court concluded, regardless of any other options the lease may contain.

We think the district court's reading of clause (b) is in error. In our view, the conclusive presumption provided under clause (b) applies only where the option to purchase for nominal consideration necessarily arises upon compliance with the lease. See 1C Secured Transactions Under UCC s 29.05(2)(b) pp. 2947-49. It does not apply where the lessee has the right to terminate the lease before that option arises with no further obligation to continue paying rent. But see In re Vaillancourt, supra, 7 UCCRep. 748; In re Royers Bakery, Inc., 1 UCCRep. 342 (Bankr.E.D.Pa.1963). For where the lessee has the right to terminate the transaction, it is not a conditional sale.

Moreover, to hold that a lease containing such an option is intended as security, even though the lessee has no contractual obligation to pay the full amount contemplated by the agreement, would lead to clearly erroneous results under other provisions of the Code. Under section 9-506 of the Code, for example, a debtor in default on his obligation to a secured party has a right to redeem the collateral by tendering full payment of that obligation. The same right is also enjoyed by a lessee under a lease intended as security. A lessee who defaults on a lease intended as security is entitled to purchase the leased goods by paying the full amount of his obligation under the lease. But if the lessee has the right to terminate the lease at any time during the lease term, his obligation under the lease may be only a small part of the total purchase price of the goods leased. To afford the lessee a right of redemption under such circumstances would clearly be wrong. There is no evidence that the drafters of the Code intended such a result.

We therefore hold that while section 1-201(37)(b) does provide a conclusive test of when a lease is intended as security, that test does not apply in every case in which the disputed lease contains an option to purchase for nominal or no consideration. An option of this type makes a lease one intended as security only when it necessarily arises upon compliance with the terms of the lease.

(3) Applying section 1-201(37), so construed, to the facts of this case, it is clear that the district court erred in concluding that the possibility of Marhoefer's purchasing the stuffer for one dollar at the conclusion of a second four-year term was determinative. Because Marhoefer could have fully complied with the lease without that option ever arising, the district court was mistaken in thinking that the existence of that option alone made the lease a conditional sale. Certainly, if Marhoefer had elected to renew the lease for another term, in which case the nominal purchase option would necessarily have arisen, then the clause (b) test would apply. [Reiser concedes that had Marhoefer elected to renew the lease after the first term, the transaction would have been transformed into a sale. George Vetie, Reiser's treasurer, testified that the renewal option was actually intended as a financing mechanism to allow Marhoefer to purchase the stuffer at the end of the lease if it desired to do so but was either unable or unwilling to pay the initial purchase price of $9,968.] But that is not the case we are faced with here. Marhoefer was not required to make any payments beyond the first four years. The fact that, at the conclusion of that term, it could have elected to renew the lease and obtain an option to purchase the stuffer for one dollar at the end of the second term does not transform the original transaction into a conditional sale. This fact does not end our inquiry under clause (b), however, for the trustee also argues that, even if the district court erred in considering the one dollar purchase option as determinative, the lease should nevertheless be considered a conditional sale because the initial option price of $9,968 is also nominal when all of the operative facts are properly considered. We agree that if the clause (b) test is to apply at all in this case, this is the option that must be considered. For this is the option that was to arise automatically upon Marhoefer's compliance with the lease. We do not agree, however, that under the circumstances presented here the $9,968 option price can properly be considered nominal. It is true that an option price may be more than a few dollars and still be considered nominal within the meaning of section 1-201(37). Because clause (b) speaks of nominal "consideration" and not a nominal "sum" or "amount," it has been held to apply not only where the option price is very small in absolute terms, but also where the price is insubstantial in relation to the fair market value of the leased goods at the time the option arises.

The trustee argues that the determination of whether the option price is nominal is to be made by comparing it to the fair market value of the equipment at the time the parties enter into the lease, instead of the date the option arises. Although some courts have applied such a test, the better approach is to compare the option price with the fair market value of the goods at the time the option was to be exercised.

Here, however, the evidence revealed that the initial option price of $9,968 was not nominal even under this standard. George Vetie, Reiser's treasurer and the person chiefly responsible for the terms of the lease, testified at trial that the purchase price for the Vemag stuffer at the time the parties entered into the transaction was $33,225. He testified that the initial option price of $9,968 was arrived at by taking thirty percent of the purchase price, which was what he felt a four-year-old Vemag stuffer would be worth based on Reiser's past experience.

The trustee, relying on the testimony of its expert appraiser, argues that in fact the stuffer would have been worth between eighteen and twenty thousand dollars at the end of the first four-year term. Because the initial option price is substantially less than this amount, he claims that it is nominal within the meaning of clause (b) and the lease is therefore one intended as security.

Even assuming this appraisal to be accurate, an issue on which the bankruptcy court made no finding, we would not find the initial option price of $9,968 so small by comparison that the clause (b) presumption would apply. While it is difficult to state any bright line percentage test for determining when an option price could properly be considered nominal as compared to the fair market value of the leased goods, an option price of almost ten thousand dollars, which amounts to fifty percent of the fair market value, is not nominal by any standard.

Furthermore, in determining whether an option price is nominal, the proper figure to compare it with is not the actual fair market value of the leased goods at the time the option arises, but their fair market value at that time as anticipated by the parties when the lease is signed. Here, for example, Vetie testified that his estimate of the fair market value of a four-year-old Vemag stuffer was based on records from a period of time in which the economy was relatively stable. Since that time, a high rate of inflation has caused the machines to lose their value more slowly. As a result, the actual fair market value of a machine may turn out to be significantly more than the parties anticipated it would be several years earlier. When this occurs, the lessee's option to purchase the leased goods may be much more favorable than either party intended, but it does not change the true character of the transaction.

We conclude, therefore, that neither option to purchase contained in the lease between Marhoefer and Reiser gives rise to a conclusive presumption under section 1-201(37)(b) that the lease is one intended as security. This being so, we now turn to the other facts surrounding the transaction.

III

Although section 1-201(37) states that "(w)hether a lease is intended as security is to be determined by the facts of each case," it is completely silent as to what facts, other than the option to purchase, are to be considered in making that determination. Facts that the courts have found relevant include the total amount of rent the lessee is required to pay under the lease, whether the lessee acquires any equity in the leased property, the useful life of the leased goods, the nature of the lessor's business, and the payment of taxes, insurance and other charges normally imposed on ownership. Consideration of the facts of this case in light of these factors leads us to conclude that the lease in question was not intended as security.

First, Marhoefer was under no obligation to pay the full purchase price for the stuffer. Over the first four-year term, its payments under the lease were to have amounted to $31,920. Although this amount may not be substantially less than the original purchase price of $33,225 in absolute terms, it becomes so when one factors in the interest rate over four years that would have been charged had Marhoefer elected to purchase the machine under a conditional sale contract. The fact that the total amount of rent Marhoefer was to pay under the lease was substantially less than that amount shows that a sale was not intended.

It is also significant that the useful life of the Vemag stuffer exceeded the term of the lease. An essential characteristic of a true lease is that there be something of value to return to the lessor after the term. Where the term of the lease is substantially equal to the life of the leased property such that there will be nothing of value to return at the end of the lease, the transaction is in essence a sale. Here, the evidence revealed that the useful life of a Vemag stuffer was eight to ten years.

Finally, the bankruptcy court specifically found that "there was no express or implied provision in the lease agreement dated February 28, 1977, which gave Marhoefer any equity interest in the leased Vemag stuffer." This fact clearly reveals the agreement between Marhoefer and Reiser to be a true lease. Had Marhoefer remained solvent and elected not to exercise its option to renew its lease with Reiser, it would have received nothing for its previous lease payments. And in order to exercise that option, Marhoefer would have had to pay what Reiser anticipated would then be the machine's fair market value. An option of this kind is not the mark of a lease intended as security.

Although Marhoefer was required to pay state and local taxes and the cost of repairs, this fact does not require a contrary result. Costs such as taxes, insurance and repairs are necessarily borne by one party or the other. They reflect less the true character of the transaction than the strength of the parties' respective bargaining positions. See also Rainier National Bank, supra, 631 P.2d at 395 ("The lessor is either going to include those costs within the rental charge or agree to a lower rent if the lessee takes responsibility for them.").

IV

We conclude from the foregoing that the district court erred in its application of section 1-201(37) of the Uniform Commercial Code to the facts of this case. Neither the option to purchase the Vemag stuffer for one dollar at the conclusion of a second four-year term, nor the initial option to purchase it for $9,968 after the first four years, gives rise to a conclusive presumption under clause (b) of section 1-201(37) that the lease is intended as security. From all of the facts surrounding the transaction, we conclude that the agreement between Marhoefer and Reiser is a true lease. The judgment of the district court is therefore reversed.

## 2.2 Excluded Transactions

Section 9-109(d) lists thirteen transactions that are excluded from its scope. Several exclusions limit the breadth of the scope provision that would otherwise include the sale of accounts, chattel paper, payment intangibles or promissory notes. For example, sections 9-109(d)(4) and (5) except an assignment of such assets as part of the sale of a business out of which they arose or that is made for purposes of collection only. Official Comment 12 explains that these transactions are excluded because "by their nature, [they] do not concern commercial financing transactions." Regardless of whether your initial application of section 9-109(a) suggests that Article 9 will apply, be sure to double check against the exclusions in section 9-109(d).

For most commercial loan transactions, it is enough to know that (i) security interests in real property, including security interests in leases or rents (but not promissory notes that are themselves secured by real estate), are governed by real property law; (ii) if another state statute governs the creation, perfection, priority, or enforcement of a security interest created by the state, those security interests are excluded from the scope of Article 9; (iii) security interests in insurance policies are not subject to Article 9 under the law of most states[4] — and in some states, such as New York, contracts for annuities, including variable annuities, are expressly excluded from the operation of Article 9.

---

4. In most states, the creation and perfection of a security interest in an insurance policy is governed by common law; however, some states, such as California, include insurance policies within the scope of Article 9 (in California, Division 9). This difference highlights the importance of doing state-specific research rather than relying on the Uniform Commercial Code, when you are in practice.

## 2.3 Transactions to Which Article 9 Applies to a Limited Extent Only

Unlike the transactions listed in section 9-109(d), which are totally excluded from Article 9's scope, some transactions are governed both by other laws to the extent that those other laws so provide, and by Article 9 to a more limited extent. Security interests in certain types of property (such as ships, aircraft, railcars, copyrights, trademarks and patents) are governed, at least to some extent, by federal law. Security interest granted by governmental units may be governed by statutes other than the UCC. Applicable federal law may address issues of creation and perfection, but not other issues, such as issues of priority. Similarly, certain statutory liens that arise by operation of state law may not be governed by Article 9's creation rules, but are covered by its priority rules.

# 3. Other Bodies of Law Applicable to Secured Transactions

Although this course concentrates on UCC Article 9, students should be aware of some of the other bodies of law that may be applicable. First, where Article 9 does not specifically displace common law, principles of law and equity supplement its provisions.[5] Second, as discussed above, some "transactions" are true leases, whose analysis is now governed by Uniform Commercial Code Article 2A. Third, as indicated above, applicable federal law will supersede otherwise applicable provisions of the UCC in some instances and supplement the UCC in others.

Finally, UCC section 9-201(b) provides generally that a transaction subject to Article 9 remains subject to any applicable consumer protection laws.[6] This course is limited to the UCC, however, and, while many of the examples and exercises in this text involve consumer transactions, they are presented, and should be understood and analyzed, as if no law other than the UCC applied. An attorney representing a creditor in the documentation of a consumer loan, on the other hand, should take care to learn, and to comply with, the consumer protection regime applicable to the jurisdiction in which she practices.

---

5. UCC § 1-103.

6. In California, for example, consumers are entitled to the protection of several laws, among them the Retail Installment Sales Act ("Unruh Act"), California Civil Code Sections 1801-1812.20; The Automobile Sales Finance Act ("Rees-Levering Act"), Civil Code Sections 2981-2984.5; the Manufactured Housing Act of 1980, California Health & Safety Code Sections 18000-18153; and the California Finance Lenders Law, California Financial Code Sections 22000-22780. One provision of the Unruh Act, for example—Section 1804.3(a)—provides that no contract subject to that Act, except a contract for services, "shall provide for a security interest in any goods theretofore paid for or which have not been sold by the seller." Federal consumer protection law likewise provides protections to which the UCC is subject. FDIC Rule AA, for example, applicable to national banks, 12 CFR 227, at Section 227.17(d), declares that it is "an unfair act or practice for a bank to enter into a consumer credit obligation that contains, or to enforce in a consumer credit obligation purchased by the bank," a provision that creates "[a] nonpossessory security interest in household goods other than a purchase money security interest."

As you can see, in practice a lawyer cannot confine her analysis of a secured transactions problem to the Uniform Commercial Code.

# Additional Resources

Erwin S. Barbre, J.D., Annotation, *Equipment leases as security interest within Uniform Commercial Code § 1–201(37)*, 76 A.L.R.3d 11 (1977).

Richard L. Barnes, *Distinguishing Sales and Leases: A Primer on the Scope and Purpose of UCC Article 2A*, 25 U. Mem. L. Rev. 873, 891 (1995).

Ronald M. Bayer, *Personal Property Leasing: Article 2A of the Uniform Commercial Code*, 43 Bus. Law. 1491, 1498 (1988).

Penelope L. Christophorou, Kenneth C. Kettering, Lynn A. Soukup, and Steven O. Weise, *Under the Surface of Revised Article 9: Selected Variations in State Enactments from the Official Text of Revised Article 9*, 34 UCC L. J. 331 (2002).

Penelope L. Christophorou, Kenneth C. Kettering, Lynn A. Soukup, and Steven O. Weise, *Analysis of State Variations*, 34 UCC L. J. 358 (2002).

Barkley Clark, *Revised Article 9 of the UCC: Scope, Perfection, Priorities, and Default*, 4 N.C. Banking Inst. 129, 180 (2000).

Michael W. Gaines, *Security Interest Confusion in the Leasing Arena*, 18 Stetson L. Rev. 69, 69 (1988).

Edwin E. Huddleson, *Old Wine in New Bottles: UCC Article 2A — Leases*, 39 Ala. L. Rev. 615, 623–39 (1988).

David A. Lander, *Understanding the Expanded Scope of Revised Article 9 of the UCC*, 2000 No. 9 Norton Bankr. L. Adviser 1 (Sept. 2000).

J. P. Ludington & A. L. Schwartz, Annotation, *Construction and effect of UCC art 9, dealing with secured transactions, sales of accounts, contract rights, and chattel paper*, 30 A.L.R.3d 9 (1970).

C. Scott Pryor, *Revised Uniform Commercial Code Article 9: Impact in Bankruptcy*, 7 Am. Bankr. Inst. L. Rev. 465, 465 n. 5 (1999).

C. Scott Pryor, *How Revised Article 9 will turn the trustee's strong-arm into a weak finger: A potpourri of cases*, 9 Am. Bankr. Inst. L. Rev. 229 (2001).

Edwin E. Smith, *Overview of Revised Article 9*, 73 Am. Bankr. L.J. 1, 53 (1999).

Gary D. Spivey, J.D., Annotation, *Consignment Transactions Under Uniform Commercial Code Article 9 on Secured Transactions*, 58 A.L.R. 6th 289 (2010).

John F. Wagner, Jr., J.D., Annotation, *Applicability of Article 9 of Uniform Commercial Code to assignment of rights under real-estate sales contract, lease agreement, or mortgage as collateral for separate transaction*, 76 A.L.R.4th 765 (1989).

# Chapter 5

# Creation of Security Interest

**Figure 5-1: Article Graphic Organizer**

```
                    ┌──────────────────┐
                    │   Scope of       │
                    │   Article 9      │
                    └──────────────────┘
                             │
                             ▼
                ┌───────────────────────────┐
                │    Creation of            │
                │    Security Interest      │
                │ (Attachment and           │
                │  Enforceability)          │
                └───────────────────────────┘
                             │
              ┌──────────────┴──────────────┐
              ▼                              ▼
   ┌────────────────────┐        ┌────────────────────┐
   │ Issues Arising     │        │ Issues Arising     │
   │ Out of Relationship│        │ Out of Presence of │
   │ between Debtor     │        │ Competing Claims   │
   │ and Secured Party  │        │ to Same Collateral │
   └────────────────────┘        └────────────────────┘
              │                              │
              ▼                              ▼
      ┌──────────────┐              ┌──────────────┐
      │   Default    │              │  Perfection  │
      └──────────────┘              └──────────────┘
              │                              │
              ▼                              ▼
      ┌──────────────┐              ┌──────────────────┐
      │   Remedies   │              │ Priority Disputes│
      └──────────────┘              └──────────────────┘
                                             │
                                             ▼
                                    ┌──────────────────┐
                                    │   Bankruptcy     │
                                    │   Considerations │
                                    └──────────────────┘
```

## Chapter Problem

Carefully review the Security Agreement in Appendix B, and answer the following questions. If you cannot find a provision in the Security Agreement that answers the question, explain what information you need and what type of provision you would add to it to accomplish your purpose.

1. Which provision(s) in the Security Agreement are necessary for the creation of a security interest in the Collateral? Be sure to include an explanation of (1) how the lender will give "value," and (2) how the debtor will have "rights in the collateral." Explain fully.

2. Now carefully read paragraphs 2, 3, and 9. For each of those paragraphs explain (a) the meaning of the paragraph, and (b) why it has been included in the Security Agreement.

---

# Code Sections

1-204, 9-108, 9-201 9-203, 9-204, 9-206

# 1. Introduction

Article 9 does not have a section entitled "How to Create a Security Interest." Instead, part 2 of Article 9 uses terms like "effectiveness of a security agreement," "attachment of a security interest," and "rights of parties to the security agreement." Students should recognize that this part of Article 9 includes all of the rules they need to know regarding how to create a security interest. Importantly, it introduces new terminology and establishes the basic rules about the relationship between a borrower and a personal property secured lender. In addition to the applicable code sections, students will need to learn all of the Article 9 definitions of different types of collateral. (See *Figure 5-3*, below.)

As illustrated in the Graphic Organizer (*Figure 5-1*), to create a security interest under the UCC, you should first confirm that the transaction is governed by the rules of Article 9. (See Chapter 4, Scope.) Simply stated, an Article 9 security interest is created (comes into effect) when (1) value has been given *by the lender to the borrower* (e.g., in the commercial loan context, the lender should have entered into a loan agreement with the borrower, should have entered into a commitment to make a loan to the borrower, or should already have lent money to the borrower);[1] (2) the debtor must have rights in the collateral or the power to transfer rights in the collateral to the secured party (in general, the debtor will own the property that is to serve as collateral); and (3) there is a voluntary agreement to grant a lien (or some substitute, such as the list of identified transactions in the scope provision, section 9-109), which provides a description of the collateral. See *Figure 5-2*.

When all of these steps have taken place, section 9-203 states that the security interest is enforceable against the debtor and third parties with respect to the collateral. At that point, in proper Article 9 terminology, the security interest "attaches" to the collateral.

---

1. But note that the person granting the security interest need not be the borrower. See discussion in section 4.2, below.

**Figure 5-2: Enforceability**

```
                         ┌─────────────────────┐
                         │   Enforceability    │
                         └─────────────────────┘
                                    │
        ┌───────────────────┬───────┴──────────────┐
        ▼                   ▼                       ▼
┌───────────────┐  ┌───────────────┐   ┌─────────────────────┐
│ Value has been│  │  Debtor has   │   │ One of the following│
│    given      │  │  rights in the│   │      is met:        │
│  (§ 1-204)    │  │   collateral  │   └─────────────────────┘
└───────────────┘  └───────────────┘             │
          ┌──────────────┬─────────┴────┬──────────────┐
          ▼              ▼              ▼              ▼
   ┌────────────┐ ┌────────────┐ ┌────────────┐ ┌────────────┐
   │            │ │Collateral in│ │ Delivery of│ │ Control of │
   │  Security  │ │possession of│ │ certificated│ │  certain   │
   │  Agreement │ │Secured Party│ │  security  │ │ collateral │
   └────────────┘ └────────────┘ └────────────┘ └────────────┘
```

There are no additional requirements for a security interest to be enforceable. Once a security interest has attached, it is enforceable.

This chapter focuses on the most common method of creating a security interest: the authentication of a security agreement that provides a description of the collateral. A security agreement is simply a contract between the parties wherein the debtor "grants" a security interest in the collateral as security for the payment or performance of specified obligations. A sample security agreement is included in this book in Appendix B. The chapter then discusses how a security interest granted in a security agreement extends beyond the original collateral to proceeds of that collateral. Finally, it explains how a security interest granted by one debtor can continue to encumber collateral when the original debtor changes its legal structure, without the need for a consensual agreement with the new debtor.

# 2. Value

The first requirement for attachment of a security interest is that the lender has given value.[2] Students sometimes think that a lender can only give value by lending money to the borrower. However, a more common method of giving value is for a lender to make a commitment to lend.[3] Another common situation is when a seller, such as a car dealership, sells goods on credit and "takes back" a security interest in the product sold. In such a situation, the seller gives "value" by extending credit to the buyer. Although there is

---

2. The borrower's obligation to the lender is often evidenced by a promissory note. For a sample form of promissory note, see Appendix A.

3. The distinction is significant because it will affect the *time* of attachment and ultimately the *time* of perfection, which, as you will see, will ultimately affect priority issues. Accordingly, a lender can establish a priority in time before it is actually out-of-pocket any money at all.

generally no issue with respect to *whether* a secured party has given value, the analysis of *when* value is given may be important in analyzing some priority disputes, which will be discussed later in this book.

---

### Exercise 5-1: "Value"

In which of the following situations has a lender given "value" to a borrower?

1. Lender loans borrower $10,000.

2. Grandmother gives grandson money with which to purchase a car. No

3. Vendor sells furniture to buyer on credit. Yes

4. Jake owes Mary $500. He is unable to repay her, so he gives her his watch to hold on to until he is able to repay the loan. Yes

5. Lender agrees to lend $10,000 to borrower to be used for a specific purpose, but only after borrower satisfies certain conditions. Yes
   Subject to conditions .. ok

---

# 3. Rights in the Collateral

The second requirement for attachment of a security interest is that the debtor has rights in the collateral. Article 9 does not define "rights." At a minimum, it is understood that a debtor has "rights" in collateral when the debtor owns the collateral. This requirement often necessitates an understanding of UCC Article 2. Under Article 2, for example, a buyer of goods can have rights in goods that have been identified to a contract for sale of goods.[4] Another situation in which a debtor who does not own property has sufficient rights in the collateral to transfer an interest in it is where a debtor sells property in a transaction subject to Article 9 (*e.g.*, accounts), but the buyer fails to properly perfect its interest in the collateral acquired. In that situation, the debtor can effectively transfer that same property to a second purchaser, whose interest can take priority over the interest of the initial buyer.[5]

Under section 9-203, the security interest attaches to the collateral when all of the three requirements have been met; hence, it attaches when the last of the three events occurs. In loan transactions involving collateral owned by the debtor, the last event is usually the giving of value by the lender. In transactions where the lender (or seller) is financing the acquisition of goods, the last event is usually the debtor acquiring rights in the collateral. While a debtor generally cannot encumber another's property with the debtor's own debt, a debtor may do so under certain circumstances. For example, if the owner of property consents to the debtor using the property as collateral, the borrower has acquired sufficient rights in that property to use it as collateral under a security agreement.[6]

---

4. UCC § 2-501.

5. §9-318(b). See, *e.g.*, Thomas E. Plank, *Assignments of Receivables Under Article 9: Structural Incoherence and Wasteful Filing* 68 Ohio L.J. 231 (2007).

6. The owner will then be a "debtor" as defined in Article 9. See, *e.g.*, *In re Whatley*, 874 F.2d 997 (5th Cir. 1989); *In re Atchison*, 832 F.2d 1236 (11th Cir. 1987). See also discussion in section 4.2.

**Exercise 5-2:  Rights in the Collateral**

Each of the following questions describes a set of facts, identifying a potential debtor and the collateral the debtor wants to use for a loan. In each case, determine whether, and, if so, when, the debtor will have "rights in the collateral" for purposes of section 9-203.

1. Mary will inherit some valuable jewelry under her mother's will. If Mary wants to use the jewelry as collateral for a loan before her mother dies, when will Mary have rights in the collateral?  *[handwritten]*

2. George enters into a contract with Seller Corporation for the manufacture of custom furniture. If George wants to use the furniture as collateral for a loan, when will George have rights in the collateral?

3. Jane owns stock in SYC Corporation. SYC Corporation owns various pieces of heavy equipment. If Jane wants to use the heavy equipment as collateral for a loan, when will Jane have rights in the collateral?  *No.*

# 4.  An Authenticated Security Agreement Which Provides a Description of the Collateral

With certain exceptions, the vast majority of Article 9 transactions begin with a voluntary agreement between a debtor and a secured party that has at its core the grant of a voluntary lien (security interest) in collateral. The voluntary agreement is a contract, generally known as a "security agreement," although the constituent documents in a personal property secured transaction may include instead purchase agreements, credit sale agreements, loan agreements, and other forms of agreement as well.

A security agreement need not be a formal contract. Courts have looked at various documents to determine whether they satisfy the requirements of a security agreement. Some examples of the types of documents found to satisfy the requirements of a security agreement include (1) a letter signed by the debtor,[7] (2) a settlement agreement between parties,[8] and (3) a contract for the sale of air conditioning equipment where the passage of title to equipment was expressly conditioned on the debtor's payment of the entire purchase price.[9] Official Comment 4 to UCC section 9-203 provides that even "a bill of sale, although absolute in form, may be shown to have been in fact given as security." A creditor, therefore, is permitted to show by parol evidence that a transfer purporting to be absolute was in fact for security.

Although there is no particular form required for a security agreement, certain elements must be present. These include (1) a description of the collateral; (2)

---

7. *In re Fibre Glass Boat Corp.*, 324 F.Supp. 1054 (S.D. Fla. 1971), *aff'd* 448 F.2d 781.
8. *In the Matter of Kids Stop of America, Inc.*, 64 B.R. 397 (Bankr. M.D. Fla. 1986).
9. *In re Consolidated Steel Corp.*, 11 UCC Rep. 408 (M.D. Fla. 1972); *Suburbia Federal Savings & Loan Association v. Bel-Air Conditioning Co.*, 385 So.2d 1151 (Fla. 4th DCA 1980).

identification of the parties; and (3) a description of the obligations secured. Typically, a security agreement includes a formal grant of a security interest, but — as explained in the preceding paragraph — a specific grant is not essential, if it can be established — or if it is deemed as a matter of law — that the agreement was intended to provide security for an obligation.

## 4.1 Description and Classification of Collateral

Because the voluntary agreement is the source of the lien, it is important that the security agreement describe the collateral upon which the secured party obtains a lien. Indeed, one of the most important parts of the security agreement is the description of the collateral. The security agreement is the contract that defines the secured party's right to specific property; its principal function is to enable the parties themselves or their successors in interest to identify it, particularly if the secured party has to repossess the collateral or reclaim it in a legal proceeding.[10]

When a lender takes a security interest in all of a debtor's assets, or in all of its assets of a specific type, it is usually sufficient to use descriptions by category or type of collateral defined in the UCC.[11] Therefore, the lawyer drafting the security agreement must be able to "classify the collateral" into Article 9 categories. Classification is particularly important because it will dictate how the security interest that is created will later be perfected.[12] In the real world, that process means taking the real-world facts that identify the property that will be collateral, and assigning them to the appropriate Article 9 category. *Figure 5-3* provides a visual guide to the broad classifications of collateral under Article 9.

Some of the Article 9 collateral classifications are quite broad. For example, "goods" includes all things that are movable at the time the security interest attaches, as well as "fixtures"; standing timber that is to be cut and removed under a conveyance or contract for sale; the unborn young of animals; crops grown, growing, or to be grown (including crops produced on trees, vines or bushes); and manufactured homes;[13] "goods" are further subdivided into "consumer goods," "equipment," "farm products," and "inventory" (which includes, in addition to goods held for sale, goods held for lease or to be furnished under contract of service, goods out on lease or furnished under contract, and raw materials, work in process, and materials used or consumed in a business).[14]

Some of these terms may be familiar to you if you have already studied other UCC articles, such as 2, 3 and 4. Students with a background in business may recognize additional terms. For other students, the long list of types of collateral may be daunting.

---

10. *Talcott, Inc. v. Franklin National Bank of Minneapolis*, 292 Minn. 277, 286-87, 194 N.W. 2d 775, 782 (1972) quoted in *World Wide Tracers, Inc. v. Metropolitan Protection, Inc.*, 373 N.W.2d 839 (Minn. 1985).

11. "All personal property" or "all assets" descriptions are insufficient. Note as well that, under UCC § 9-108(e), a generic reference to "all commercial tort claims" will be ineffective; *any* description of a commercial tort claim must describe the claim with sufficient particularity to satisfy the general requirement of § 9-108(a) that it "reasonably [identify] what is described."

12. Perfection is discussed in Chapters 7 and 8, below.

13. § 9-102(a)(44).

14. § 9-102(a)(48). The term also includes a computer program embedded in goods if the program is associated with the goods in such a manner that it is customarily considered a part of the goods, or if, by becoming the owner of the goods, a person acquires the right to use the program in connection with the goods — but not a computer program embedded in goods (*e.g.*, diskettes) that consist solely of the medium in which the program is embedded.

## Figure 5-3:  Article 9 Classifications of Collateral

| Tangible Property | Quasi-Intangible Property | Intangible Property | Proceeds |
|---|---|---|---|
| Goods<br>§ 9-102(a)(44) | Instruments<br>§ 9-102(a)(47) | Accounts<br>§ 9-102(a)(2) | Cash Proceeds<br>§ 9-102(a)(9) |
| Consumer Goods<br>§ 9-102(a)(23) | Investment Property<br>§ 9-102(a)(49) | Health-Care Insurance<br>Receivables<br>§ 9-102(a)(46) | Non-Cash Proceeds<br>§ 9-102(a)(64) |
| Equipment<br>§ 9-102(a)(33) | Documents<br>§ 9-102(a)(30) | Deposit Accounts<br>§ 9-102(a)(29) | |
| Farm Products<br>§ 9-102(a)(34) | Chattel Paper<br>§ 9-102(a)(11) | General Intangibles<br>§ 9-102(a)(42) | |
| Inventory<br>§ 9-102(a)(48) | Letter of Credit Rights<br>§ 9-102(a)(51) | Payment Intangibles<br>§ 9-102(a)(61) | |
| Money<br>§ 9-102(a)(24) | | | |

Even though the Code defines these terms, the definitions themselves may be difficult. Therefore, we give examples below of the more challenging terms in "plain English":

"Accounts": The most common type of account (also referred to as "accounts receivable") is a business's claim to be paid by its customers for goods sold and delivered. These are typically represented by invoices sent by the business when goods are sold, and delivered to the customer for payment within an agreed time frame.

"Chattel Paper": Retail installment contracts, such as the paper you sign when you buy a car. A sample of such a contract is contained in Appendix H.

"Deposit Accounts": Generally, a bank account, including savings, passbook, and similar accounts at a bank or other financial institution.

"Documents": Warehouse receipts, bills of lading, and other records used in commerce that represent commodities in storage or transportation.

"General Intangibles": A catch-all category for intangible personal property. Some of the types of general intangibles in which lenders may be especially interested include partnership interests, tax refunds, trademarks, patents, copyrights, and rights under specific agreements.

"Instrument": The most common examples are promissory notes, checks, and drafts.

"Investment Property": Stocks and bonds.

"Letter of Credit Rights": A letter of credit is a promise to pay, commonly issued by a bank or similar financial institution, on the condition that certain documents have been presented to the issuer. A sample letter of credit is contained in Appendix 3. "Letter of Credit Rights" means the right to payment or performance under a letter of credit.

Although the Code acknowledges the principle that a creditor may be given a continuing general lien on the debtor's property, to avoid later disputes the description of collateral should state that the collateral includes after-acquired property and proceeds and products of, substitutions and exchanges for, and accessions to, the collateral. No specific definition of "after-acquired collateral" is found in the Code. The term implies, however, that a debtor may grant a lien not only on existing property as collateral for a loan, but also on property the debtor may acquire later. This right is not automatic, however. If a creditor wishes to obtain a security interest in the debtor's after-acquired property, the creditor must mention it specifically in the security agreement.

---

### Exercise 5-3:  Questions to Consider

As you work on the material in this chapter, try to answer the following questions:

1. What are the UCC classifications of collateral?

2. Why is it important to classify collateral?

3. What determines the classification of collateral?

4. At what point in time is the classification determined?

---

### Exercise 5-4:  Classifying Collateral

In each of the following fact patterns, determine how each item of personal property would be classified if it were used as collateral for a loan.

1. The guitar that Beth Buyer purchased from Mega-Mart so Beth could play at a night club with a friend's band. (She joined the band to earn some extra money since her business was not doing well.)

2. Arial Augustine's personal jewelry collection.

3. Chickens that Frank Farmer is currently raising and the eggs from the chickens that he plans to sell to SuperFarmer's Market.

4. Chickens that Frank Farmer is currently raising and the eggs from the chickens that he plans to feed his family.

5. Chickens and eggs that SuperFarmer's Market bought from Frank Farmer.

6. A mobile home held for sale by Homestead Mobile Home Dealer.

7. A mobile home that Ben Buyer purchased from Homestead Mobile Home Dealer to live in.

8. A mobile home that Ben Buyer purchased from Homestead Mobile Home Dealer to use as his office at a construction site.

9. The notes and security agreements received by Homestead from Ben for the sale of the mobile home.

10. A truck purchased by Phil Phoenix to make deliveries for his company, Phoenix Pet Supply Outlet.

11. Richard Rockstar's rights to royalty payments from his last album.

12. Carl Contractor's right to payment under a construction contract to build Connie Consumer a pool.

13. Donald Debtor's 100 shares of stock held in AmeriCorp Corporation.

14. Jenna Jetson's personal checking account at BigBank.

15. The receipt issued to Warren Widget, by a warehouse man from the deposit of 1,000 widgets at StorageRUs.

16. A person's automobile, used for everyday purposes.

17. Automobiles held for sale by the local Toyota dealer.

18. Automobiles held for lease by the local Enterprise Rent-A-Car office.

19. A laptop computer used by a college professor.

20. Cattle fattened by a farmer for sale in the hands of the farmer.

21. Milk from the farmer's dairy herd in the hands of one who buys it.

22. A law firm's supply of toner cartridges for a printer.

23. Office Depot's supply of toner cartridges.

24. A car dealer's right to payment from a consumer for an automobile purchased on credit and for which the consumer signed a piece of paper promising to pay the purchase price in 60 days.

25. A car dealer's right to payment from a consumer for an automobile purchased on credit and for which the consumer signed a piece of paper promising to pay the purchase price in installments for 3 years, and granting Car Dealer a right to repossess the automobile if the consumer fails to make the promised payments.

26. A lawyer's right to payment from clients for work to be performed.

27. The right to receive a tax refund.

28. 100 shares of Apple stock held in "street name" at a brokerage house.

29. 100 shares of McDonald's stock represented by a stock certificate.

---

## 4.2  Identification of the Parties

In this book, we have referred to the party who makes a loan as the lender and the party who incurs the obligation as the borrower. Typically, in an Article 9 transaction, the borrower will also be a "debtor" under section 9-102(a)(28). However, Article 9 takes into account the possibility that sometimes someone other than the borrower will own property that will serve as collateral. Therefore, under Article 9, any party who has an interest in the collateral is known as the "debtor." The party who is obligated to the lender in respect of the obligation that is secured by the collateral is known as the "obligor."[15] One common situation in which a non-obligor grants a security interest in collateral is when the obligor is a corporation and the assets that are collateral are owned individually by a shareholder of the corporation. Although the individual is not personally obligated on the loan, by permitting the lender to have a security interest in her assets, the individual becomes a "debtor" under Article 9.

---

15. §9-102(a)(59).

## Exercise 5-5:  Attachment and Enforceability of Security Interest

1. Dennis owns a small, successful landscaping business, and wants to expand. He applies for a loan from Big Bank. Big Bank notifies Dennis that he is eligible for a loan, provided that he has collateral for the loan. Dennis currently owns two trucks, various pieces of landscaping equipment, and an antique lawn mower, which he keeps and showcases at home.

    1.1. On January 2, Dennis signs a security agreement stating that Big Bank has a security interest in "all of the Debtor's personal property." Big Bank gives Dennis the $20,000 loan proceeds when he signs the security agreement. Does Big Bank have an enforceable security interest in Dennis's personal property? Why or why not?

    1.2. In exercise 1.1, how would you advise Big Bank to describe the collateral in its security agreement?

    1.3. Assuming that the description of collateral in the security agreement is sufficient, when would Big Bank's security interest attach?

    1.4. Assume the same facts as exercise 1.3, except that Dennis does not receive the loan proceeds until January 5. Also assume that the security agreement provides that Big Bank promises to make the $20,000 loan. When would Big Bank's security interest attach?

    1.5. What would be the legal effect of the Bank's including the following language in the security agreement: "The collateral, as described in this agreement, also secures any loans the Secured Party may make to the Debtor in the future"?

2. Alley Bank loaned Mary's business $50,000, in an authenticated agreement that recited that the loan was secured by "inventory and all now owned and after acquired equipment." On March 2, Mary ordered several touch screen displays to entertain her customers at her dessert bar. On March 4, Screenz, the company Mary ordered from, packaged the screens and labeled the box with Mary's business's name and address, but due to a mix up the package was not mailed until March 8. On March 7, Mary was forced to file for bankruptcy.

    2.1. Does Alley Bank have an enforceable security interest in the screen displays? Why or why not?

    2.2. Assume that before filing for bankruptcy, Mary made one last effort to save her business. Mary asked Susan, her sister, for a $75,000 loan. Susan agreed, on the condition that Mary secure the loan with jewelry Mary had inherited from their grandmother. Mary agreed, and Susan kept the jewelry in a safe at her home. Does Susan have an enforceable security interest in the jewelry? If so, when did the security interest attach?

3. Danny Debtor owned and operated three separate businesses as sole proprietorships. Secured Party loaned Debtor money to purchase certain business equipment for Debtor's decal business. The security agreement granted the Secured Party a security interest in, among other things, Debtor's equipment. Did the security interest attach to all of the equipment used in Danny's three businesses, or was it limited to the equipment that the loan proceeds were used to purchase?

# 5.  Proceeds and Supporting Obligations

In general, **proceeds** are whatever is acquired upon the sale, lease, license, exchange or other disposition of collateral.[16] Under section 9-203, the attachment of a security interest in collateral also gives the secured party the rights to proceeds. Nevertheless, most lawyers expressly include proceeds (and some include a definition of the term) in their description of collateral in the security agreement.

The definition of "supporting obligations" is a relatively recent addition to Article 9.[17] The term includes different types of credit enhancements that support obligations owed to the debtor that are themselves collateral for a loan being made to the debtor. Typical supporting obligations include letters of credit and guaranties that support obligations such as leases of personal property, student loans, automobile loans, etc.[18] Under section 9-203, the attachment of a security interest in collateral is also attachment of a security interest in a supporting obligation for the collateral.

---

## Exercise 5-6:  Proceeds

1. Games & More, the operators of a gaming arcade, obtained a loan from Loaner Bank to purchase 20 different arcade games. The security agreement described the collateral as the arcade games purchased by Games & More, specifically describing each arcade game. Does Loaner Bank's security interest extend to the money Games & More receives from its customers' use of the games? Why or why not?

2. Though thorough in describing the arcade games as the collateral in the security agreement, Loaner Bank failed to include any language to the effect of "proceeds of the described collateral." If Games & More were to sell those arcade games, would Loaner Bank have a security interest in the money received from the sale of the arcade games?

3. Loaner Bank had a security interest in Fred Farm's crops. Consider the following situations.

   3.1 Due to an unforeseen and severe drought, all of Fred Farm's crops were destroyed. Fred Farm received a disaster relief payment from the government. Loaner Bank's security agreement sufficiently described the crops as collateral, but did not mention proceeds. Does Loaner Bank have a security interest in the disaster relief payment funds?

   3.2 Assume that Loaner Bank's security agreement described the collateral as "all farm products, including contract rights and accounts." Under the Department of Agriculture's Payment-in-Kind program, Fred Farm was paid to not plant crops. Does Loaner Bank have a security interest in the funds Fred received from that program?

4. Loaner Bank loaned Compu-Sales $75,000 to replenish its stock of inventory—computers. According to the security agreement, the loan was secured

---

16. §9-102(a)(64) contains the complete definition of "proceeds."

17. See §9-102(a)(77).

18. An example of a personal guaranty used in connection with a secured loan transaction is contained in Appendix C.

by Compu-Sales' inventory. When Compu-Sales sells a computer from its inventory to a customer, what happens to Loaner Bank's security interest? What is Loaner Bank's collateral after the sale is completed?

---

# 6. "New Debtors" under Article 9

Before the 2010 revisions to Article 9, problems sometimes arose when the original debtor changed its legal structure (*e.g.*, from a corporation to a limited liability company, or a corporation merged into another corporation or a corporation was acquired by another corporation). To address these types of situations, the 2010 Code introduced the concept of a "new debtor," and sections 9-203 (d) and (e) specifically address the creation, attachment, and enforceability issues in this context. Official Comment 7 to section 9-203 explains that "Subsection (e) makes clear that the enforceability requirements of subsection (b) (3) are met when a new debtor becomes bound under an original debtor's security agreement.... Subsection (d) explains when a new debtor becomes bound."

---

### Exercise 5-7: New Debtors

American Bank loaned Pets & More the money necessary to start up operations as a retail pet and pet supply store. The loan was secured by collateral described as "inventory, and now or after acquired equipment." Within a year, Pets Unlimited, a much larger competitor, purchased Pets & More, and agreed by contract to become obligated for all of Pets & More's obligations.

1. If Pets & More ceases to exist, is American Bank's loan still secured? Who is the debtor?

2. Is it necessary for American Bank to have Pets Unlimited sign a new security agreement?

3. Without any new documentation, what is American Bank's collateral after the sale of Pets & More?

---

# 7. Rights of Third Parties

Another issue that practitioners must become familiar with involves the enforceability of a security interest against *other parties to the collateral*—for example, what if a contract between the debtor and one of its customers—or even a law applicable to the contract in question—prohibits the transfer or encumbrance by the debtor of its rights under that contract? By and large, Part 4 of Article 9 implements a policy of free assignability of rights to payment: section 9-406(d) provides that prohibitions against assignment contained in most agreements evidencing rights to payment, and laws restricting their assignment, are ineffective; section 9-407(a) provides parallel protections to secured lenders taking assignments of leases. Sections 9-408 and 9-409, which apply to (i) sales of payment intangibles and promissory notes and assignments of rights under general intangibles and health-care-insurance receivables, and (ii) assignments of rights to payment under letters of credit, respectively, permit the attachment of a security interest, but—if other law would give effect to an underlying contractual prohibition on assignment—prohibit enforcement of the security interest directly against the debtor's counterparty. (In other words, the secured party may have a perfected security interest in the collateral, but not be able to collect payments directly from, or enforce performance by, the counterparty.)[19]

Other sections of Part 4 address other effects on the debtor's contractual counterparties of the grant of a security interest in a debtor's rights against them—whether a lender becomes obligated to perform a contract in which it has a security interest (9-402); the effect of an agreement by the counterparty not to assert against a secured party claims or defenses it might have against the debtor and the rights of an assignee generally (9-403, 9-404); the effect of the grant of security interest in a contract on the ability to modify the contract (9-405). Article 9's provisions relating to assignability tend to be adopted with relatively less uniformity than other provisions of Article 9.

As always, the Official Comments are an invaluable guide to the understanding of Part 4, and you must always consult local law to see what version of these codes sections has been adopted.

# Additional Resources

Annotation, *Secured Transactions: What constitutes "inventory" under UCC § 9-109(4)*, 77 A.L.R. 3d 1266 (1977).

Annotation, *Secured Transactions: What constitutes "consumer goods" under UCC § 9-109(1)*, 77 A.L.R. 3d 1225 (1977).

Ralph C. Anzivino, *When Does a Debtor Have Rights in the Collateral Under Article 9 of the Uniform Commercial Code?*, 61 Marq. L. Rev. 23 (1977).

Erwin S. Barbre, Annotation, *Sufficiency of description of crops under UCC §§ 9-203(1)(b) and 9-402(1)*, 67 A.L.R. 3d 308 (1975).

Cindy J. Chernuchin, *Understanding the terms of security agreements,* 57 No. 3 Prac. Law. 39 (2011).

Margit Livingston, *Certainty, Efficiency and Realism: Rights in Collateral Under Article 9 of the Uniform Commercial Code,* 73 N.C. L. Rev. 115 (1994).

Steven W. Sanford, *Debtor's Rights in Collateral as a Requirement for Attachment of a Security Interest Under the Uniform Commercial Code,* 26 S.D. L. Rev. 163 (1981).

Joseph W. Turner, Comment, *Rights in Collateral Under U.C.C. § 9-203*, 54 Mo. L. Rev. 677 (1989).

---

19. Some secured parties deal with issues raised by Part 4 by obtaining consents from counterparties whose obligations to the debtor are important components of the secured party's collateral package; in other cases, secured parties sometimes expressly exclude from their collateral the debtor's rights in respect of any contract that includes an enforceable restriction on assignment or encumbrance. And some states vary the general rule to give effect to some prohibitions on assignment or encumbrance—Delaware, for example, expressly excludes interests in limited partnerships or limited liability companies from the operation of § 9-408.

# Chapter 6

# Default and Secured Party Remedies

**Figure 6-1:  Article 9 Graphic Organizer**

```
                    ┌─────────────────┐
                    │    Scope of     │
                    │    Article 9    │
                    └────────┬────────┘
                             │
                             ▼
              ┌──────────────────────────────┐
              │         Creation of          │
              │       Security Interest      │
              │ (Attachment and Enforceability)│
              └──────────────┬───────────────┘
                  ┌──────────┴──────────┐
                  ▼                     ▼
      ┌───────────────────┐  ┌───────────────────┐
      │  Issues Arising   │  │  Issues Arising   │
      │ Out of Relationship│  │ Out of Presence of│
      │  between Debtor   │  │ Competing Claims  │
      │ and Secured Party │  │ to Same Collateral│
      └─────────┬─────────┘  └─────────┬─────────┘
                ▼                      ▼
         ┌───────────┐          ┌───────────┐
         │  Default  │          │ Perfection│
         └─────┬─────┘          └─────┬─────┘
               ▼                      ▼
         ┌───────────┐          ┌───────────────┐
         │ Remedies  │          │Priority Disputes│
         └───────────┘          └───────┬───────┘
                                        ▼
                                ┌───────────────┐
                                │  Bankruptcy   │
                                │Considerations │
                                └───────────────┘
```

## Chapter Problem

---

**INTRA-OFFICE MEMORANDUM**

**Date:**     February 25
**To:**       Ann Associate
**From:**     Ima Partner
**Subject:**  Mertz's Mezzanine Loans

Your client, Mertz's Mezzanine Loans, LLC, has made a loan to a Penny Rios, one of three members in Century Ventures, LLC, a limited liability company formed under the Delaware Limited Liability Company Act. As security for the loan, Penny has granted to Mertz's a security interest in her "limited liability company interest" in Century Ventures. Century Ventures was formed to acquire land with the intent to hold it for investment. The security agreement granting the security interest (a copy of which is in Appendix G) defines an "Event of Default" as "any 'Event of Default' under, and as defined in, the Note [the promissory note evidencing the loan to Penny]." The Note defines "Event of Default" to include, among other things, Penny's failure to pay any amount due under the Note and the continuation of that failure for a period of 10 days after notice from Lender advising Penny of that failure and demanding that it be cured.

Yesterday, approximately one year after the loan was funded, Penny failed to pay the installment of principal and interest due on the Note. A representative of Mertz's tried calling Penny this morning to ask about the payment, but was informed that her phone had been disconnected. The loan officer at Mertz's has become concerned, and has called you to find out what they should do now. He has also expressed an interest in simply taking over Penny's interest in Century Ventures, as that company's land has recently been rezoned for commercial development, and has appreciated greatly in value since Mertz's first made the loan. The loan officer has asked you to prepare for a phone call with him and his supervisor in three days' time, during which they'd like you to discuss what steps they must take to realize upon their collateral.

Prepare an outline of the points you think should be discussed on the call — of the steps you would recommend that Mertz's take immediately, based on facts currently known, of the ways in which Mertz's might realize on their collateral (including the standards that would apply and the procedures that would be involved), and of other facts, not currently known, that could affect your ultimate recommendation to Mertz's, explaining why they are important.

---

Students who are familiar with reading and briefing cases are sometimes at a loss when asked to think about preparing for a client interview. You may find the following approach helpful as you analyze what you know and what you do not know about the chapter problem.

## Figure 6-2: Preparing for a Client Interview

| Known Facts | Issue | Rule of Law | Application of Law to Known Facts | Identification of Unknown Facts | |
|---|---|---|---|---|---|
| | | | | Questions for Client | Documents to Review |
| | | | | | |
| | | | | | |
| | | | | | |

## Code Sections

1-103(b) 9-207, 9-208, 9-209, 9-210, 9-601, 9-602, 9-603, 9-604, 9-605, 9-606, 9-607, 9-608, 9-609, 9-610, 9-611, 9-612, 9-613, 9-614, 9-615, 9-616, 9-617, 9-618, 9-619, 9-620, 9-621, 9-622, 9-623, 9-624, 9-625, 9-626, 9-627, 9-628

# 1.  Default

Article 9 does not define default; accordingly, loan documents typically will pay careful attention to a definition of default, as well as describing the secured party's remedies when the debtor defaults. In the relatively unusual case where there is no agreement that defines default, under section 1-103 and case law, the ordinary meaning of default — failure to pay — is usually applied.[1] Failure to pay is only the starting point in loan documents that list "events of default." One of the most litigated types of default provisions is known as an "insecurity clause." Such a provision is typically used in concert with an acceleration clause, which allows the lender to declare an obligation immediately due and payable. Notwithstanding the Code's willingness to permit such clauses (see, *e.g.*, section 1-309), courts have policed such provisions, looking at both the lender's good faith in finding itself "insecure," as well as the materiality of the borrower's alleged default.

---

1. See, *e.g, Cofield v. Randolph County Comm'n*, 90 F.3d 468 (11th Cir. 1996).

Upon the debtor's default, the secured party has the rights provided in the security agreement, as well as those set forth in part 6 of Article 9, subject to limitations also set forth in part 6.[2]

---

### Exercise 6-1:  Security Agreement Default Provisions

Review the default provisions in the sample Security Agreement, in Appendix B. List each separate event of default. Be prepared to explain what each means. Next, list the secured party's rights upon default under the Security Agreement. Compare the list to the secured party's rights upon default under part 6 of Article 9. Be prepared to discuss why you think the author of the Security Agreement included rights that are already given by the statute.

---

### Exercise 6-2:  Default

Sydney's Sidecars is a corporation in the business of providing rides to pedestrians along the beach. On June 1, BigBank loaned Sydney's $50,000, and Sydney's signed a valid security agreement granting BigBank a security interest in all of Sydney's sidecars, listing each sidecar by individual VIN number, make, model, and year. The security agreement stated that if the debtor, Sydney's, failed to make the agreed monthly payments BigBank had the right to declare the debtor "in default" on the loan. One month later, Sydney's failed to make the first monthly payment when it was due.

1. Has Sydney's defaulted on the loan? If so, what was its default?

2. What are BigBank's rights, and when do they arise?

3. If BigBank had inadvertently failed to define "default" in its security agreement, could BigBank nevertheless declare that a default had occurred? Upon what legal authority could it rely?

---

# 2. Judicial Enforcement

A secured creditor always has the option of filing suit when a debtor defaults. Even though this option involves the same judicial process as that required of an unsecured creditor,[3] a secured creditor may have an easier time proving its case. Moreover, upon the conclusion of the lawsuit, the secured party gains another significant advantage. The lien of any levy made by an ordinary judgment creditor is effective only as of the date of the actual levy. The lien of any levy that may be made by a secured creditor upon its collateral is effective as of the date the security interest was originally perfected.[4] As we will discuss in Chapter 7, the effective date of the lien can be very important in a priority dispute.

---

2. See UCC § 9-602 and § 9-603.
3. See Chapter 3 for a discussion of that process.
4. UCC § 9-601(e).

# 3. Collection and Enforcement by Secured Party

Official Comment 2 to UCC section 9-607 explains that collateral consisting of rights to payment is the most liquid asset of a typical debtor's business. It is also a type of property that may be collected without interference with the debtor's business (as distinguished from collateral that is inventory or equipment, whose removal may bring the business to a halt). Therefore, section 9-607 permits the secured party, after the debtor's default and without judicial process, to liquidate this type of collateral by collecting whatever may become due on the collateral. For example, for collateral that is accounts receivable, chattel paper or general intangibles, the secured party may notify an account debtor or other person obligated on the collateral to make payments or otherwise render performance directly to the secured party instead of the debtor.

Some security agreements will anticipate the debtor's default and seek to avoid a subsequent need to notify account debtors by providing, among other things, for a "lock box" arrangement, pursuant to which account debtors are directed to make payments to a lock box rather than to the debtor's business address. The directions provide that they cannot be revoked without the secured party's consent. In the event of default, the secured party can then take over control of the lock box, and collect the accounts, without any need to contact account debtors and without the need for the debtor's cooperation. For an example of this type of agreement, see Appendix D.

# 4. Secured Party's Right to Take Possession of Collateral after Default

UCC section 9-609 provides that after default a secured party may take possession of collateral, or, without removal, render equipment unusable, and dispose of collateral on the debtor's premises. Such action may be taken with or without judicial process; however, a secured party acting without judicial process *must* proceed without breach of the peace. Because it is greatly beneficial to the secured party to take possession of collateral as soon as possible, and without the necessity of a lawsuit, it is important to understand what "without breach of the peace" means. The phrase has been interpreted very broadly in litigation. Many of these cases involve the repossession of consumer property, such as cars and boats; courts in those cases have consistently taken the position that if a secured party proceeds to take possession of collateral after even a mildly expressed protest by the debtor, the secured party has breached the peace.[5]

In a commercial setting, it is possible that the debtor will voluntarily give possession of collateral to the secured party. In such situations, the prudent secured party will require the debtor to sign a "peaceable possession agreement," to document the fact that possession was relinquished voluntarily and accomplished without a breach of the peace. *Figure 6-3* is an example of a peaceable possession agreement.

---

5. For a discussion of how courts have interpreted the meaning of "breach of the peace" and applied it to repossessions see *Giles v. First Virginia Credit Services, Inc.*, following exercise 6-3 and the articles listed under Additional Resources at the end of this Chapter.

## Figure 6-3:  Peaceable Possession Agreement

Gentlemen:

During the first quarter of _____ you have advanced a total of $_____ to the undersigned (the "Debt"). Of the Debt, a sum of $_____ plus interest and costs, which are payable on demand, were memorialized by the terms of that certain Secured Promissory Note of _____ (the "Note") and the Security Agreement of even date therewith (the "Security Agreement"), providing that all such obligations are secured by all or substantially all of the assets of the undersigned. The undersigned further acknowledges that (i) it received written notice of demand under the Note on _____ (ii) it has failed to pay the amount due, and therefore (iii) it has defaulted in the payment of the Debt to you. Because that default has occurred and is continuing, you have demanded, in accordance with Section 9-609(a)(1) of the Uniform Commercial Code, and the undersigned herewith grants to you, as of the date hereof, all rights of possession in and to the collateral set forth on Exhibit 1 hereto (the "Collateral").

This letter also serves as an authorization to any employee of the undersigned, or any third party, to grant you and/or your designee, and the undersigned hereby (i) grants you and/or your designee, full and complete access to any premises and all properties and assets where the Collateral is located to allow you to take possession of any such Collateral in order to enforce your rights against and collect from the undersigned, and (ii) appoints you as its attorney in fact for the purposes of this letter.

The undersigned knowingly and intelligently waives any rights it may have to notice and a hearing before a court of competent jurisdiction and consents to your entry on the premises where the aforesaid Collateral is located for the purposes set forth herein.

This letter agreement may be executed in multiple counterparts, each of which shall be deemed an original, but all of which together shall constitute one and the same agreement.[6]

## Exercise 6-3:  *Giles v. First Virginia Credit Services, Inc.*

In the following case arising out of the repossession of an automobile, the North Carolina Court of Appeals reviews a trial court's grant of a summary judgment. As you read the case, consider the following questions:

1. Was the debtor "in default" at the time of the repossession?

2. How does the court explain the meaning of a "breach of the peace"?

3. What are the consequences if a repossession resulted in a breach of the peace?

---

6. PEACEFUL POSSESSION LETTER AGREEMENT dated June 6, 2010 http://www.faqs.org/sec-filings/100624/ECLIPS-ENERGY-TECHNOLOGIES-INC_8-K/c02772exv10w6.htm#ixzz2ava8oeo7 .

# Giles v. First Virginia Credit Services, Inc.

## 149 N.C. App. 89 (2002)

McGee, Judge.

Richard Giles and Joann Giles (plaintiffs) appeal the trial court's order granting First Virginia Credit Services, Inc.'s (First Virginia) motion for summary judgment in part.

Plaintiffs filed a complaint against defendants First Virginia and Professional Auto Recovery, Inc. (Professional Auto Recovery) for wrongful repossession of an automobile. Plaintiffs alleged in an amended complaint that: (1) First Virginia and Professional Auto Recovery wrongfully converted and/or repossessed the automobile and plaintiffs' personal property located within the automobile; (2) plaintiffs made a payment on the account which First Virginia accepted immediately prior to First Virginia's repossession of the automobile and which First Virginia subsequently cashed and applied to plaintiffs' account after the repossession; (3) removal of the automobile constituted breach of the peace in violation of N.C. Gen. Stat. § 25-9-503; (4) N.C. Gen. Stat. § 25-9-503 is unconstitutional; and (5) First Virginia was negligent in hiring Professional Auto Recovery and committed unfair or deceptive trade practices entitling plaintiffs to treble damages.

First Virginia filed an answer stating the automobile was repossessed due to the default of Joann Giles in making the payments to First Virginia on a loan secured by the automobile. First Virginia stated that N.C. Gen. Stat. § 25-9-503 permitted a secured lender to peaceably repossess its collateral upon default by a debtor and that such repossession could not, as a matter of law, constitute conversion of the collateral or an unfair or deceptive trade practice. First Virginia moved to dismiss plaintiffs' complaint for failure to state a claim pursuant to N.C. Gen. Stat. § 1A-1, Rule 12(b)(6).

Joann Giles entered into an installment sale contract on or about 18 January 1997 for the purchase of an automobile. The contract was assigned to First Virginia, which obtained a senior perfected purchase money security interest in the automobile. The terms of the contract required Joann Giles to make sixty regular monthly payments to First Virginia. The contract stated that Joann Giles' failure to make any payment due under the contract within ten days after its due date would be a default. The contract contained an additional provision agreed to by Joann Giles that stated:

> If I am in default, you may consider all my remaining payments to be due and payable, without giving me notice. I agree that your rights of possession will be greater than mine. I will deliver the property to you at your request, or you may use lawful means to take it yourself without notice or other legal action.... If you excuse one default by me, that will not excuse later defaults.

During the early morning hours of 27 June 1999, Professional Auto Recovery, at the request of First Virginia, repossessed the locked automobile from plaintiffs' front driveway. According to First Virginia, the account of Joann Giles was in arrears for payments due on 2 May 1999 and 2 June 1999, and pursuant to the terms of the contract, repossession was permitted.

In an affidavit filed by plaintiffs in opposition to First Virginia's motion for summary judgment, plaintiffs' neighbor, Glenn A. Mosteller (Mr. Mosteller), stated that he was awakened around 4:00 a.m.

> by the running of a loud diesel truck engine on the road outside my house. Evidentially [sic] the truck was stopped because I lay in bed for a while and did not get up. I then became concerned and went to the window to see what was

going on. At this time I saw a large rollback diesel truck with a little pickup truck on the truck bed behind it. The truck only had its parking lights on. The truck . . . started going toward the Giles' yard. It still only had its parking lights on. About that time, a man jumped out of the truck and ran up the Giles' driveway. Their car was parked up at their house. Then the car came flying out back down the driveway making a loud noise and started screeching off. . . . At about the same time, the rollback also pulled off real fast making a real loud diesel noise and went down [the road]. . . . I got to the phone, called the Giles and told them someone was stealing their car. . . . My lights were on. . . . and the Giles' lights were on and that portion of our neighborhood had woken up. Richard Giles came out in his yard and we hollared a few words back and forth and I jumped in my truck. . . . to try to get the police. About 5 minutes later a police car came up and pulled into the Giles' yard. Then another police car came then a Sheriff's Deputy car came. Then another police car came. . . . There was a great commotion going on out in the street and in our yard all to the disturbance of the quietness and tranquility of our neighborhood. . . . It scared me and it scared the Giles.

Joann Giles stated in a deposition that she was awakened by Mr. Mosteller's telephone call in which he told her that someone was stealing her car. She stated she ran to see if the automobile was parked outside and confirmed that it was gone. Joann Giles testified she woke up her husband and gave him the telephone; he ran outside into the yard and heard Mr. Mosteller "hollering" at him from across the street. Plaintiffs testified in their depositions that neither of them saw the car being repossessed but were only awakened by their neighbor after the automobile was gone. During the actual repossession, no contact was made between Professional Auto Recovery and plaintiffs, nor between Professional Auto Recovery and Mr. Mosteller.

First Virginia filed a motion for summary judgment pursuant to N.C. Gen. Stat. § 1A-1, Rule 56. Plaintiffs filed a motion to amend their complaint pursuant to N.C. Gen. Stat. § 1A-1, Rule 15. These motions were heard by the trial court on 17 May 2000. In an order dated 15 June 2000, the trial court: (1) granted plaintiffs' motion to amend their complaint; (2) granted First Virginia's motion for summary judgment in part, stating there was no genuine issue as to any material fact as to the conversion or repossession of the motor vehicle; (3) denied First Virginia's motion for summary judgment in part, concluding that there were genuine issues of material fact as to the reasonableness of the taking into possession or conversion of plaintiffs' personal property located within the automobile and related damages; (4) declined plaintiffs' request to declare N.C. Gen. Stat. § 25-9-503 unconstitutional; and (5) ruled on other motions not at issue in this appeal. The trial court certified in an order filed 6 July 2000 that its decisions in the 15 June 2000 order constituted a final judgment as to some of plaintiffs' claims and found the order was immediately appealable pursuant to N.C. Gen. Stat. § 1A-1, Rule 54(b). Plaintiffs appeal.

I. [Discussion of interlocutory appeal has been purposely omitted.]

II

By their first assignment of error, plaintiffs argue the trial court erred in granting in part First Virginia's motion for summary judgment dismissing plaintiffs' claim for wrongful conversion and/or repossession of their automobile. Plaintiffs specifically argue that (1) the determination of whether a breach of the peace occurred in violation of N.C. Gen. Stat. § 25-9-503 is a question for the jury and not one to be determined by summary judgment, and (2) there is a dispute as to whether plaintiffs were in default. . . .

A.

Plaintiffs first argue the trial court erred in granting partial summary judgment to First Virginia because the issue of whether a breach of the peace occurred is a question for the jury.

Our Courts have long recognized the right of secured parties to repossess collateral from a defaulting debtor without resort to judicial process, so long as the repossession is effected peaceably. See e.g., Rea v. Credit Corp., 257 N.C. 639, 641, 127 S.E.2d 225, 227 (1962); Freeman v. Acceptance Corp., 205 N.C. 257, 258, 171 S.E. 63, 63 (1933). Our General Assembly codified procedures for self-help repossessions, including this common law restriction, in the North Carolina Uniform Commercial Code (UCC). N.C. Gen. Stat. § 25-9-503 (1999), in effect at the time of the repossession in this case, reads in part,

> Unless otherwise agreed a secured party has on default the right to take possession of the collateral. In taking possession a secured party may proceed without judicial process if this can be done without breach of the peace or may proceed by action.

The General Assembly did not define breach of the peace but instead left this task to our Courts, and although a number of our appellate decisions have considered this self-help right of secured parties, none have clarified what actions constitute a breach of the peace.

N.C. Gen. Stat. § 25-9-503, at issue in this appeal, has been replaced by N.C. Gen. Stat. § 25-9-609 (Interim Supp. 2000) (Effective 1 July 2001), which states that a secured party, after default, may take possession of the collateral without judicial process, if the secured party proceeds without breach of the peace. In Number 3. of the Official Comment to the new statutory provision, our General Assembly continued to state that, "like former Section 9-503, this section does not define or explain the conduct that will constitute a breach of the peace, leaving that matter for continuing development by the courts." N.C.G.S. § 25-9-609. The General Assembly clearly may further define and/or limit the time, place and conditions under which a repossession is permitted, but it has not yet done so.

In a pre-UCC case, Rea v. Credit Corp., 257 N.C. 639, 127 S.E.2d 225 (1962), a defaulting debtor left his locked automobile on his front lawn. An agent of the mortgagee went to the debtor's home to repossess the automobile, saw the automobile parked on the lawn, found no one at home, and asked a neighbor where the debtor was. The agent was told no one was at home and he thereafter opened the automobile door with a coat hanger and removed the automobile on a wrecker. Our Supreme Court found that this evidence could not warrant a finding by a jury that the mortgagee's agent wrongfully took possession of the automobile because no breach of the peace occurred. In Rea, although our Supreme Court did not define breach of the peace, it reiterated the common law rule that the right of self-help repossession "must be exercised without provoking a breach of the peace[.]" Id. at 641-42, 127 S.E.2d at 227. Our Supreme Court thought the law "well stated" by the South Carolina Supreme Court in the case of Willis v. Whittle, that

> "if the mortgagee finds that he cannot get possession without committing a breach of the peace, he must stay his hand, and resort to the law, for the preservation of the public peace is of more importance to society than the right of the owner of a chattel to get possession of it."

Rea, 257 N.C. at 641-42, 127 S.E.2d at 227 (quoting Willis v. Whittle, 82 S.C. 500, 64 S.E. 410 (1909)).

In a case addressing the issue of whether prior notice of repossession is required under N.C. Gen. Stat. § 25-9-503, our Court stated that repossession can be accomplished under the statute without prior notice so long as the repossession is peaceable. Everett v. U.S. Life Credit Corp., 74 N.C. App. 142, 144, 327 S.E.2d 269, 269 (1985). Without specifically defining breach of the peace, our Court explained that "of course, if there is confrontation at the time of the attempted repossession, the secured party must cease the attempted repossession and proceed by court action in order to avoid a 'breach of the peace.'" Id. at 144, 327 S.E.2d at 270. This indicates, as argued by First Virginia, that confrontation is at least an element of a breach of the peace analysis.

In that breach of the peace has not heretofore been clarified by our appellate courts, but instead only vaguely referred to, we must construe this term as the drafters intended. "In construing statutes the court should always give effect to the legislative intent." Electric Service v. City of Rocky Mount, 20 N.C. App. 347, 348, 201 S.E.2d 508, [98] 509, aff'd, 285 N.C. 135, 203 S.E.2d 838 (1974). "The intent of the Legislature may be ascertained from the phraseology of the statute as well as the nature and purpose of the act and the consequences which would follow from a construction one way or another." Campbell v. Church, 298 N.C. 476, 484, 259 S.E.2d 558, 564 (1979). In determining what conduct constitutes a breach of the peace we consider each of these contributing elements.

The phrase "breach of the peace" is defined in Black's Law Dictionary as the "criminal offense of creating a public disturbance or engaging in disorderly conduct, particularly by an unnecessary or distracting noise." Black's Law Dictionary 183 (7th ed. 1999). The phrase is also commonly understood to mean a "violation of the public order as amounts to a disturbance of the public tranquility, by act or conduct either directly having this effect, or by inciting or tending to incite such a disturbance of the public tranquility." 12 Am. Jur. 2d Breach of Peace § 5 (1997).

In a criminal case, our Supreme Court defined breach of the peace as "a disturbance of public order and tranquility by act or conduct not merely amounting to unlawfulness but tending also to create public tumult and incite others to break the peace." State v. Mobley, 240 N.C. 476, 482, 83 S.E.2d 100, 104 (1954). See also Perry v. Gibson, 247 N.C. 212, 100 S.E.2d 341 (1957) (wrongful death case stating the same definition for breach of the peace). Such "'[a] breach of the peace may be occasioned by an affray or assault, by the use [17] of profane and abusive language by one person toward another on a public street and in the presence of others, [564] or by a person needlessly shouting and making loud noise.'" Mobley, 240 N.C. at 482, 83 S.E.2d at 104 (quoting 4 Am. Jur. Arrest § 30). A breach of the peace, as used in Chapter 19 of our General Statutes, entitled "Offenses Against Public Morals," is defined as "repeated acts that disturb the public order including, but not limited to, homicide, assault, affray, communicating threats, unlawful possession of dangerous or deadly weapons, and discharging firearms." N.C. Gen. Stat. § 19-1.1(1) (1999).

We must also consider the nature and purpose of Chapter 25 of the North Carolina General Statutes, the UCC, which is to be "liberally construed and applied to promote its underlying purposes and policies." N.C. Gen. Stat. § 25-1-102 (1999). Its stated purposes are:

(a) to simplify, clarify and modernize the law governing commercial transactions;

(b) to permit the continued expansion of commercial practices through custom, usage and agreement of the parties;

(c) to make uniform the law among the various jurisdictions.

Id.

In carrying out the policy of uniformity with other jurisdictions, we consider their treatment of the term of breach of the peace. While cases from other jurisdictions are not binding on our courts, they provide insight into how this term has been analyzed by other courts and therefore are instructive.

The courts in many states have examined whether a breach of the peace in the context of the UCC has occurred. Courts have found a breach of the peace when actions by a creditor incite violence or are likely to incite violence. Birrell v. Indiana Auto Sales & Repair, 698 N.E.2d 6, 8 (Ind. App. 1998) (a creditor cannot use threats, enter a residence without debtor's consent and cannot seize property over a debtor's objections); Wade v. Ford Motor Credit Co., 668 P.2d 183, 189 (Kan. App. 1983) (a breach of the peace may be caused by an act likely to produce violence); Morris v. First National Bank & Trust Co. of Ravena, 254 N.E.2d 683, 686-87 (Ohio 1970) (a physical confrontation coupled with an oral protest constitutes a breach of the peace).

Other courts have expanded the phrase breach of the peace beyond the criminal law context to include occurrences where a debtor or his family protest the repossession. Fulton v. Anchor Sav. Bank, FSB, 452 S.E.2d 208, 213 (Ga. App. 1994) (a breach of the peace can be created by an unequivocal oral protest); Census Federal Credit Union v. Wann, 403 N.E.2d 348, 352 (Ind. App. 1980) ("if a repossession is ... contested at the actual time ... of the attempted repossession by the defaulting party or other person in control of the chattel, the secured party must desist and pursue his remedy in court"); Hollibush v. Ford Motor Credit Co., 508 N.W.2d 449, 453-55 (Wis. App. 1993) (in the face of an oral protest the repossessing creditor must desist). Some courts, however, have determined that a mere oral protest is not sufficient to constitute a breach of the peace. Clarin v. Minnesota Repossessors, Inc., 198 F.3d 661, 664 (8th Cir. 1999) (oral protest, followed by pleading with repossessors in public parking lot does not rise to level of breach of the peace); Chrysler Credit Corp. v. Koontz, 661 N.E.2d 1171, 1173-74 (Ill. App. 1996) (yelling "Don't take it" is insufficient).

If a creditor removes collateral by an unauthorized breaking and entering of a debtor's dwelling, courts generally hold this conduct to be a breach of the peace. Davenport v. Chrysler Credit Corp., 818 S.W.2d 23, 29 (Tenn. App. 1991) and General Elec. Credit Corp. v. Timbrook, 291 S.E.2d 383, 385 (W. Va. 1982) (both cases stating that breaking and entering, despite the absence of violence or physical confrontation, is a breach of the peace). Removal of collateral from a private driveway, without more however, has been found not to constitute a breach of the peace. Hester v. Bandy, 627 So.2d 833, 840 (Miss. 1993). Additionally, noise alone has been determined to not rise to the level of a breach of the peace. Ragde v. People's Bank, 767 P.2d 949, 951 (Wash. App. 1989) (unwilling to hold that making noise is an act likely to breach the peace).

Many courts have used a balancing test to determine if a repossession was undertaken at a reasonable time and in a reasonable manner, and to balance the interests of debtors and creditors. See e.g., Clarin v. Minnesota Repossessors, Inc., 198 F.3d 661, 664 (8th Cir. 1999); Davenport v. Chrysler Credit Corp., 818 S.W.2d 23, 29 (Tenn. App. 1991). Five relevant factors considered in this balancing test are: "(1) where the repossession took place, (2) the debtor's express or constructive consent, (3) the reactions of third parties, (4) the type of premises entered, and (5) the creditor's use of deception." Davenport, 818 S.W.2d at 29 (citing 2 J. White & R. Summers, Uniform Commercial Code § 27-6, at 575-76 (3d ed. 1988)).

Relying on the language of our Supreme Court in Rea, plaintiffs argue that the "guiding star" in determining whether a breach of the peace occurred should be whether or not the public peace was preserved during the repossession. Rea, 257 N.C. at 641-42, 127 S.E.2d at 228. Plaintiffs contend "the elements as to what constitutes a breach of the peace should be liberally construed" and urge our Court to adopt a subjective standard considering the totality of the circumstances as to whether a breach of the peace occurred.

Plaintiffs claim that adopting a subjective standard for N.C. Gen. Stat. § 25-9-503 cases will protect unwitting consumers from the "widespread use of no notice repossessions, clandestine and after midnight repossessions" and will protect "our State's commitment to law and order and opposition to vigilante policies, opposition to violence and acts from which violence could reasonably flow[.]" If a lender is not held to such a high subjective standard, plaintiffs contend that self-help repossessions should be disallowed altogether.

First Virginia, in contrast, argues that a breach of the peace did not occur in this case, as a matter of law, because there was no confrontation between the parties. Therefore, because the facts in this case are undisputed concerning the events during the actual repossession of the automobile, the trial court did not err in its partial grant of summary judgment.

First Virginia disputes plaintiffs' contention that a determination of whether a breach of the peace occurred should be a wholly subjective standard, because if such a standard is adopted, every determination of whether a breach of the peace occurred would hereafter be a jury question and "would run directly contrary to the fundamental purpose of the Uniform Commercial Code, which is to provide some degree of certainty to the parties engaging in various commercial transactions." Further, First Virginia argues that applying a subjective standard to a breach of the peace analysis could be detrimental to borrowers, with lenders likely increasing the price of credit to borrowers to cover the costs of having to resort to the courts in every instance to recover their collateral upon default. The standard advocated by plaintiffs would "eviscerate" the self-help rights granted to lenders by the General Assembly, leaving lenders "with no safe choice except to simply abandon their 'self help' rights altogether, since every repossession case could [result] in the time and expense of a jury trial on the issue of 'breach of the peace[.]'" Finally, First Virginia argues that a subjective standard would be detrimental to the judicial system as a whole because "with a case-by-case, wholly subjective standard ... the number of lawsuits being filed over property repossessions could increase dramatically[.]"

Based upon our review of our appellate courts' treatment of breach of the peace in pre-UCC and UCC cases, as well as in other areas of the law, the purposes and policies of the UCC, and the treatment other jurisdictions have given the phrase, we find that a breach of the peace, when used in the context of N.C. Gen. Stat. § 25-9-503, is broader than the criminal law definition. A confrontation is not always required, but we do not agree with plaintiffs that every repossession should be analyzed subjectively, thus bringing every repossession into the purview of the jury so as to eviscerate the self-help rights duly given to creditors by the General Assembly. Rather, a breach of the peace analysis should be based upon the reasonableness of the time and manner of the repossession. We therefore adopt a balancing test using the five factors discussed above to determine whether a breach of the peace occurs when there is no confrontation.

In applying these factors to the undisputed evidence in the case before us, we affirm the trial court's determination that there was no breach of the peace, as a matter of law. Professional Auto Recovery went onto plaintiffs' driveway in the early morning hours, when presumably no one would be outside, thus decreasing the possibility of confrontation. Professional Auto Recovery did not enter into plaintiffs' home or any enclosed area. Consent to repossession was expressly given in the contract with First Virginia signed by

Joann Giles. Although a third party, Mr. Mosteller, was awakened by the noise of Professional Auto Recovery's truck, Mr. Mosteller did not speak with anyone from Professional Auto Recovery, nor did he go outside until Professional Auto Recovery had departed with the Giles' automobile. Further, neither of the plaintiffs were awakened by the noise of the truck, and there was no confrontation between either of them with any representative of Professional Auto Recovery. By the time Mr. Mosteller and plaintiffs went outside, the automobile was gone. Finally, there is no evidence, nor did plaintiffs allege, that First Virginia or Professional Auto Recovery employed any type of deception when repossessing the automobile.

There is no factual dispute as to what happened during the repossession in this case, and the trial court did not err in granting summary judgment to First Virginia on this issue.

B.

Plaintiffs next argue there was a factual dispute over whether or not a default occurred in the repayment of the note and therefore summary judgment was improper.

N.C. Gen. Stat. §25-9-503 [26] states that "unless otherwise agreed a secured party has on default the right to take possession of the collateral." The contract signed by Joann Giles stated that she would be in default if she "failed to make any payment within 10 days after its due date." Additionally, she agreed that if the bank chose to excuse a default, that would not excuse later defaults.

Plaintiffs argue in their brief to this Court that Joann Giles was "one payment behind" when her automobile was repossessed on 27 June 1999. They claim a payment was made to First Virginia before the automobile was repossessed, bringing her account up to date, but that payment was cashed and credited to Joann Giles' account two days after the repossession. Plaintiffs thus imply that because the check was ultimately received and cashed, Joann Giles' account was not in default when the repossession occurred. This position, however, is untenable. If a default is not cured before repossession, the fact that the check was mailed before repossession is immaterial when it is not received until after the collateral is repossessed. 10 Ronald A. Anderson, Anderson on The Uniform Commercial Code, §9-503:52 (3d ed. 1999 Revision).

Plaintiffs also argue in their brief that Credit Co. v. Jordan, 5 N.C. App. 249, 168 S.E.2d 229 (1968) "espouses the proposition that acceptance of late payments along with evidence of unconscionable or improper action on the part of the financial institution would constitute waiver or estoppel." Plaintiffs contend that First Virginia had accepted late payments in the past from Joann Giles and that First Virginia's repossession of the automobile was unconscionable; therefore, First Virginia was estopped from repossessing her automobile on 27 June 1999.

Plaintiffs' reliance on Credit Co., however, is misplaced because the proposition stated by plaintiffs is taken from dicta in that case and is not binding on this Court in the case before us. Further, plaintiffs do not direct us to any evidence in the record supporting a conclusion that First Virginia intended to forbear plaintiffs' payments or that First Virginia acted unconscionably. In fact, Joann Giles agreed in the contract that acceptance of a late payment by First Virginia would not excuse a later default. Plaintiffs' argument of forbearance by First Virginia is without merit.

The trial court found, and we agree, that there is no genuine issue of material fact as to whether Joann Giles' account was in default when the automobile was repossessed. The trial court did not err in granting summary judgment to First Virginia on this issue.

Plaintiffs' first assignment of error is overruled.

II. (Discussion of constitutionality of self-help repossession omitted)

The trial court's order granting partial summary judgment for First Virginia is affirmed. Affirmed.

---

### Exercise 6-4:  Self-Help Repossession

In 2012, Brittney Buyer purchased a 2012 Jeep Cherokee from Angie's Auto Club for $35,000. To finance the purchase, Brittney borrowed $35,000 from BigBank. The loan agreement between Brittney and BigBank provided, among other things, that the debtor, Brittney Buyer, would make monthly payments of $675 on the 1st of every month, could pay off the loan in full without penalty, and in the event of default BigBank would have the authority to repossess the Jeep. Brittney Buyer failed to make her monthly payment on May 1st. On June 15th, BigBank hired Tommy of TJ's Towing to go to Brittney's home to repossess the Jeep.

On June 16th Tommy went to Brittney's residence, hooked up her Jeep and was about to start towing the Jeep away when Brittney came outside. Brittney yelled for Tommy to stop, placed her hands on her Jeep and placed herself between Tommy and his vehicle. Tommy moved Brittney aside, got in his towing vehicle and towed Brittney's Jeep away.

1. Did BigBank have the right to repossess Brittney's Jeep for only one late payment? Why or why not? Do you need any additional facts?

2. Assume that BigBank had the right to repossess Brittney's Jeep. Was the repossession of Brittney's Jeep a rightful repossession? Why or why not? Do you need any additional facts?

3. Would your answer to Question 2 change if, before Brittney noticed and objected to Tommy's actions, Tommy had towed the Jeep off of Brittney's property and was starting to drive down the street?

---

# 5.  Disposition of Collateral and Notification of Disposition

Once the secured party is in possession of collateral, the benefits of making a loan secured by personal property collateral become apparent. Instead of waiting for the conclusion of litigation and then searching for assets of the debtor, the secured party in possession of collateral may dispose of it in a commercially reasonable manner, and use the proceeds of the disposition to satisfy its debt. "Disposition" is not a defined term; however, section 9-610 broadly authorizes a secured party to "sell, lease, license or otherwise dispose of" all or any portion of the collateral. This term has also been interpreted very broadly by courts.[7] The sole limitation is that every aspect of the disposition must be commercially reasonable. In addition, section 9-611 requires a secured party that disposes of collateral under section 9-610 to send notice to specified parties before the proposed disposition. Sections 9-613 and 9-614 include forms of notice appropriate for use in a non-consumer (9-613) and consumer (9-614) goods transaction. *Figure 6-4* summarizes the secured party's obligations in connection with disposition of collateral.

### Figure 6-4:  Disposition of Collateral after Default (9-610)

|  | Consumer Goods | Non Consumer Goods |
|---|---|---|
| Notification before Disposition | 9-611 | 9-611 |
| To Whom Notice must be sent | • The debtor<br>• Any secondary obligor | • The debtor<br>• Any secondary obligor<br>• Person from whom secured party received a notification of an interest in the collateral<br>• Any other secured party or lien holder perfected by filed financing statement 10 days before notification date (or perfected under 9-311(a)) |
| Timing of Notification | Sent after default and within a reasonable time of disposition: a question of fact<br><br>9-612 | Sent after default and 10 days or more before the time of disposition set forth in the notice<br><br>9-612 |
| Contents and Form of Notification | 9-614 | 9-613 |
| Application of Proceeds of Disposition | 9-615 | 9-615 |
| Explanation of Calculation of Surplus or Deficiency | Secured Party *must* send explanation w/in 14 days after receipt of request and *before* paying any surplus or demanding any deficiency<br><br>9-616 | 9-616 |

---

7. For example, the Colorado Court of Appeals stated that "an examination of the default provisions of Article 9 of the UCC leads us to conclude that 'disposition' upon default was intended to refer to a transfer of some portion of the *creditor's* interest in the collateral *and* a transfer of the *debtor's* interest." (Emphasis in original.) *Silverberg v. Colantuno*, 991 P.2d 280, 289 (Colo.App.,1998).

# 6. Application of Proceeds of Disposition; Deficiency Rights; Surplus Obligations

After the secured party has disposed of the collateral, it may deduct authorized expenses associated with the disposition.[8] Then, except where the underlying transaction was an actual sale of accounts, chattel paper, payment intangibles or promissory notes, the secured party (absent any agreement to the contrary in the underlying transaction documents) must pay the debtor for any surplus, and the debtor will be liable to the secured party for any deficiency.

---

**Exercise 6-5:** *Hicklin v. Onyx Acceptance Corp.*

In the following case, the Supreme Court of Delaware considers whether a post-repossession private sale of collateral was commercially reasonable. As you read the case, consider the following questions:

1. Is the concept of "commercially reasonable" under the Code a rule or a standard? (Refer back to Chapter 2 for a discussion of rules and standards.)

2. What evidence must a secured creditor present to prove that a sale was commercially reasonable?

3. What are the consequences if a secured creditor makes a sale that is subsequently determined not to have been commercially reasonable?

---

# Hicklin v. Onyx Acceptance Corp.
## 970 A.2d 244 (Del. 2009)

Opinion

JACOBS, Justice:

Shannon P. Hicklin, the defendant below, appeals from a Superior Court order affirming a deficiency judgment of the Court of Common Pleas arising from the repossession and sale of a car financed by the plaintiff below, Onyx Acceptance Corporation ("Onyx"). On appeal, Hicklin argues that the Superior Court erroneously upheld the judgment of the Court of Common Pleas, because the trial court: (1) applied an incorrect standard in determining the commercial reasonableness of a sale after repossession, and (2) improperly admitted hearsay evidence. Hicklin also claims statutory damages for Onyx's alleged violation of the Delaware Uniform Commercial Code ("UCC"). We conclude that the trial court erroneously applied the UCC commercial reasonableness standard, that the trial court did not abuse its discretion in admitting hearsay evidence, and that Hicklin is not entitled to statutory damages. We therefore affirm in part and reverse in part the Superior Court order affirming the judgment of the Court of Common Pleas.

---

8. See §9-615.

## FACTUAL AND PROCEDURAL BACKGROUND

On July 6, 2000, Hicklin purchased a 1993 Ford Explorer (the "car") under an installment sales contract. Payments under that contract were assigned to Onyx. Hicklin fell behind on her payments, and on February 11, 2004, Onyx repossessed the car. At that time, Hicklin was three payments past due and owed $5,741.65 under the contract.

The car, when repossessed, had minor defects including a cracked windshield, dings, scratches, and a "check engine" message that would cost an estimated $1,365 to repair. Those defects were never repaired. According to the Kelley Blue Book, the average wholesale price of a 1993 Ford Explorer at that time was $3,700.

The repossessed car was driven to Dulles, Virginia and sold for $1,500 at a private auction operated by ABC Washington-Dulles, LLC ("ABC"). After deducting the sale proceeds from the costs of repossession and sale and the contract balance, there remained a deficiency of $5,018.88. Onyx sued Hicklin in the Court of Common Pleas to collect that deficiency. Hicklin denied liability and counterclaimed for statutory damages under 6 *Del. C.* § 9-625(c), on the ground that Onyx had failed to sell the car in a commercially reasonable manner as the UCC required.

Onyx's only witness at trial was Cesar Jimenez, an employee who worked in Onyx's Philadelphia office. Onyx is headquartered and maintains its records in California. Jimenez had worked for Onyx for 10 years, during which time he underwrote loans, made credit decisions, collected delinquent accounts and assigned delinquent accounts for repossession. At trial, Jimenez testified that Onyx sells its repossessed cars at private auction, because private auctions result in higher sale prices. Jimenez also authenticated several documents, including the repossession notice and reports describing the condition of Hicklin's repossessed car.

The Court of Common Pleas found that the fair market value of the car at the time of the sale was $2,335, using the higher of the two disputed mileage figures to determine the wholesale value, and then subtracting the repair costs. The court held that because the $1,500 auction price was greater than 50% of the car's adjudicated value, the sale was commercially reasonable. Consequently, the trial court ruled, Hicklin remained liable for Onyx's deficiency and was not entitled to statutory damages.

Hicklin timely appealed that judgment to the Superior Court. Hicklin claimed that the trial court had erroneously applied the common law "shock the conscience," rather than the UCC commercial reasonableness, standard. Hicklin also argued that the trial court misapplied the "business records exception" of D.R.E. 803(6), when admitting into evidence various documents offered by Onyx. Specifically, Hicklin claims that the trial court erroneously credited the authentication of those documents by Jimenez, who was not their custodian. Rejecting these arguments, the Superior Court held that the trial court had not relied solely on the 50% "shock the conscience" test, but also had considered Jimenez's testimony, the documentary evidence, and the inaccurate odometer reading, to conclude that the sale was commercially reasonable. On that basis, the Superior Court affirmed the judgment of the Court of Common Pleas. This appeal followed.

## ANALYSIS

### I.

On appeal from the Court of Common Pleas to the Superior Court, the standard of review is whether there is legal error, whether the trial court's factual findings are sufficiently supported by the record, and whether those findings are the product of an orderly and logical reasoning process. Factual findings of the Court of Common Pleas that are supported by the record will be upheld even if, acting independently, the Superior Court would have reached a contrary result. On further appeal to this Court we apply the same standard in reviewing independently the underlying decision of the Court of Common Pleas.

Applying a presumption that repossession sales that recover over 50% of a vehicle's value are commercially reasonable, the trial court granted Onyx a deficiency judgment. On appeal, Hicklin claims that: (1) the trial court erred in applying the common law "shock the conscience" test rather than the UCC "commercial reasonableness" test, and that (2) Onyx failed to meet its burden of proving a commercially reasonable disposition of the collateral. Hicklin urges that Onyx did not establish that the auction was commercially reasonable, because Onyx failed to: (a) introduce evidence of the prevailing practice in disposing of repossessed automobiles, or (b) show that the time, place and manner of the sale were commercially reasonable.

Onyx responds that the trial court properly applied the commercial reasonableness test, and that Onyx adequately proved that it had sold the car in a commercially reasonable manner. Onyx contends that the commercial reasonableness test is flexible and permits a secured creditor, acting in good faith, to exercise business judgment and flexibility in deciding how to dispose of collateral. Onyx further argues that it was not required to introduce evidence of the prevailing trade practice in disposing of repossessed automobiles, and that even without such evidence, it established that the time, place, and manner of the sale were commercially reasonable.

This appeal raises two issues. The first is what is a commercially reasonable disposition under the UCC, and how may a party prove commercial reasonableness. The second is what consequence flows from a secured party's failure to establish a commercially reasonable disposition of collateral. For the reasons next discussed, we conclude that: (1) the trial court applied an erroneous commercial reasonableness standard, (2) Onyx failed to adduce sufficient evidence to establish a commercially reasonable sale of Hicklin's car, (3) Onyx's failure to establish commercial reasonableness bars it from recovering any deficiency, (4) the trial court did not err in admitting certain documents into evidence, and that (5) Hicklin is not entitled to statutory damages.

## II. The Courts Below Applied An Erroneous Commercial Reasonableness Standard

Because this dispute concerns a security interest in personal property, it is governed by Article 9 of the UCC. Section 9-610 of the UCC (6 *Del. C.* §9-610) states the general rule governing the disposition of collateral:

> (a) After default, a secured party may … dispose of … the collateral in its present condition or following any commercially reasonable preparation. …
>
> (b) Every aspect of a disposition of collateral, including the method, manner, time, place, and other terms, must be commercially reasonable. …

The UCC does not specifically define the term "commercially reasonable." Whether or not a secured party's disposition of collateral action was commercially reasonable must be considered on a case by case basis. Comment 2 to 6 *Del. C.* §9-610 states that "[s]ection 9-627 provides guidance for determining the circumstances under which a disposition is 'commercially reasonable.'" Sections 9-627(b) and (c), in turn, provide the following "safe harbors" that are deemed to establish conclusively that a secured party acted in a commercially reasonable manner under Section 9-610:

> (b) A disposition of collateral is made in a commercially reasonable manner if the disposition is made:

(1) in the usual manner on any recognized market;

(2) at the current price in any recognized market at the time of disposition; or

(3) otherwise in conformity with reasonable commercial practices among dealers in the type of property that was the subject of the disposition.

(c) A ... disposition ... is commercially reasonable if it has been approved:

(1) in a judicial proceeding;

(2) by a bona fide creditors' committee;

(3) by a representative of creditors; or

(4) by an assignee for the benefit of creditors.

Our prior case law has articulated a standard substantially similar to the one established by Section 9-627(b)(3):

To be commercially reasonable the actions must be "in keeping with prevailing trade practice among reputable and responsible business and commercial enterprises engaged in the same or similar businesses."

The only safe harbor provision applicable here would be proof of "conformity with reasonable commercial practice among dealers in the type of property that was the subject of the disposition." The reason is that auctions of the kind at issue here are not "recognized markets" in which sales are conclusively deemed commercially reasonable.

Onyx could prove that its sale of Hicklin's car was commercially reasonable under 6 *Del. C.* § 9-610(a) in one of two ways. First, it could show that every aspect of the sale was conducted in a commercially reasonable manner, as Section 9-610(b) prescribes. Second, it could take advantage of the Section 9-627(b)(3) safe harbor applicable here, by showing that it sold the car in accordance with the accepted practices of reputable dealers in that type of property. Because showing conformity with the practices of reputable dealers in the trade conclusively establishes commercial reasonableness, secured parties often utilize that safe harbor. Where they do not, secured parties must meet the burden of showing that every aspect of the sale is "commercially reasonable"—a burden that requires the secured party to establish considerably more than that a presumptively fair price for the collateral was obtained.

### A. Onyx Failed to Prove the Sale of Hicklin's Car Was Commercially Reasonable in Every Aspect

The UCC affords secured parties greater rights than those available at common law the ability both to repossess collateral and to sue for a judgment on the underlying obligation rather than having to elect between those remedies. The UCC also requires the secured party to meet a high standard when disposing of collateral. Although obtaining a satisfactory price is the purpose of requiring a secured party to resell collateral in a commercially reasonable way, price is only one aspect. It is improper to reason backwards from price alone to determine the commercial reasonableness of the overall sale process. Because *every aspect* of a sale must be "commercially reasonable," showing that the sale grossed over 50% of the collateral's value, without more, will not establish the secured party's compliance with 6 *Del. C.* § 9-610(b). Therefore, the Court of Common Pleas (and, on appeal, the Superior Court) reversibly erred by holding that the sale of Hicklin's car for over 50% of its adjudicated fair market value, without more, was "commercially reasonable."

Onyx argues that a recovery of more than 50% of fair market value should establish "commercial reasonableness," citing Court of Common Pleas precedent adopting that presumption. Because those cases are inconsistent with the plain language of the UCC, they are not sound law and we overrule them.

Onyx next argues that even if the trial court made an error of law, the evidence nonetheless sufficiently establishes that Onyx sold Hicklin's car in a commercially reasonable manner. Onyx argues that private auctions generally yield higher prices, and that because Hicklin's car was sold to the highest bidder at a private auction, the sale must have perforce been "commercially reasonable." We disagree. Even if private auctions *generally* result in higher sales prices than other methods, there is no evidence that the *specific* auction procedures employed by ABC here would have resulted in higher prices. To illustrate, the sale of a car to the highest bidder at a poorly publicized, sparsely attended, and inconveniently located auction would not be meaningful; but a sale to the highest bidder at a highly-publicized, well-attended auction run by a highly-regarded auctioneer in a convenient location would be. Onyx has failed to adduce any evidence that would permit a fact-finder to determine whether the ABC auction represented the former or the latter kind of auction. Without proof of the specific auction procedures that were followed, a secured party cannot satisfy its burden of establishing commercial reasonableness.

*B. Onyx Has Failed to Establish That Its Sale of the Car Conformed With Accepted Trade Practice*

Nor has Onyx proved commercial reasonableness by establishing conformity with accepted practices in the trade. Onyx argues that 6 *Del. C.* §9-610(b) does not *require* it to prove conformity with prevailing trade practices. That is true but of no help to Onyx. To be sure, Section 9-627(b)(3), which provides that sales which conform to accepted trade practice are commercially reasonable, is not the exclusive way to prove commercial reasonableness. Accordingly, Onyx was not required to introduce any evidence of practice in the trade. But, without such evidence, Onyx cannot avail itself of that UCC provision to prove a commercially reasonable sale of Hicklin's car.

*C. Onyx's Good Faith Does Not Establish the Commercial Reasonableness of the Sale*

Onyx next implies, without directly arguing, that because it acted in good faith when it sold Hicklin's car, the sale was commercially reasonable, or alternatively, was a substantial factor that the court could consider in evaluating commercial reasonableness. That contention fails to take into account 6 *Del. C.* §1-304, which provides that "[e]very contract or duty within the Uniform Commercial Code imposes an obligation of good faith in its performance and enforcement." Good faith is a bedrock minimum standard that all secured parties must satisfy. Article 9 goes beyond that, by imposing a higher standard-commercial reasonableness. A secured party's failure to act in good faith may evidence a lack of commercial reasonableness, but the converse is not necessarily true. That is, a showing of good faith in selling repossessed collateral, without more, cannot establish the commercial reasonableness of the method, manner, time, place, and other terms of that sale.

### III. Onyx's Failure to Establish a Commercially Reasonable Sale of the Collateral Bars a Recovery of Any Deficiency

The parties do not directly address another critical issue-the consequence of a secured party's failure to establish a commercially reasonable sale of collateral. Hicklin asserts, but without making any reasoned argument, that such a failure bars a recovery of any deficiency, and Onyx does not address the issue at all. We hold that a secured party's failure to establish a commercially reasonable sale of repossessed consumer collateral bars it from recovering any deficiency.

The UCC establishes a rebuttable presumption that secured parties in non-consumer transactions are entitled to deficiency judgments, even if they fail to comply with other provisions of Article 9. That presumption, however, does not apply here, because Hicklin bought her car in a consumer transaction. 6 *Del. C.* § 9-626(b) states:

> The limitation of the rules in subsection (a) [adopting the rebuttable presumption rule] to transactions other than consumer transactions is intended to leave to the court the determination of the proper rules in consumer transactions. *The court may not infer from that limitation the nature of the proper rule in consumer transactions and may continue to apply established approaches.* (emphasis added).

Delaware adopted revised Article 9 on July 1, 2001. The former Article 9 did not directly address the consequence of a secured party's failure to comply with its provisions. Delaware case law, however, held that a failure to comply with the notice provisions of Article 9 created an absolute bar to the secured party recovering a deficiency. In a 1980 decision, this Court adopted the absolute bar rule in the context of deficient notice, for the policy reason that proper notice of the sale of collateral enables a debtor to ensure that the secured party follows procedures designed to yield the highest available sale price. Those same policy concerns are applicable in this case and under Article 9 in its current form, where the secured party has failed to establish that it sold the collateral in a commercially reasonable manner. We therefore hold that a secured party's failure to prove a commercially reasonable disposition of repossessed consumer goods will absolutely bar a recovery of any deficiency. Accordingly, the entry of a deficiency judgment in Onyx's favor (and its affirmance by the Superior Court) cannot stand.

### IV. Hicklin's Claims of Evidentiary Error

Hicklin's second claim of error is evidentiary. The Court of Common Pleas allowed Jimenez, a non-custodial Onyx employee, to lay a foundation for admitting certain business records prepared both by Onyx staff and by outside contractors retained by Onyx as business records under D.R.E. 803(6). The Superior Court affirmed that ruling. On appeal, Hicklin argues, *inter alia,* that because Jimenez an employee in Onyx's Philadelphia office was not the custodian of the business records maintained at Onyx's corporate headquarters in California, he was not qualified to establish the foundation required to authenticate those documents as business records for Rule 803(6) purposes. Onyx argues that because Jimenez had worked for Onyx for ten years in several different capacities, he could properly authenticate those documents under D.R.E. 803(6) as an "other qualified witness." Alternatively (Onyx argues) even if those records were erroneously admitted, substantial evidence supports the trial court's evidentiary ruling.

Because we conclude that the trial court erred as a matter of law by granting Onyx a deficiency judgment, and reverse the Superior Court's affirmance on that basis, we address Hicklin's evidentiary claim only insofar as is necessary to decide her counterclaim for statutory damages. We review a trial court's evidentiary rulings for abuse of discretion.

D.R.E. 803(6) provides, in relevant part:

> A ... record ... kept in the course of a regularly conducted business activity ... as shown by the testimony of the custodian or other qualified witness ... [is admissible hearsay].

The trial judge ruled that Jimenez was a qualified authenticating witness, because he had worked for Onyx for over ten years, and had underwritten loans, made credit decisions, and assigned delinquent accounts for repossession. Although Hicklin argues that Jimenez was not the document's custodian, she is unable to articulate precisely how the trial court abused its discretion in finding Jimenez to be an "other qualified witness." We conclude that Jimenez's employment history with Onyx was a sufficient basis for the trial court to find (and that the court committed no abuse of discretion in finding) that Jimenez was qualified to authenticate the repossession notice.

### V. Hicklin Is Not Entitled to Statutory Damages on Remand

The final issue concerns Hicklin's counterclaim for statutory damages based on Onyx's alleged breach of the notice provisions of 6 *Del. C.* §9-611. The Superior Court held that Hicklin had failed to offer any support for her counterclaim, and affirmed the trial court's rejection of it. On appeal to this Court, Hicklin again argues that Onyx's breach of Article 9's notice provisions entitles her to statutory damages under 6 *Del. C.* §9-625(c). Onyx responds that because it gave Hicklin proper statutory notice, she is not entitled to statutory damages.

We agree that Hicklin's statutory damages claim lacks merit. Hicklin's argument that Onyx breached the notice requirements of 6 *Del. C.* §9-611, by failing to send a proper repossession notice rests on her claim that the repossession notice was not properly authenticated by Jimenez. Hicklin does not contend that the repossession notice was substantively deficient. Because we have concluded that the notice was properly authenticated and admitted into evidence, Hicklin's claim for statutory damages fails.

### *CONCLUSION*

For the foregoing reasons, the Superior Court's order affirming the judgment of the Court of Common Pleas is: (1) affirmed, insofar as it upholds the dismissal of Hicklin's counterclaim for statutory damages, and (2) reversed insofar as it affirms the deficiency judgment entered in favor of Onyx. The case is remanded to the Superior Court, with instructions to remand it to the Court of Common Pleas, for proceedings consistent with this Opinion.

---

### Exercise 6-6:  Commercially Reasonable Disposition of Collateral

Arthur Artie, an art collector, entered into a written security agreement with BigBank pursuant to which BigBank loaned Arthur $50,000 to be paid in full by Jan 1. The loan was secured by Arthur's art collection (the security agreement listed each piece by title of the work, creator, and year made). On January 1, Arthur still owed BigBank $10,000. BigBank immediately took possession of Arthur's art collection and sold each piece at auction to cover the $10,000 Arthur owed BigBank.

1. Did BigBank have the right to sell Arthur's art collection at an auction?

2. What if a series of private sales could yield more money than the proceeds of a single auction? Is BigBank obligated to arrange for the private sales?

3. If Arthur can prove that the proceeds of BigBank's auction were significantly less than the appraised value of his art collection, can he successfully argue that the auction was not commercially reasonable?

---

### Exercise 6-7:  Notification of Disposition

On February 1, Jessica Jetsetter purchased a 2011 Ford Mustang on credit from the Franklin Ford dealership, who took back a security interest in the vehicle as security for payment of the balance due on the vehicle. Jessica was to make monthly payments of $120. She made regular payments of $120 for five months, but lost her job, and was unable to continue making payments. Franklin Ford repossessed the vehicle, and now seeks your advice regarding its rights and obligations with respect to it.

1. Can Franklin sell Jessica's car without a court order? If so, what kind of a sale should it conduct? What procedure must it follow?

2. Assume that Franklin Ford scheduled a sale and sent a notice to Jessica addressed to the proper place as indicated on the loan agreement, but Jessica did not personally receive the notification after several attempts to deliver the notice by certified mail. Has Franklin satisfied its obligation to give notice?

3. What if Franklin knew that Jessica was currently living in a different location and would not be at the address indicated in the loan documents for several months? Would the notice satisfy Franklin's notification obligations?

4. Would your answer to Question 1 be different if, instead of a Ford Mustang, the vehicle were a tractor that Jessica used on her potato farm? Why or why not?

# 7. Rights of Transferee of Collateral

Section 9-617 spells out the rights of the party to whom the secured party transfers repossessed collateral. A good faith transferee takes free of any rights of the debtor or any subordinate security interest or liens, even if the secured party failed to comply with all of the provisions of Article 9. Section 9-610 specifically provides that the secured party may disclaim any and all warranties in connection with a sale of collateral, and subsection (f) provides a safe harbor record sufficient to disclaim warranties: "There is no warranty relating to title, possession, quiet enjoyment or the like in this disposition."[9]

## Exercise 6-8: Rights of Transferee of Collateral

In March, Betty Buyer purchased a new car from Lexi's Lexus Dealership for $45,000, with a loan from BigBank, secured by her new car. BigBank obtained all of the necessary documents for the attachment of a valid security interest. In July, Betty defaulted, and relinquished possession of the car to Bank. On August 16th, Betty Buyer received a certified letter providing proper notice to Betty Buyer that BigBank planned to sell the Lexus on October 1st.

1. Before the sale of the Lexus what are Betty's Buyer's rights with respect to the vehicle?

2. Before the sale of the Lexus, what steps, if any, can Betty take to get the vehicle back from BigBank?

---

9. See UCC § 2-312.

3. After BigBank sells the Lexus at a proper public sale to Daniel Day for $50,000, if Daniel had no knowledge of Betty Buyer's delinquent loan, what are Daniel Day's and Betty Buyer's respective rights to the Lexus?

4. Would your answer to Question 3 change if Daniel knew that BigBank was selling a car it had repossessed from Betty?

---

# 8.  Acceptance of Collateral in Full or Partial Satisfaction of Obligation

Yet another option available to a secured party is to retain collateral in full or partial satisfaction of the debt. That option is subject to UCC 9-620, which (i) permits the debtor (and certain other parties with an interest in the collateral) to require that the collateral be disposed of; (ii) prohibits the secured party from retaining the collateral in only partial satisfaction of the debt in certain consumer transactions; and (iii) requires the affirmative consent of the debtor to retention of the collateral in partial satisfaction of the debt in all cases. (A debtor can be deemed to have consented to retention of the collateral in full satisfaction of the debt if the secured party properly fulfills the applicable requirements of UCC 9-620.)

# 9.  Waivers

Although many of the provisions of the Code may be varied by agreement of the parties,[10] Article 9 specifically provides that neither the debtor nor the obligor may waive or vary certain rules stated in part 6 that protect the debtor. These include the right to: (a) require that the secured party use the collateral only in the manner and to the extent agreed to by the debtor; (b) request an accounting from the secured party regarding the collateral and any surplus from the sale of the collateral; (c) require that the secured party proceed in a commercially reasonable manner when enforcing the obligation against the debtor; (d) have the secured party apply the proceeds from the collateral to the debtor's obligation under the loan; (e) receive timely notice upon disposition of the collateral by the secured party; (f) a calculation and explanation of the surplus or deficiency on disposition of the collateral; (g) redeem the collateral; and (h) remedies when the secured party fails to comply with the requirements of part 6. While these rights can never be waived at the inception of a loan, the debtor is entitled to waive certain of them *after* an event of default. Official Comment to UCC 9-602 explains that the "legal system traditionally has looked with suspicion on agreements that limit the debtor's rights and free the secured party of its duties.... The specified rights of the debtor and duties of the secured party may not be waived or varied except as stated."

---

10.  UCC § 1-201(3).

### Exercise 6-9:  Waivers under Part 6 of Article 9

Create a graphic representation, such as a table, to illustrate which rights under part 6 can never be waived, and which rights can be waived after an event of default occurs.

# 10.  Noncompliance with Article 9

Official Comment 2 to UCC 9-625 explains that "the principal limitations under Article 9 on a secured party's right to enforce its security interest against collateral are the requirements that it proceed in good faith (section 1-203), in a commercially reasonable manner (sections 9-607 and 9-610) and, in most cases, with reasonable notification (sections 9-611 through 9-614)." UCC 9-625 outlines specific remedies if it is established that a secured party is not complying with the requirements of Article 9, including (1) injunctive relief; (2) damages according to proof; and (3) in consumer goods transactions, the award of statutory damages to the debtor — and, sometimes, the secured party's loss of all right to recover the unpaid balance of the debt.

### Exercise 6-10:  *In re Schwalb*

The following case, set in a bankruptcy court, demonstrates the entire "first story" of a secured transaction, discussing the issues you have learned in the order you have learned them: (1) scope (inclusions and exclusions); (2) characterization of collateral; and (3) creation of a security interest. Because the case was heard in a bankruptcy court, the Court actually reviewed the second story, but these portions of the case have been omitted. To determine the validity of the secured creditor's claim in bankruptcy, the court thoroughly analyzes the debtor's default, and whether the secured creditor's claim will be reduced for failure to comply with proper foreclosure procedures. As you read the case, identify the approach the Court followed. Then use that same approach to analyze the Chapter Problem.

## In re Schwalb

### 347 B.R. 726 (D. Nev. 2006)

Opinion

AMENDED OPINION REGARDING CONFIRMATION OF CHAPTER 13 PLAN

BRUCE A. MARKELL, Bankruptcy Judge.

### I. INTRODUCTION

"Then the bird does not belong to any of you?" Spade asked, "but to a General Kemidov?"

"Belong?" the fat man said jovially, "Well, sir, you might say it belonged to the King of Spain, but I don't see how you can honestly grant anybody else clear title to it—except by right of possession." He clucked. "An article of that value that has passed from hand to hand by such means is clearly the property of whoever can get hold of it." [Dashiell Hammett, *The Maltese Falcon*, reprinted in THE NOVELS OF DASHIELL HAMMETT 397 (1965).]

Possession is the central theme in this case. Pioneer Loan & Jewelry, a pawnbroker, possesses two certificates of title that list it as the owner of two motor vehicles. Michelle Schwalb, the debtor, possesses those vehicles. Pioneer claims exclusive ownership, and that Ms. Schwalb has no legal or equitable interest in the vehicles beyond mere possession. Schwalb counters that Pioneer has no interest in the vehicles because she never transferred title or granted any other interest in them to Pioneer.

Pioneer seeks possession of the vehicles, and has asked this court to force Ms. Schwalb to turn them over to it. Ms. Schwalb seeks to keep the vehicles and pay Pioneer nothing under her chapter 13 plan, the confirmation of which is the subject of this opinion.

Both parties' fallback position is that Pioneer's interest is that of a secured creditor, as it is not disputed that Pioneer originally lent money to Ms. Schwalb on the strength of the vehicles as collateral. But this presents a different problem: the documents under which Pioneer lent Ms. Schwalb money provided for an annual interest rate of approximately 120%. As a result, by the time Ms. Schwalb filed her bankruptcy, Pioneer's claim had grown to more than double the original loan. Pioneer thus believes that Ms. Schwalb has insufficient resources to pay this claim over the life of her chapter 13 plan. Ms. Schwalb responds that Pioneer's secured claim is less than Pioneer alleges. She offered evidence that she can afford plan payments at the current plan value. She also asserts, and Pioneer does not dispute, that Pioneer's failure to file a proof of claim prevents Pioneer from asserting any unsecured claim related to its loans.

All of these issues were tried to the court during a confirmation hearing on March 20, 2006. After hearing the testimony, and reviewing all the evidence and the pleadings, the court finds that Pioneer is a secured creditor, and that Ms. Schwalb can fund a chapter 13 plan given the findings regarding value (after offsets for statutory damages). The court will thus require the debtor to file an amended plan consistent with this opinion, and when it is filed, the court will confirm that plan.

## II. RELEVANT FACTS

Michelle Schwalb is not a typical chapter 13 debtor. She holds no job, because she can't hold one. Seven years ago she had a brain tumor removed, leaving her unsteady and unable to concentrate for extended periods of time. Social Security disability payments are her only regular income. She is 34 years old, diabetic, has a non-working pituitary gland, and has initial symptoms of Grave's disease. She must take steroids to live. Ms. Schwalb lives with a man who fathered her only child, and they have been together as a family for thirteen or fourteen years. He works outside the home, and pays most of the household expenses.

Ms. Schwalb's chapter 13 plan is being funded entirely from her monthly disability payments, which are currently $580, and from contributions by her father. Her father's current monthly contribution is $640. Ms. Schwalb's father testified at confirmation that he is doing so out of a desire to take care of his daughter and his grandchild. He also testified that, before his daughter filed this chapter 13 case, he regularly contributed between $600 and $800 per month towards her support.

Ms. Schwalb's father gave her the two vehicles at issue, a 1997 Infiniti QX4 Sport Utility Vehicle and a 2002 Cadillac Escalade. Before dealing with Pioneer, Ms. Schwalb had clean title to both vehicles. Then, sometime during 2004, the debtor, her father and her partner decided they needed to contribute funds to a business that Ms. Schwalb's partner ran. They went to Pioneer and obtained two loans totaling $20,000.

The business, however, failed. Ms. Schwalb had no way to repay Pioneer. At this point, Pioneer began to take action to obtain the vehicles. To understand the actions Pioneer took, however, it is necessary to review the transactions by which Ms. Schwalb obtained the $20,000.

Ms. Schwalb and her father initially approached Pioneer in June of 2004. Mr. Schwalb had done business with Pioneer and, at that time, enjoyed some goodwill with it. Ms. Schwalb's Infiniti QX4 Sport Utility Vehicle was offered as collateral, and Pioneer advanced $4,000 against possession of the certificate of title for the vehicle. The parties testified that Ms. Schwalb gave Pioneer her certificate of title after she signed it as seller. The buyer's name was left blank.

When she received the $4,000 in loan proceeds, Ms. Schwalb signed a document referred to by the parties as a pawn ticket. The pawn ticket is a preprinted form used by Pioneer in its pawnbroker business. It is a simple 5-inch by 8-inch form, with text front and back. Among other things, the front has blanks for describing the property pawned, for the amount of the loan and for the repayment date.

On Ms. Schwalb's pawn ticket, the parties designated the property pawned as an Infiniti QX4 Sport Utility Vehicle, and included its Vehicle Identification Number (VIN). The ticket also contained the loan terms. Ms. Schwalb was to repay the $4,000 in 120 days, plus $1,605 interest. The disclosed annual interest rate was 122.04%. If Ms. Schwalb did not "redeem" the pawn and pay the loan within the 120 days, the pawn ticket indicated that "you shall … forfeit all right and interest in the pawned property to the pawnbroker who shall hereby acquire an absolute title to the same." Just before the blank on the pawn ticket in which the parties inserted the description of the Infiniti and its VIN, the pawn ticket indicated, in very small five-point type, "You are giving a security interest in the following property: " Pioneer did not retain possession of the vehicle. Ms. Schwalb drove off in it with her $4,000. Pioneer put the signed certificate of title in a safe on its premises.

The transaction with the Cadillac was essentially the same, except Pioneer advanced $16,000 against possession of the signed certificate of title, and the interest rate was 121.76%. This transaction occurred on August 19, 2004. In each case, Pioneer's representative testified that the amount Pioneer lent against the certificates of title was within Pioneer's general practice of lending no more than 30% to 40% of the retail value of the vehicle offered as collateral.

Approximately $1,605 in interest on the Infiniti loan was paid on or around November 6, 2004, thus extending the redemption period to March 6, 2005. No interest was ever paid on the Cadillac loan. The final 120-day term expired on the Infiniti loan on March 6, 2005, and on December 17, 2004, for the Cadillac loan.

When Ms. Schwalb did not repay either loan, Pioneer took both certificates of title to the Nevada Department of Motor Vehicles ("DMV") where, sometime in April 2005, Pioneer requested that the DMV reissue the certificates showing Ms. Schwalb as the owner and Pioneer as the "lienholder." The DMV complied. After Pioneer's initial efforts to obtain the vehicles were unsuccessful, Pioneer then presented the newly reissued certificates of title to the DMV, this time requesting that the DMV reissue the certificates of title without any mention of Ms Schwalb, and listing Pioneer as the sole owner. Again the DMV complied. Pioneer then filed a state court lawsuit apparently alleging conversion and seeking recovery of both vehicles. There was testimony that Pioneer consulted with the local police regarding the necessity of changing the certificates of title to facilitate its legal action seeking recovery of the vehicles.

Ms. Schwalb filed her chapter 13 case on August 9, 2005. Pioneer elected not to file a proof of claim, instead opting to claim ownership of the vehicles. Pioneer attempted to obtain relief from stay so that it could obtain the vehicles, but withdrew that motion for procedural reasons.

Ms. Schwalb's plan, filed with her chapter 13 petition, proposes to pay her creditors over 36 months. Her monthly payment is $555 for the first 12 months of her plan, and $709 per month for the remaining 24 months of her plan.

Initially, Ms. Schwalb contends that Pioneer is not a secured creditor, and is barred from participating in her case as an unsecured creditor. Her initial proposal is thus to pay Pioneer nothing under her plan. If Pioneer is found to be a secured creditor despite her objection, she proposes to value the collateral for the secured claims at $16,000 for the Cadillac loan and $4,000 for the Infiniti loan. The plan would then pay these two secured claims full over the life of the plan, together with 10% simple interest.

### III. PIONEER'S PROPERTY INTERESTS

The parties have focused on the nature of Pioneer's property interest, if any, in the two vehicles. Relying on its pawn ticket and the laws of other states, Pioneer contends that it owns both vehicles, and that Ms. Schwalb has no legal or equitable interest in them. Ms. Schwalb counters that Pioneer is not a pawnbroker with respect to the vehicles since it did not retain possession of them after making the loans. Ms. Schwalb further argues that the language of the pawn ticket is insufficient to create an Article 9 security interest under Nevada's version of the Uniform Commercial Code (UCC).

Pioneer, if forced to yield on its ownership claims, contends that the language in the pawn ticket is sufficient under Nevada's version of Article 9 to create a security interest, and that it has not violated any of Article 9's requirements or restrictions. Ms. Schwalb, however, contends that Pioneer did not comply with significant and mandatory provisions of Article 9, and requests that this court reduce Pioneer's claim.

#### A. Pawnbrokers and the Pawning of Goods Generally

> All around the cobbler's bench
> The monkey chased the weasel
> The monkey thought that all was fun
> Pop! Goes the weasel!
> A penny for a spool of thread
> A penny for a needle
> That's the way the money goes
> Pop! Goes the weasel!

[Nursery rhyme it may be, but its origins are in pawnbroking. In English slang (and the English version of the rhyme is printed above), to "pop" something is to pawn it; and a "weasel" was slang for a hatter's tool. WILLIAM MORRIS & MARY MORRIS, MORRIS DICTIONARY OF WORD AND PHRASE ORIGINS 457–58 (1977); BREWER'S DICTIONARY OF PHRASE AND FABLE 929 (16th ed., Adrian Room, rev. 1999).]

Under Nevada law, a pawnbroker is a "person engaged, in whole or in part, in the business of loaning money on the security of pledges, deposits or other secured transactions in personal property." NEV. REV. STAT. § 646.010. The parties agree that Pioneer is a licensed pawnbroker under this law. They disagree, however, on the significance of Pioneer's status, and to resolve those differences the court must investigate the history and current status of pawnbrokers, and the impact of pawnbroker status with respect to a nonpossessory vehicle loan.

### 1. Short History of Pawnbroking

Pawnbrokers engage in transactions in which a debtor pawns goods in return for a short-term loan. Pawnbroking has a significant and positive place in the history of lending. *Italian Banks and Pawnbroking: In Hock,* THE ECONOMIST, May 27, 2006, at 73 (reporting that pawnbroking is a 500-year old business and stating that the bank claiming to be the world's oldest bank, the Monte dei Paschi di Siena, began in the pawn business). According to some accounts, Queen Isabella of Spain pawned her jewels to finance Columbus' trip of discovery. Jarret C. Oeltjen, *Florida Pawnbroking: An Industry in Transition,* 23 FLA. ST. U.L. REV. 995, 996 (1996). At various times in our history, pawning one's clothes and other possessions was an ordinary and common occurrence.

Pawning one's goods differs from lending against them; in a typical pawn, a debtor deposits goods with the pawnbroker, and receives money in return. If the customer does not "redeem" his pawn within a specified time, tradition has it that the power to sell the goods deposited automatically passes to the pawnbroker. If the pawnbroker's subsequent sale of the goods does not cover the loan, the pawnbroker takes the loss; conversely, if the pawnbroker sells the goods for more than the money lent, custom allows the pawnbroker to keep the surplus. CASKEY, *supra* note 7, at 1. Another way to characterize the transaction is as a nonrecourse loan by the pawnbroker to the customer, with agreed strict foreclosure on the redemption date.

### 2. Recent History, and the Advent of "Title Pawns"

Despite its venerable history, pawnbroking has lately experienced something of a public relations crisis. Pawnbrokers are regulated in a manner designed to deter personal property theft, and often are found in low-income neighborhoods on the fringe of respectability. Despite efforts to improve this image, "the negative portrait lingers; pawnshops continue to be cast as 'nuisance businesses,' in the company of tattoo shops and massage parlors, and somewhere in rank between liquor stores and houses of prostitution." Oeltjen, *supra,* at 1001.

This negative perception has not been helped by the type of loans present here. As noted in a recent report sponsored in part by the Consumer Federation of America, "car title loans are marketed as small emergency loans, but in reality these loans trap borrowers in a cycle of debt. Car title loans put at high risk an asset that is essential to the well-being of working families—their vehicle." AMANDA QUESTER & JEAN ANN FOX, CAR TITLE LENDING: DRIVING BORROWERS TO FINANCIAL RUIN 2 (2005). As noted by Quester and Fox, some states have passed laws favorable to the title loan industry, *id.* at 10, while others have specifically prohibited pawnbrokers from engaging in "title pawn" transactions, *id* at 11 & n. 101. *See id.* at App. A, pp. 32–34 (collecting state statutes permitting and regulating title loans).

### 3. Nevada's Regulation of Pawnbrokers and Title Pawn Transactions

Nevada has not directly enacted legislation regarding the relationship between traditional pawnbroking and title lending. As a consequence, Pioneer attempts to support its position with extrapolations of existing state and local regulations, as well as of recent Nevada Attorney General opinions. As will be seen, however, these arguments are unavailing.

### a. State

Nevada regulates pawnbrokers through a series of provisions found in Chapter 646 of the Nevada Revised Statutes. NEV. REV. STAT. §§ 646.002 to 646.060. Most of these provisions regulate the business and accounting side of pawnbroking; for example, pawnbrokers are required to keep detailed records of their transactions, *id,* § 646.020, and are required each day to turn over records of the previous day's transactions to law enforcement officials. *Id.* § 646.030.

Of all the sections in Chapter 646, only one — Section 646.050 — provides substantive restrictions on the terms of a loan made by pawnbrokers. It requires that pawnbrokers cannot charge more than 10% per month on their loans, and must offer a redemption period of at least 120 days to their customers. *Id.* § 646.050.1. The criminal provisions of the chapter, however, do not refer to this rate regulation; rather, they are concerned with compliance with the recordkeeping provisions. *Id.* § 646.060. This limitation underscores the basic fact that the main purpose of Chapter 646 is not consumer protection, but law enforcement.

Chapter 646 also covers "motor vehicles received in pledge," and permits the storage of such vehicles at a location apart from the pawnbroker's principal place of business. In the late 1990s, when title pawns began to expand in Nevada, the state attorney general was asked to opine on the appropriate classification of such activity. In two opinions cited by counsel, the attorney general found that nonpossessory lending against the strength of a vehicle's title fit within the definition of "pawnbroker" for regulatory purposes because, although it was not the typical possessory lending historically associated with pawnbrokers, it did fit the statutory definition of someone in the business of "loaning money on the security of pledges, deposits or *other secured transactions in personal property.*" NEV. REV. STAT. § 646.010 (emphasis supplied). *See* OP. NEV. ATT'Y GEN. 97–03 (1997); OP. NEV. ATT'Y GEN. 95–20 (1995). *See also* OP. NEV. ATT'Y GEN. 97–13 (1997) (clarifying that opinions were meant to aid in the proper regulations of such lending). The attorney general apparently assumed that such nonpossessory lending was subject to Article 9 of Nevada's version of the UCC, *see, e.g.,* OP. NEV. ATT'Y GEN. 95–20 ("Since pawn transactions authorized by NRS Chapter 646 allow the pawnbroker to engage in 'other secured transactions in personal property....'"), but opined that when practiced with the traditional pledge of personal property, it was within the business of pawnbroking, at least for purposes of exempting pawnbrokers from regulation under the installment lending provisions of Chapter 675 of the Nevada Revised Statutes. *Id.*

### b. City

Nevada pawnbrokers are also regulated by municipal governments, and Pioneer was (and is) subject to regulation by the City of Las Vegas. Chapter 6.60 of the Las Vegas Municipal Code in most parts copies and expands on Chapter 646 of the Nevada Revised Statutes. It also requires a pawnbroker to be licensed, and requires a separate license if the person "accepts a motor vehicle as pledged property or in any other matter allows the use of a motor vehicle as collateral or security for a loan." LAS VEGAS MUNICIPAL CODE, §§ 6.6.020 (definition of "auto-pawnbroker"); 6.60.035 (requirement of a separate license for auto-pawnbroker).

The municipal provisions applicable to Pioneer are also primarily related to law enforcement, and not to consumer protection. The municipal code, however, does contain certain disclosure requirements for borrowers, and also makes it unlawful for the pawnbroker to charge or receive more than 10% interest per month.

### B. Application of Article 9

Neither the state nor the local regulation specifically refers to the applicability of the primary statute related to personal property collateral — Article 9 of the UCC. Conversely, Nevada has not explicitly excluded pawnbroking from the scope of Article 9. The initial question is thus easily stated: Does Article 9 apply to Pioneer's two transactions with Ms. Schwalb?

### 1. Does Article 9 Apply to Traditional Pawnbroking Activities?

Pioneer contends (and often assumes without argument) that pawnbroking is excluded from Article 9. That contention is false as a matter of statutory construction. Article 9 is intended to be the primary statute regarding the consensual personal property security. It is a marvel of drafting that consolidates and resolves many issues into one single statute. And it is intentionally broad; as noted in the comments, "all consensual security interests in personal property and fixtures are covered by this Article.... When a security interest is created, this Article applies regardless of the form of the transaction or the name that parties have given to it." Cmt. 2 to UCC §9–109.

To achieve this breadth of coverage, Article 9 looks to substance over form. This is confirmed by its text: Article 9 states that it applies to any "transaction, *regardless of its form,* that creates a security interest in personal property or fixtures by contract." NEV. REV. STAT. §104.9109.1(a) (emphasis supplied).

Given this broad scope, some states have altered the breadth of Article 9 by either expanding the list of exclusions to Section 9–109 as adopted, or by restricting the effect Article 9 gives to security interests in Section 9–201. *Compare* NEV. REV. STAT. §104.9109.4(n) (excluding "[a] transfer by a government or governmental unit" from scope of Nevada's Article 9) *and* NEV. REV. STAT. §104.9201.2 (excluding consumer transactions under Chapters 97 and 97A from Article 9's section validating security agreements) *with* UCC §9–109(d) (containing no exclusion for governmental transfers) *and* UCC §9–201(b) (containing generic exclusion for consumer protection laws from Article 9's section validating security agreements generally). *See also* UCC §9–109(c)(2) (permitting exception for categories of transactions expressly provided by another state statute).

In the area of pawnbroking, however, Nevada has not adopted other states' practice of excluding some or all of pawnbroking's practices from Article 9. *See, e.g.,* CAL. COMM. CODE §9201(b) (2006) (exempting California's Pawnbroker Law, CAL. FIN. CODE §§21000 *et. seq.* from Article 9); 810 ILL. COMP. STATT §5/9–201(b)(5) (2006) (exempting Illinois' Pawnbroker Regulation Act); N.C. GEN. STAT. 25–9–201(b) (2006) (exempting North Carolina's Pawnbrokers Modernization Act of 1989 (Chapter 91A of North Carolina's General Statutes)).

Given this lack of express exclusion, the court believes that Nevada would join the other states and commentators who have examined the issue, and concluded that pawnbroking is an activity governed by Article 9 of the UCC that neither the parties' contrary language nor an industry's contrary practice can alter. *In re Davis,* 269 B.R. 914 (Bankr.M.D.Ala.2001) (applying Alabama law); *In re Jones,* 206 B.R. 569 (Bankr.M.D.Ala.1997) (applying Alabama law); *Mattheiss v. Title Loan Express* (*In re Mattheiss*), 214 B.R. 20, 28 (Bankr.N.D.Ala.1997) (applying Alabama law); *In re Lopez,* 163 B.R. 189, 191 (Bankr.D.Colo.1994) (despite language of forfeiture in pawn agreement, pawn relationship created a secured transaction capable of being modified in a chapter 13 plan); *Lynn v. Financial Solutions Corp. (In re Lynn)*, 173 B.R. 894, 900–01 (Bankr.M.D.Tenn.1994) (applying Tennessee law); *Harkness v. EZ Pawn Alabama, Inc.*, 724 So.2d 32 (Ala.Civ.App.1998) (on referral from Alabama Supreme Court); *Reeves v. Foutz & Tanner, Inc.*, 94 N.M. 760, 617 P.2d 149 (1980) (applying Article 9's provisions regarding a surplus following disposition applied to pawn transactions); 4 JAMES J. WHITE & ROBERT S. SUMMERS, UNIFORM COMMERCIAL CODE § 30–1(b), at 4 (5th ed. 2002) ("When a pawnshop takes possession of a debtor's clarinet, the parties are entering into a perfected secured transaction."); 8A LAWRENCE'S ANDERSON ON THE UNIFORM COMMERCIAL CODE § 9–102:152 (3d ed. Lary Lawrence, ed. 2005) ("Pawn transactions are Article 9 secured transactions.") [hereinafter "ANDERSON"].

### 2. Pioneer's Transactions Are Not Traditional Pawn Transactions

Even if the court held that pawnbroking's practices are impliedly exempt from Article 9, Pioneer would not prevail for the simple reason that the transactions at issue are not those of a traditional pawnbroker. Pawnbrokers are bailees of personal property held as collateral for loans. If the loan is not paid — or, in the argot of pawnbroking, if the pawn is not redeemed — then the pawnbroker sells the goods held, and keeps the proceeds; the debtor is not liable for any deficiency, and the pawnbroker is not accountable for any surplus. *See* Oeltjen, *supra*, at 996–97.

As a result, a true pawn requires a pledge, and a pledge requires delivery of the collateral to the pawnbroker. *See, e.g., Pendleton v. American Title Brokers, Inc.*, 754 F.Supp. 860, 864 (S.D.Ala.1991); *Lynn v. Financial Solutions Corp. (In re Lynn)*, 173 B.R. 894, 898 (Bankr.M.D.Tenn.1994); *State ex rel McGraw v. Pawn Am.*, 205 W.Va. 431, 433–34, 518 S.E.2d 859, 861–62 (1998). *Cf.* 18 U.S.C. § 921(a)(12) (defining pawnbroker, for purpose of regulating sale of firearms, as "any person whose business or occupation includes the taking or receiving, by way of pledge or pawn, of any firearm or ammunition as security for the payment or repayment of money."); NEB. OP. ATTY. GEN. No. 98027, 1998 Westlaw 344508, at 1 (June 19, 1998) ("[W]e believe that a pawnbroker is required to have actual possession of the automobile in order for the lending arrangement to constitute a pawnbroking transaction under Nebraska law.").

Here, of course, Pioneer did not possess the vehicles (although state law permitted it to do so); at best, it was a bailee of the certificates of title, for whatever good holding on to pieces of officially issued paper did it. As such, the issue as to the exempt status of traditional pawnbroking activities is not directly raised by this case.

Pioneer argues that actual possession was not necessary. Since it had possession of the certificates of title, it has "constructive" possession of the vehicles, and that this constructive possession was sufficient to bring it under the protective reach of pawnbroking status. Nothing in the Nevada statutory scheme authorizes this view, and pre-UCC cases rejected it. *See, e.g., Casey v. Cavaroc*, 96 U.S. 467, 477, 24 L.Ed. 779 (1877); (noting that "possession may be considered as of the very essence of a pledge," and that "constructive delivery cannot be effected without doing what amounts to a transfer of the property," using keys to a warehouse and bills of lading as examples); *Commercial Bank of Jacksonville v. Flowers*, 116 Ga. 219, 42 S.E. 474 (1902) (constructive possession of goods not accomplished by possession of receipt from wharfinger who had actual possession of goods). *See also* Section III.C.1.b, *infra*.

### C. Applicability of Article 9 to Pioneer's Loans

As indicated above, Section 9–109 makes Pioneer's transactions with Ms. Schwalb subject to Nevada's version of Article 9. This was not unexpected. Pioneer's form of pawnbroking ticket expressly states that Ms. Schwalb was "giving a security interest" in the two vehicles to Pioneer. Although more will be said about this language below, it is a clear indication that Pioneer was both aware of the term "security interest," and wanted to use it in the two transactions. And if a "security interest" is involved, the default statute of applicability is Article 9 of the UCC.

Beyond that, however, as the courts and commentators cited above have found, each transaction here fits within the text of Section 9–109 — that it be a "transaction ... that creates a security interest in personal property or fixtures by contract." NEV. REV. STAT. § 104.9109.1(a). This can be seen from an analysis of the components of Section 9–109.

The component most obviously present is a contract — a provision that requires that transaction to be consensual. "Contract," as defined in the UCC is "the total legal obligation that results from the parties' agreement ..." NEV. REV. STAT. § 104.1201.2(*l*). The UCC defines the term "agreement" as "the bargain of the parties in fact, as found in their language or inferred from other circumstances...." *Id.* § 104.1201.2(c).

Here, Ms. Schwalb and Pioneer had an "agreement" — Pioneer would lend money to her on the security of her two vehicles. That was their bargain in fact. This agreement gave rise to legal obligations — that is, rights that courts would vindicate — some supplied by Nevada's common law of contracts, and others by Nevada's version of Article 9. This consensual agreement combined with the attendant legal consequences form the necessary contract; or, put another way, the transaction was consensual, and breach of it implied various legal consequences.

Was it a contract to create or provide for a security interest? "Security interest" is defined in Article 1 as "an interest in personal property ... which secures payment or performance of an obligation." NEV. REV. STAT. § 104.1201.2(ii). Here, Ms. Schwalb gave Pioneer an interest in her vehicles as a condition of obtaining the two loans, and Pioneer held onto the title to ensure repayment. When Ms. Schwalb did not repay the loans within the 120–day redemption period, Pioneer's position is that exclusive ownership of the vehicles passed to it. This type of arrangement — in which rights to possession of personal property arise upon failure to repay debt or honor some other obligation — is a classic security interest and fits the definition of "an interest in personal property [that] secure[d] payment ... of an obligation." NEV. REV. STAT. § 104.9201.2(ii).

As a result, the transactions here were covered by Article 9 of the UCC. This conclusion has serious repercussions for the parties.

## 1. Attachment Generally

The initial consequence of Article 9's applicability is that the creation and status of Pioneer's interest is governed by a combination of the common law of contract law and the statutory provisions of Article 9. For an Article 9 security interest to be enforceable, it must "attach." NEV. REV. STAT. § 104.9203.

Attachment, in turn, has three requirements: (1) value has to have been given; (2) the debtor must have rights in the collateral; and (3) either (a) the debtor has authenticated a security agreement that provides a description of the collateral, or (b) the secured party possesses the collateral pursuant to a security agreement. NEV. REV. STAT. § 104.9203.2(a)-(c).

Value is present in the form of the loans extended by Pioneer to Ms. Schwalb. NEV. REV. STAT. § 104.1204. Similarly, there is no doubt that, at the time of each transaction,

Ms. Schwalb's ownership rights in the vehicles were sufficient "rights in the collateral" for a security interest to attach. *Foothill Capital Corp. v. Clare's Food Market, Inc. (In re Coupon Clearing Service, Inc.)*, 113 F.3d 1091, 1103 (9th Cir.1997) ("Where a debtor has rights to collateral beyond naked possession, a security interest may attach to such rights."), citing *Morton Booth Co. v. Tiara Furniture, Inc.*, 564 P.2d 210, 214 (Okla.1977).

The issue thus boils down to whether the "debtor authenticated a security agreement that provides a description of the collateral," or whether the collateral was "in the possession of the secured party under NRS 104.9313 pursuant to the debtor's security agreement." *Id.* § 104.9203.2(c)(1)-(2).

### a. Authenticated Agreement

Ms. Schwalb contends that the pawn ticket is legally insufficient as a security agreement. At trial, she testified that she did not know what she was signing at the time she received each of the two loans. Each pawn ticket used, however, contained the following preprinted language just before a description of the automobile involved as well as its VIN: "You are giving a security interest in the following property:"

Under Article 9, a "security agreement" is "an agreement that creates or provides for a security interest." NEV. REV. STAT. § 104.9102.1(ttt). The pawn ticket was clearly an "agreement" as the UCC uses that term. It contained "the bargain of the parties in fact," as expressed in "their language or [as could be] inferred from other circumstances ..." *Id.* § 104.1201.2(c). The bargain was simple and standard: Ms. Schwalb borrowed money at interest, and agreed to repay it within 120 days.

Thus, the only question is whether the agreement also included collateral as security for repayment of the loan. Each pawn ticket definitively described the vehicle at issue, by make, model and VIN. The issue is thus whether the words "[y]ou are giving" adequately "create [ ] or provide [ ]" for a security interest in the vehicles. The safest and traditional words to accomplish this task are words of grant or assignment, such as "I hereby grant a security interest in X to secure repayment of my debt to you" or "I assign this property to you to secure what I owe you."

In these phrases, the operative verbs—grant, assign, etc.—are in the present tense and indicate a present act. But the word used by the pawn ticket—"giving"—is not in the present tense but instead is the present participle of the verb "to give." Ms. Schwalb contends that use of the participle "giving" can only be read to refer to Pioneer's description of what Pioneer thought Ms. Schwalb had done or was doing—not as Ms. Schwalb's acknowledgment that she was engaging in a legally significant act. The analogy would be to something like noting that the statement "You are falling" describes an action taken by another rather than separately constituting the act of falling.

But this is a quibble. While a description may not be the act it describes, by signing the pawn ticket Ms. Schwalb acknowledged and adopted the act it described—giving a security interest. Moreover, the statutory verbs are "creates" *or* "provides." Even if the language did not "create" the security interest as Ms. Schwalb contends, it certainly did provide for "giving" one.

The insistence on formal words of grant or transfer is inconsistent with the structure and intent of Article 9. As the Idaho Supreme Court noted with respect to the original version of Article 9:

> Courts have often repeated that no magic words are necessary to create a security interest and that the agreement itself need not even contain the term 'security

interest.' This is in keeping with the policy of the code that form should not prevail over substance and that, whenever possible, effect should be given to the parties' intent.

*Simplot v. Owens,* 119 Idaho 243, 245–46, 805 P.2d 449, 451–52 (1990), *quoting Idaho Bank and Trust Co. v. Cargill,* 105 Idaho 83, 87, 665 P.2d 1093, 1097 (Ct.App.1983). *See also Nolden v. Plant Reclamation (In re Amex–Protein Dev. Corp.),* 504 F.2d 1056, 1059–60 (9th Cir.1974) ("There is no support in legislative history or grammatical logic for the substitution of the word 'grant' for the phrase 'creates or provides for.'").

The proper policy considerations are well stated by a leading commentator on Article 9: "There is no requirement for words of grant. In fact, such a requirement smacks of the antiquated formalism the drafters were trying to avoid." 1 CLARK & CLARK, *supra,* at ¶ 2.02[1][c], at p. 2–16. *See also* 4 WHITE & SUMMERS, *supra,* at § 31–3 ("the drafters did not intend that specific 'words of grant' be required.").

Ms. Schwalb's further argument that she did not understand the import of the words she subscribed to is also unavailing. Even though they appear in tiny five-point type, the words are discernible as an integral part of the pawn ticket. It has long been the common law rule that signing a document authenticates and adopts the words it contains, even if there was a lack of subjective understanding of the words or their legal effect. In essence, people are presumed to be bound by what they sign. *Campanelli v. Conservas Altamira, S.A.,* 86 Nev. 838, 841, 477 P.2d 870, 872 (1970) ("when a party to a written contract accepts it is (*sic*) a contract he is bound by the stipulations and conditions expressed in it whether he reads them or not. Ignorance through negligence or inexcusable trustfulness will not relieve a party from his contract obligations. He who signs or accepts a written contract, in the absence of fraud or other wrongful act on the part of another contracting party, is conclusively presumed to know its contents and to assent to them....."), *quoting Level Export Corp. v. Wolz, Aiken & Co.,* 305 N.Y. 82, 87, 111 N.E.2d 218, 221 (1953), *quoting Metzger v. Aetna Ins. Co.,* 227 N.Y. 411, 416, 125 N.E. 814, 816 (1920).

Ms. Schwalb contends that cases such as *Expeditors Int'l of Washington, Inc. v. Official Creditors Comm. (In re CFLC, Inc.),* 166 F.3d 1012 (9th Cir.1999) require a finding of a subjective intent to grant security, an intent that she contends is lacking here. In particular, she points to the following quotation from *CFLC* in support of her position:

> Determining whether the parties intended to create a security interest is a two-step process. The court must find both language in a written agreement that objectively indicates the parties' intent to create a security interest and the presence of a subjective intent by the parties to create a security interest.

*Id.* at 1016.

This quotation appears at odds with Nevada's common law of contracts set forth above. Yet upon examination, this antinomy dissolves. In *CFLC,* a shipping concern, Expeditors, handled CFLC's domestic and international shipping needs. Concurrently with Expeditors' receipt of goods to ship, Expeditors issued invoices to the debtor, CFLC, Inc., that contained the following language: "The Company [Expeditors] shall have a general lien on any and all property (and documents relating thereto) of the Customer [CFLC], in its possession, custody or control or en route, for all claims for charges, expenses or advances incurred by the company in connection with any shipments of the Customer...." *Id.* at 1014.

Over the course of several years, Expeditors sent 330 such invoices to CFLC. CFLC never signed any of them, and it did not discuss or take special note of the terms found in them. *Id.* When CFLC filed for bankruptcy, Expeditors had possession of goods it was transporting for CFLC, and Expeditors ultimately sued to assert its claimed lien on those goods. *Id.* at 1014–15.

The Ninth Circuit found that the unsigned invoices did not meet the requirements of California's version of Section 9-203. Initially, and most importantly, CFLC did not sign any of the invoices, so the requirement of a signed security agreement was not met. *Id.* at 1016. When pressed with the argument that CFLC had evidenced an intent to be bound by the invoice's provision of a security interest, the Ninth Circuit responded:

> [W]e decline to apply course of dealing analysis to non-Article 2 transactions in which there has been only a tacit acceptance of a contract term repeatedly sent to the offeree on a pre-printed form. Even under the common law, "silence in the face of an offer is not an acceptance, unless there is a relationship between the parties or a previous course of dealing pursuant to which silence would be understood as acceptance." *Id.* at 1018, *quoting Southern Cal. Acoustics Co. v. C.V. Holder, Inc.,* 71 Cal.2d 719, 722, 79 Cal.Rptr. 319, 456 P.2d 975, 978 (1969). Put another way, the Ninth Circuit was unwilling to find either objective or subjective manifestation of intent to be bound from a course of dealing.

In the present case, of course, Ms. Schwalb signed each pawn ticket, distinguishing this case from *CFLC.* Her signatures were each authentications; that is, each signature signaled her assent to the contract and her agreement to be bound by its terms; that is the common law understanding of what it is to "sign" a contract. *See, e.g., Campanelli,* 477 P.2d at 872; FARNSWORTH, *supra,* at § 3.7. As "signing" is "authentication" under the UCC, § 9–102(a)(7)(A), Ms. Schwalb's signatures effectively authenticated each pawn ticket within the meaning of Section 9–203. Because each pawn ticket adequately described the collateral covered by listing its VIN number, see § 9–108(b), Ms. Schwalb's signature thus completed the requirements of Section 9–203(b)(3)(A). Under *CFLC* and the UCC, then, Pioneer's interest attached upon such authentication.

### b. Attachment Based on "Constructive Possession" of the Certificates of Title

Pioneer argues in the alternative that its security interest attached through constructive possession of the vehicles, which was accomplished by possession of the certificates of title. Although at least one court has accepted a form of this argument, *Floyd v. Title Exch. & Pawn of Anniston, Inc.,* 620 So.2d 576 (Ala.1993), it does not square with tradition, commercial practice or Nevada law.

In commercial parlance, a record or writing stands proxy for goods it covers only if it is a "document of title" as defined in Article 1 of the UCC. That definition states:

> "Document of title" means a record:
>
> (1) That in the regular course of business or financing is treated as adequately evidencing that the person in possession or control of the record is entitled to receive, control, hold and dispose of the record and the goods the record covers; and
>
> (2) That purports to be issued by or addressed to a bailee and to cover goods in the bailee's possession which are either identified or are fungible portions of an identified mass....

NEV. REV. STAT. § 104.1201.2(p).

Documents of title, as defined, include warehouse receipts, bills of lading and the like. *Id.* Commercial parties deal with these documents as if they were dealing with the goods themselves; indeed, Article 9 allows perfection of goods covered by a negotiable document to be perfected by possession of that document. NEV. REV. STAT. § 104.9312.3.

But the automobile certificates of title here bear little resemblance to the documents of title described in Article 1. Certificates of title do not serve the commercial purpose of standing proxy for vehicles; they are generally held by the owner or lienholder of the car, not a bailee who controls the goods as its business. This is not particularly surprising. Certificate of title statutes were not designed to facilitate commerce; rather, they are regulatory and anticrime statutes that allow "big-ticket" items such as cars to be tracked by law enforcement authorities. LYNN M. LOPUCKI & ELIZABETH WARREN, SECURED CREDIT: A SYSTEMS APPROACH 406 (6th ed. 2006) ("Certificates of title are part of a complex system that serves a variety of purposes, most unrelated to secured credit. Certificates of title are part of the system by which the police identify the owner of a vehicle that is involved in an accident, lost, stolen, or used in the commission of a crime. Certificates of title are also used to transfer ownership of motor vehicles and to keep track of successive annual registrations and taxation of vehicles.").

Indeed, although Article 9 brings certificates of title into its system, it is only to provide a proxy for the financing statement, not the vehicle. In most states, the only way to perfect an interest in a car or other vehicle is to note the secured party's interest on the certificate of title. Except in rare circumstances, possession of the car will not perfect the already-attached secured party's security interest. NEV. REV. STAT. § 104.9313.2. The upshot of this is that mere possession of the certificate of title is of little legal significance under Article 9; that possession neither creates a security interest nor perfects one otherwise granted in the vehicles. *See, e.g., Lee v. Cox,* 18 U.C.C. Rep. Serv. 807, 21 Fed. R. Serv.2d 828 (M.D.Tenn.1976) (possession of registration certificates for eight Arabian horses did not perfect interest in horses). At best, Pioneer possessed the certificates of title for what they were worth—which is not much, as it turns out; their possession facilitated Pioneer's perfection of its interests as will be seen, but it did not assist Pioneer in divesting Ms. Schwalb of her interests.

Pioneer's interests were thus attached, but that alone is insufficient in this case. While attachment may make the security interest enforceable against the debtor, more is needed when the debtor is a debtor in bankruptcy. What is required in the later case is that the security interest be good against the world. The process by which such validity is obtained is referred to in Article 9 as perfection.

## 2. Perfection (intentionally omitted)

## 3. Enforcement

Perhaps the key difference that attends the application of Article 9 to the transactions at issue lies in how Pioneer may enforce its security interest. Its contract, the pawn ticket, is explicit. It states that:

> In the event of failure to pay the loan with 120 days from date hereof, you shall thereby forfeit all right and title unto such pawned property to the pawnbroker who shall thereby acquire an absolute title to the same.

Before Ms. Schwalb filed her case, Pioneer sought to enforce this clause by first applying to be listed as the owner on the certificates of title, and then by filing a state court action seeking possession of the vehicles.

### a. Unenforceable Forfeiture Clause

Pioneer continues to seek enforcement of this forfeiture clause as written. It asserts that both vehicles belong, in all senses of that word, to it and to it alone. This assertion is misguided. Article 9 prohibits the waiver by debtors of certain provisions. In particular, Section 9–602 contains a long list of provisions that "the debtor … may not waive or vary." NEV. REV. STAT. § 104.9602. These include the provisions regarding: the obligation to proceed in a commercially reasonable manner, *id.* § 104.9602.7, strict foreclosure, *id.* § 104.9602.10, and the debtor's right to redeem the collateral, *id.* § 104.9602.11.

If the parties sign a security agreement containing prohibited waivers, and then seek to enforce them, courts most often remedy violations of Section 9–602 by simply reading the relevant documents as if the offending clause had never been included. They then assess the parties' conduct under the remaining provisions and the default standards set forth in Article 9. *See, e.g., AAR Aircraft & Engine Group, Inc. v. Edwards,* 272 F.3d 468, 472 (7th Cir.2001) (waiver of duty to proceed in commercially reasonable manner unenforceable); *Tropical Jewelers, Inc. v. NationsBank, N.A.,* 781 So.2d 381, 384 (Fla.Dist.Ct.App.2000) (same); *Fleming v. Carroll Pub. Co.,* 581 A.2d 1219, 1223 (D.C.1990) (parties signed document denominated a "lease" that allowed lessor to take leased goods without notice; court finds that Article 9 applies, and that lessor/secured party could not rely on provision dispensing with notice, and held that provision to be unenforceable); *Prescott v. Thompson Tractor Co.,* 495 So.2d 513, 517 (Ala.1986) (predecessor to Section 9–602 precludes waiver by a debtor of the right to notification of the disposition of collateral); *Barber v. LeRoy,* 40 Cal.App.3d 336, 342–43, 115 Cal.Rptr. 272, 277 (1974) (provision allowing secured party to bid at private sale void as against public policy and unenforceable); *C.I.T. Corp. v. Haynes,* 161 Me. 353, 356, 212 A.2d 436, 438 (1965) (waiver of right of redemption in conditional sales contract subject to Article 9 unenforceable as against public policy).

These provisions are of special concern in consumer transactions. As noted in the official comments to Section 9–602:

> our legal system traditionally has looked with suspicion on agreements that limit the debtor's rights and free the secured party of its duties. As stated in former Section 9–501, Comment 4, "no mortgage clause has ever been allowed to clog the equity of redemption." The context of default offers great opportunity for overreaching. The suspicious attitudes of the courts have been grounded in common sense. This section, like former Section 9–501(3), codifies this long-standing and deeply rooted attitude. The specified rights of the debtor and duties of the secured party may not be waived or varied except as stated.

Cmt. 2, UCC § 9–602.

This wariness has been, for the most part, reflected in academic commentary on this subject. *See, e.g.,* Barkley Clark, *Default, Repossession, Foreclosure and Deficiency: A Journey to the Underworld And a Proposed Salvation,* 51 ORE. L. REV..302, 303 (1972) (noting that a consumer "is as likely to read (let alone understand) [a security agreement] as he is to run windsprints in Red Square"); Michael M. Greenfield, *The Role of Assent in Article 2 and Article 9,* 75 WASH. U.L.Q..289, 300 (1997) (arguing that a consumer's waiver of a statutory right at the time of contract formation "is highly suspect" and that the "small-print boilerplate" language of the waiver makes a consumer's assent "a fiction").

### *b. Violations of Part 6 of Nevada's Article 9*

If enforced as written, the pawn ticket forfeiture provisions would not only have waived and varied, but they would have effectively obliterated, Ms. Schwalb's right to prohibit Pioneer's strict foreclosure of her interest in the vehicles, as well as her right to redeem the vehicles after default and repossession. NEV. REV. STAT. §§ 104.9602.10; 104.9602.11. But under Section 9–602, these rights may not be waived or varied by private agreement. The result of this clash is that, in accordance with the prevailing law under Article 9 cited above, the pawn tickets will have to be enforced without reference to their forfeiture provisions.

What effect does that erasure have? Initially, it makes Article 9's default standards, rather than the pawn tickets' forfeiture provisions, applicable to Pioneer's action in attempting to dispose of the vehicles. Given the parties' prepetition dealings, this legal conclusion has bite, as will be seen later. *See* Section IV.B.2, *infra.* But for the present analysis, it means that Pioneer was obligated to proceed as to the vehicles in the manner required by Part 6 of Article 9. This it did not do. Because violations of Part 6 take on a significant role later in this opinion, it is appropriate to catalog the more egregious of Pioneer's violations.

The cornerstone duty placed on every secured party is the obligation to proceed in a commercially reasonable manner. Article 9 expresses this by requiring that "[e]very aspect of a disposition of collateral, including the method, manner, time, place and other terms, must be commercially reasonable." NEV. REV. STAT. § 104.9610.2.

Although proceeding by judicial action may be commercially reasonable in some case, the manner in which Pioneer proceeded here was not. It sought judicial vindication as the sole owner of the vehicles, a status it claimed through operation of the forfeiture clause in its pawn ticket. Such forfeitures are authorized in some circumstances, and are referred to as "strict foreclosures." *See* NEV. REV. STAT. § 104.9620.

But a secured party's ability to engage in a strict foreclosure with respect to a consumer is heavily circumscribed. In particular, a secured creditor may not strictly foreclose on consumer goods without the consumer's consent, NEV. REV. STAT. § 104.9620.1(a), and may not strictly foreclose on any collateral that it does not possess, *id.* § 104.9620.1(c). Neither of these conditions is present here, thus making Pioneer's attempts to strictly foreclose on the vehicles violations of Part 6 of Nevada's Article 9.

In addition, when Pioneer proceeded in state court as if the vehicles were its sole property, Pioneer violated its duty to give Ms. Schwalb the option to force a public disposition, and deprived her of the opportunity to redeem. NEV. REV. STAT. §§ 104.9602.10; 104.9602.11. Proceeding in this contrary-to-law manner was perforce not commercially reasonable.

There were other violations. Article 9 is explicit that a secured party must notify a debtor before any disposition, NEV. REV. STAT. § 104.9611.2, and is explicit on what that notice must contain. *Id.* § 104.9613.1. But Pioneer could not produce any notice that it sent to Ms. Schwalb, and she could not locate any notice she received from Pioneer. The parties, however, stipulated that Pioneer generally sends a notice to its borrowers on a standard form, and that they had no reason to believe that Pioneer did not send a notice on this standard form to Ms. Schwalb. Pioneer then produced an exemplar of that standard form. While the form appears to contain many of the required disclosures, it does not contain all of the required provisions. In particular, the notice violates NEV. REV. STAT. § 104.9612.1(d), which requires that any notice contain a statement that "the debtor is entitled to an accounting of the unpaid indebtedness and states the charge, if any, for an accounting."

Pioneer omitted this required disclosure, of course, because of Pioneer's belief in the validity of its forfeiture provisions, which did not mention any accounting. Pioneer's erroneous belief, even if in good faith, does not save it; there is no good faith defense to the failure to provide sufficient notice of a proposed disposition. *See, e.g., Kruse v. Voyager Ins. Cos.,* 72 Ohio St.3d 192, 196–97, 648 N.E.2d 814, 817 (Ohio 1995) (failure to send notice to debtor was a violation of Article 9's notice provisions); *Wilmington Trust Co. v. Conner,* 415 A.2d 773, 776 (Del.1980) (failure to give credit for finance charges paid but unearned in notice of disposition was violation of Article 9's notice provisions).

### c. The Irrelevance of Non–Nevada Statutory Law *(intentionally omitted)*

### D. Summary

Pioneer entered into two transactions with Ms. Schwalb that were and are subject to Article 9 of the UCC. Pioneer believed that each transaction was a pawn of the vehicle, and thus thought that Article 9 did not apply. Both of these beliefs were mistaken. First, the transaction was not a traditional pawn of the vehicles. Throughout her case and this litigation, Ms. Schwalb has retained possession of the vehicles. Thus, the traditional basis of pawnbroking — possession of the collateral by the pawnbroker — is absent.

This absence also has significant consequences for Pioneer with respect to the applicability of Article 9. Although the court expresses no opinion on the applicability of Article 9 to traditional possessory pawns, the nonpossessory financing in this case does come within Article 9. Although Pioneer did not believe that Article 9 applies, the "substance over form" rules of Article 9 render that belief irrelevant.

Applying Article 9 to the parties' agreement — the pawn ticket — shows that some of its key provisions are unenforceable, and that Pioneer violated Article 9 in the manner in which it has proceeded in this matter. The impact of those violations will be explored later ...

### 2. Effect of Pioneer's Violation of Article 9 ...

### a. Statutory Recovery Under NEV. REV. STAT. § 104.9625

Under Article 9, there are significant consequences for failure to follow Article 9's provisions. Section 104.9625.2 provides that "a person is liable for damages in the amount of any loss caused by a failure to comply with this article." Ms. Schwalb offered to prove damages under this section, but did not introduce any evidence on this point.

Notwithstanding this failure of proof, Ms. Schwalb may still have a remedy for Pioneer's failure to comply with the enforcement provisions of Article 9. The record firmly establishes numerous instances of Pioneer's noncompliance with Part 6 of Article 9. See Section III.C.3.b, *supra.* When such noncompliance exists, Section 104.9625.3(b) provides as follows:

> If the collateral is consumer goods, a person that was a debtor ... at the time a secured party failed to comply with this part may recover for that failure in any event an amount not less than the credit service charge plus 10 percent of the principal amount of the obligation ...

As characterized by Barkley and Barbara Clark, leading commentators on Article 9:

> This sanction has been characterized as both a minimum civil penalty and a liquidated damages provision. Its appeal is that it requires no showing of actual loss.... This minimum civil penalty, quietly tucked away in a corner of the statute, is probably the most glittering nugget of consumer protection found in all of Article 9.

CLARK & CLARK, *supra,* at ¶ 4.12[4], at pp. 4–335 to 4–336; *see also* 10 ANDERSON, *supra,* at § 9–507:166 ("Even if the consumer debtor cannot prove the actual damages sustained by the noncomplying sale of the collateral, the consumer debtor may recover the statutory minimum damages."); *Davenport v. Chrysler Credit Corp.*, 818 S.W.2d 23 (Tenn.Ct.App.1991).

Does Section 9–625 apply in this case? Initially, it requires the collateral to be consumer goods. Article 9 defines these as goods held or used for "personal, family or household purposes." NEV. REV. STAT. § 104.9201.1(w). Ms. Schwalb testified that she used the vehicles to go to doctors, to run errands and to transport her daughter, and that her partner used them to go to work. This use qualifies as family, if not personal, use.

There is also no doubt that Pioneer, as a secured party, failed to comply with Part 6 of Article 9. *See* Part III.C.3.b *supra*. This noncompliance can form the basis of an award under Section 9–625. *Cf. Kruse v. Voyager Ins. Cos.*, 72 Ohio St.3d 192, 648 N.E.2d 814 (1995) (even if disposition of collateral is commercially reasonable, when collateral is consumer goods, debtor may recover under predecessor of Section 9–625 if secured party fails to provide debtor with reasonable notice of sale of collateral as required by UCC); *Erdmann v. Rants*, 442 N.W.2d 441 (N.D.1989) (award of statutory damages under predecessor of Section 9–625 when secured party failed to give notice, despite fact that sale was made in commercially reasonable manner); *Garza v. Brazos County Fed. Credit Union*, 603 S.W.2d 298 (Tex.Civ.App.1980) (though secured party made small error with respect to notice and debtor proved, noncompliance with notice requirements justified penalty under predecessor to Section 9–625); *Conti Causeway Ford v. Jarossy*, 114 N.J.Super. 382, 276 A.2d 402 (Dist.Ct.1971), *aff'd* 118 N.J.Super. 521, 288 A.2d 872 (Ct.App.Div.1972) (failure of notice justified penalty against seller under predecessor of Section 9–625).

Thus, the statutory minimum penalty of NEV. REV. STAT. § 104.9625.3 is applicable. That means that the "credit service charge[s]" — essentially all the paid and accrued interest here — are damages to which Ms. Schwalb is entitled. *See, e.g., Knights of Columbus Credit Union v. Stock*, 814 S.W.2d 427, 432 (Tex.App.1991); *Davenport v. Chrysler Credit Corp.*, 818 S.W.2d 23, 32 & n. 7 (Tenn.Ct.App.1991); 4 WHITE & SUMMERS, *supra*, at § 34–14(c) ("We interpret that sentence to grant damages equal to the total interest charge (irrespective of the amount that has been paid) in addition to 10% of the original principal amount of the debt, irrespective of how much of the principal has been repaid."). *See also* ZINNECKER, *supra*, at 170–71.

For the two loans, there is $22,303.56 of "credit service charge[s]." These charges consist of accrued but unpaid interest on both loans as of the filing, and $1,600 in interest actually paid on the Infiniti loan. In addition, the statutory damages include 10% of the principal amount of each loan. These amounts would be $400 for the Infiniti and $1,600 for the Cadillac. When added together, the interest and principal components of the statutory damages equals $25,903.56 …

## VI. CONCLUSION

Article 9 governs this case. As a result, Pioneer loses on its ownership claims as to the two vehicles. In addition, the application of Article 9 means that all Pioneer has by way of a property interest in the vehicles is a perfected security interest. This application of Article 9, however, also has a second, and similarly adverse, consequence: because of Pioneer's violations of Article 9, Pioneer's claim against Ms. Schwalb will be significantly reduced.

---

### Exercise 6-11: *Schwalb* Approach Analysis

Following is the suggested approach to analysis that you have learned in this text. Identify where in the opinion the Schwalb court discussed these same issues.

Scope

Characterization of Collateral

Creation of Security Interest

Value

Debtor Rights in Collateral

Authenticated Agreement (or substitute) with description of collateral

Debtor's Default

Secured Party Remedies

(Remedies for Debtor if Secured Party Failed to Follow Rules)

---

### Exercise 6-12: Question from a Practicing Lawyer

If a lender takes a security interest in all stock of a borrower's corporation, and the corporation's sole asset is real estate, does that make the security interest really a mortgage? If the debtor defaults, could the lender in possession of the stock conduct a public sale of stock under the UCC, potentially acquire ownership of the stock via purchase at that sale and thereby acquire ownership of the realty without need of mortgage foreclosure suit?

---

# Additional Resources

D.E. Evins, Annotation, *What conduct by repossessing chattel mortgagee or conditional vendor entails tort liability*, 99 A.L.R. 2d 358 (1965).

Donald W. Garland, *Breach of the peace guidelines for vehicle self-help repossessions*, http://www.aabri.com/manuscripts/111066.pdf.

Lori J. Henkel, Annotation, *Bank's liability for breach of implied contract of good faith and fair dealing*, 55 A.L.R. 4th 1026.

Wendell H. Holmes, *"Involuntary Strict Foreclosure" under Section 9-505(2) of the Uniform Commercial Code: Tarpit for the Tardy Creditor*, 26 Wake Forest L. Rev. 289 (1991).

Ryan McRobert, *Comment, Defining "Breach of the Peace" in Self Help Repossessions*, 87 Wash. L. Rev. 569 (2012).

Boyd J. Peterson, Annotation, *Secured Transactions: What is "public" or "private" sale under UCC § 9-504(3)*, 60 A.L.R. 4th 1012 (1988).

James D. Prendergast, Real Estate Mezzanine Lending Collateral Foreclosure, 27 no. 6 Prac. Real Est. Law 11. (2011).

Gary D. Spivey, Annotation, *Replevin or claim and delivery: modern view as to validity of statute or contractual provision authorizing summary repossession of consumer goods sold under retail installment sales contract*, 45 A.L.R. 3d 1233 (1972).

Gary D. Spivey, Annotation, *Repossession by secured seller as affecting his right to recover on note or other obligation given as a downpayment*, 49 A.L.R. 3d 364 (1973).

Gary D. Spivey, Annotation, *Validity, under Federal Constitution and laws, of self-help re-possession provision of § 9-503 of Uniform Commercial Code*, 29 A.L.R. Fed. 418 (1976).

Richard C. Tinney, Annotation, *Loss or modification of right to notification of sale of repossessed collateral under Uniform Commercial Code § 9-504*, 9 A.L.R. 4th 552 (1981).

Richard C. Tinney, Annotation, *Nature of collateral which secured party may sell or otherwise dispose of without giving notice to defaulting debtor under UCC § 9-504(3)*, 11 A.L.R. 4th 1060 (1982).

Richard C. Tinney, Annotation, *Sufficiency of secured party's notification of sale or other intended disposition of collateral under UCC § 9–504(3)*, 11 A.L.R. 4th 241 (1982).

Richard C. Tinney, Annotation, *What is "commercially reasonable" disposition of collateral required by UCC § 9–504(3)*, 7 A.L.R. 4th 308 (1981).

Jay M. Zitter, Annotation, *What constitutes "good faith" under UCC § 1-208 dealing with "insecure" or "at will" acceleration clauses*, 85 A.L.R. 4th 284.

Jay M. Zitter, Annotation, *Secured transactions: right of secured party to take possession of collateral on default under UCC § 9-503*, 25 A.L.R. 5th 696 (1994).

# Chapter 7

# Perfection of Security Interest (Filing)

**Figure 7-1: Article 9 Graphic Organizer**

```
                    ┌─────────────────┐
                    │    Scope of     │
                    │    Article 9    │
                    └────────┬────────┘
                             │
                    ┌────────▼─────────────────┐
                    │      Creation of         │
                    │    Security Interest     │
                    │ (Attachment and Enforceability) │
                    └──────────┬───────────────┘
            ┌──────────────────┴────────────────────┐
            │                                        │
  ┌─────────▼──────────┐              ┌──────────────▼─────────┐
  │   Issues Arising   │              │     Issues Arising     │
  │ Out of Relationship│              │    Out of Presence of  │
  │   between Debtor   │              │    Competing Claims    │
  │ and Secured Party  │              │    to Same Collateral  │
  └─────────┬──────────┘              └──────────────┬─────────┘
            │                                        │
    ┌───────▼───────┐                       ┌────────▼───────┐
    │    Default    │                       │   Perfection   │
    └───────┬───────┘                       └────────┬───────┘
            │                                        │
    ┌───────▼───────┐                       ┌────────▼─────────┐
    │   Remedies    │                       │ Priority Disputes│
    └───────────────┘                       └────────┬─────────┘
                                                      │
                                            ┌─────────▼──────────┐
                                            │     Bankruptcy     │
                                            │   Considerations   │
                                            └────────────────────┘
```

## Chapter Problem

Remember Ben Boxer, whom you first met in Chapter 3? Now assume that Ben has been conducting business under the fictitious name "B and B Boxes," and you represent Commercey Bank, who has entered into a secured financing transaction with Ben. Several months after the loan funded, while casually reading the legal notices in the local newspaper, Laura Loan Officer noticed a filing for B and B Boxes. It reflected that the business was being conducted by a corporation! Laura immediately called Ben, who confirmed that he had incorporated. At Laura's request, Ben has forwarded copies of the relevant legal documents directly to you. You must review those documents, analyze the Bank's legal position, and determine what steps, if any, you must take to protect Bank's legal position in light of the fact that Ben has incorporated. You have identified the following relevant provisions of the security agreement. Review them carefully, and then answer the questions set below.

---

12   Events of Default

12.1 The term "Default" as used herein shall mean an Event of Default, or any fact or circumstance which, upon the lapse of time, or giving of notice, or both, would constitute, an Event of Default. Each of the following events, unless cured within any applicable grace period set forth or referred to below in this Section 12.1 or in Section 12.2, shall constitute an "Event of Default."

(a) <u>Generally</u>. A Default by Borrower [Ben Boxer] in the performance of any term, provision or condition of this Agreement to be performed by Borrower, or a breach of, or other failure to comply with or observe, any other term, provision, covenant or warranty under this Agreement, and such default, breach or other failure remains uncured beyond any applicable specific grace period provided for in this Agreement, or as set forth in Section 12.2.

(b) <u>Note</u>. A default by Borrower in the performance of any term or provision of the Note, or any Related Documents, or a breach of, or other failure to comply with or observe, any other term provision, condition or warranty under the Note, and the specific grace period, if any, allowed under this Agreement for the default, breach or failure in question shall have expired without such default having been cured.

(c) <u>Financial Status and Insolvency</u>. (i) Borrower shall: (A) admit in writing its inability to pay its debts generally as they become due; (B) file a petition in bankruptcy or a petition to take advantage of any insolvency act; (C) make an assignment for the benefit of creditors (D) consent to, or acquiesce in, the appointment of a receiver, liquidator or trustee of itself or of the whole of any substantial part of its properties or assets; (E) file a petition or answer seeking reorganization, arrangement, composition, readjustment liquidation, dissolution or similar relief under the Federal Bankruptcy Code or any other applicable law; (F) have a court of competent jurisdiction enter an order, judgment or decree appointing a receiver, liquidator or trustee of Borrower, or of the whole or any substantial part of the property or sets of Borrower, and such order, judgment or decree shall remain unvacated or not set aside or unstayed for sixty (60) days;

(G) have a petition filed against it seeking reorganization, arrangement, composition, readjustment, liquidation, dissolution or similar relief under the Federal Bankruptcy Code or any other applicable law and such petition shall remain undismissed for sixty (60) days; (H) have, under the provisions of any other law for the relief or aid of debtors, any court of competent jurisdiction assume custody or control of Borrower or of the whole or any substantial part of its property or assets and such custody or control shall remain unterminated or unstayed for sixty (60) days; (I) have an attachment or execution levied against any substantial portion of the property of Borrower or against any portion of the Collateral which is not discharged or dissolved by a bond within thirty (30) days; (J) have an uninsured judgment entered against it in the amount of $1,500,000 or more for Borrower which has not been stayed, discharged or satisfied within thirty (30) days after the date that judgment was entered against it; or (I) breach any of its covenants in Section 10.

(d) <u>Breach of Representation or Warranty</u>. Any material representation or warranty made by Borrower shall at the time made or deemed restated pursuant to the terms of this Agreement be false or misleading in any material respect, or any warranty shall be breached in any material respect.

(e) <u>Ownership Changes</u>. A sale or other transfer of Borrower's interest in the Collateral shall occur and such default is not cured or waived by Lender (in its sole discretion) within thirty (30) days after written notice from Lender. It is noted that this section is not intended to waive any rights that Lender has regarding any other Defaults or Events of Default that may exist at that time.

12.2 <u>Grace Periods and Notice</u>. As to each of the foregoing events the following provisions relating to grace periods and notice shall apply:

(a) <u>No Notice or Grace Period</u>. There shall be no grace period and no notice provision with respect to the payment of principal at maturity and no grace period and no notice provision with respect to defaults related to the voluntary filing of bankruptcy or reorganization proceedings or an assignment for the benefit of creditors.

(b) <u>Nonpayment of Interest and Principal</u>. As to the nonpayment of principal or interest, there shall be a ten (10) day grace period without any requirement of notice from Lender.

(c) <u>Other Monetary Defaults</u>. All other monetary defaults shall have a ten (10) day grace period following notice from Lender, unless there is a specific shorter or longer grace period provided for in this Agreement.

(d) <u>Nonmonetary Defaults Capable of Cure</u>. As to nonmonetary defaults which are reasonably capable of being cured or remedied, unless there is a specific shorter or longer grace period provided for in this Agreement there shall be a thirty (30) day cure period following notice from Lender or, if such default would reasonably require more than thirty (30) days to cure or remedy, such longer period of time not to exceed a total of ninety (90) days from Lender's notice as may be reasonably required so long as Borrower shall commence reasonable actions to remedy or cure the default within thirty (30) days following such notice and shall diligently prosecute such curative action to completion within such ninety (90) day period.

1. It appears from the facts that Commercey Bank was lucky to have discovered that Ben had incorporated. Does a lender care if its debtor changes its name, identity or corporate structure? Why or why not? Can a lender prevent such changes from taking place? If not, what can a lender do to try to prevent the debtor from making such changes without its knowledge?

2. Is Ben's change in legal entity a default under Bank's existing security agreement?

3. Now that Ben has incorporated, who is Bank's debtor? Assuming that Bank had a perfected security interest in B and B Boxes' accounts before Ben incorporated, does Bank still have a security interest in B and B Boxes' accounts that arose after the date of incorporation?

4. Does Bank need to prepare a new security agreement? Why or why not? Explain fully.

5. Assume that Bank properly perfected its original security interest by filing a proper financing statement in the proper place, that identifies the debtor with the name on Ben's driver's license. Does Bank need to file a new UCC-1? Why or why not? Explain fully.

6. What additional information should you request from your client and other sources of information for review before you begin to analyze Bank's existing loan documents?

7. Assume that you have advised Bank that new loan documents must be prepared. Will you prepare amendments to the existing loan documents or will you prepare new loan documents? Explain fully.

## Code Sections

9-301, 9-303, 9-307, 9-308, 9-310, 9-501, 9-502, 9-503, 9-504, 9-505, 9-506, 9-507, 9-508, 9-509, 9-510, 9-511, 9-512, 9-513, 9-514, 9-515, 9-516, 9-517, 9-518, 9-519, 9-520, 9-521, 9-522, 9-523, 9-524, 9-525, 9-526

# 1. Introduction

In Chapter 3, we introduced the two stories that Article 9 tells. We have now finished the first story, the story of how a lender makes a loan secured by personal property collateral, and we have explored the relationship between the lender and the borrower. As we explained in Chapter 3, in the real world, the second story dominates the stage. That is the story we now unfold.

The second story starts, like the first story, with an analysis of scope, classification of collateral, and creation of a security interest. But the star of the second story is the concept of perfection.[1] It is so important that we devote two chapters to it. This chapter addresses the most common method of perfection—filing. Chapter 8 addresses the many other methods of perfection. The important thing to remember is that a security interest that

---

1. See Chapter 3, footnote 5.

### Figure 7-2: Law Governing Perfection, Effect of Perfection and Priority

| What Law Governs Perfection Issue | 9-301, 9-303 |
|---|---|
| In general | Debtor's location (9-301(a)) [See 9-307] |
| Possessory security interest in collateral | Location of collateral (9-301(b)) |
| SI in goods perfected by fixtures filing | Location of the fixtures (9-301(3)(A)) |
| SI in timber to be cut | Location of timber to be cut (9-301(3)(B)) |
| SI in as-extracted collateral | Location of wellhead or minehead (9-301(4)) |
| Goods covered by a certificate of title | 9-303 : Generally, the local law of the jurisdiction that issued the most recent certificate of title |
| Deposit accounts | 9-304: The local law of depositary bank's jurisdiction |
| Investment property | 9-305 |
| Letter of credit rights | 9-306 |

has attached pursuant to section 9-203 is enforceable as between the debtor and the secured party, and against third parties, from the time of attachment. However, unless the security interest is perfected, the rights of the secured party may become subject to the rights of a variety of third parties.[2]

## 2. Governing Law

Although most states in the United States have adopted a relatively uniform version of Article 9, it is still important to determine which state's law will govern the important issues of perfection, the effect of perfection, and priority. The general rule, set forth in section 9-301, is that the law of the state where the debtor is located governs those crucial questions. As you learn in this chapter, the most common method of perfection is by filing a financing statement in the place directed by that state's version of the UCC. Most filings are done in a central filing office, such as the Office of the California Secretary of State or the Washington State Department of Licensing. Certain special types of collateral, such as fixtures (when perfected by a fixture filing), timber to be cut, or as-extracted collateral, require filing "locally" (usually where real estate records will be recorded within a particular state). *Figure 7-2* summarizes the basic choice of law rules in Article 9.

---

### Exercise 7-1: Governing Law

In each of the following problems, identify the state law that will govern the issues of perfection and the effect of perfection.

---

2. *Cf.* §9-317. We study the possible conflicting claimants to collateral and potential priority disputes in Chapters 9 and 10.

1. Joe lived in the state of Arizona. He borrowed money from Easy Loans Lender, secured by a lien on Joe's motor vehicle. The lien was properly perfected under Arizona's certificate of title law. Joe and his vehicle then moved to the state of California. He did not bother to get a California certificate of title. Six months after he moved to California, what law governs the determination of whether Easy Loans lien is perfected?

2. Mary was a resident of the state of Missouri. She purchased a snowmobile on credit from SnowSales Inc., in Minnesota, under a retail installment sales contract that provided that SnowSales retained a security interest in the snowmobile. A snowmobile is not a motor vehicle for purposes of the Minnesota certificate of title law. She stored and used the snowmobile exclusively at her brother's house in Minnesota. What law governs the perfection of SnowSales' security interest in the snowmobile?

3. Mark was a resident of the state of Colorado. He purchased a horse trailer from Horzes Inc, which retained a security interest in the horse trailer. Mark obtained a certificate of title from the state of Colorado, which noted Horzes Inc as lienholder, as required by Colorado law. Mark then moved to Oklahoma. Under Oklahoma law the trailer was not a good covered by a certificate of title, so Mark did not obtain a new certificate of title. What law governs the issue of whether Horzes' lien was perfected?

4. Huge National Bank ("HNB") made a loan to YZ Corporation, a Delaware corporation, secured by a lien on YZ's equipment, which was located in the state of Kansas. What law governs the perfection of HNB's security interest in YZ's equipment?

5. Farmer's Friend lent money to Farmer, secured by a security interest on Farmer's sugar beet crop. What law will govern the perfection of Farmers Friend's security interest in the sugar beet crop?

6. Debtor granted Lender a security interest in Debtor's deposit account located at FNB National Bank. What law will govern the perfection of Lender's security interest in the deposit account?

7. Floorplanner provided financing to Big Star Dealership, a Delaware corporation, whose automobile dealership was located in the state of Texas. What state's law will govern the perfection of Floorplanner's security interest in, among other things, Big Star's general intangibles and chattel paper?

8. Would your answer to #7 change if the security agreement between Floorplanner and Big Star provided that it would be governed by Texas law?

---

# 3.  Perfection by Filing

After you have determined the law that governs the issue of perfection, you must consult additional code sections to determine the proper method of perfection. *Figure 7-3* is a "roadmap" that illllustrates how to link the code sections that must be consulted.

## Figure 7-3: Roadmap to Perfection by Filing

|  | In General | Specific Rules for Special Types of Collateral |
|---|---|---|
| **Governing Law** | 9-301 | 9-302, 9-303, 9-304, 9-305, 9-306 |
| **When Filing Is Required** | 9-310 |  |
| **Where to File (Filing Office)** | 9-501(a)(2) "central" filing office (e.g., in California, the Office of the Secretary of State in Sacramento) | 9-501(a)(1) for fixtures filing, as-extracted collateral or timber: the office designated for recording real estate interests |
| **What to File (Contents of Financing Statement)** | 9-502 | Real property related financing statements 9-502(b) |
| **Name of Debtor** | 9-503 |  |
| **Indication of Collateral** | 9-504 (See also 9-108) |  |
| **What Constitutes Filing; Effectiveness of Filing** | 9-516 |  |
| **Effect of Errors or Omissions** | 9-506 |  |

As *Figure 7-4* illustrates, the filing of a financing statement is the single most common method of perfecting a security interest.[3] In addition, most financing statements are filed "centrally" in the office designated by the applicable state law. A financing statement is often referred to as a "UCC-1," which is the name of the form that most financing statements take. *Figure 7-5* (on pages 114–115) is a copy of the current version of the national form UCC-1 financing statement.

The essence of filing as a method of perfection is that it gives notice to third parties of the claimed security interest. Filing involves two distinct processes: (1) the actual filing in the public record of a creditor's financing statement, and (2) the ability to search those records to determine whether a creditor has filed a financing statement against particular collateral. Anyone who is interested in the status of potential liens against personal property collateral may conduct a "UCC Search" to find such claims. Searches are run based on varying computer search logic used by the state agencies. Many states follow the search logic sponsored by the International Association of Commercial Administrators ("IACA"). The IACA search logic is described in IACA's model administrative rules (2010 edition), available on IACA's website.[4]

---

3. Exceptions to this rule are set forth in § 9-310(b) and § 9-312(b). These exceptions are discussed in Chapter 8.

4. http://www.law.indiana.edu/instruction/dhlong/5452/doc/iaca_search_logic.pdf.

## Figure 7-4: How to Perfect Security Interest

| | Automatic 9-309 | Filing 9-310 | Compliance with Other Laws 9-311 | Temporary 9-312 | Possession 9-313 | Control 9-314 |
|---|---|---|---|---|---|---|
| Accounts | | X | | | | |
| Certificated Securities | | X | | | X | X |
| Chattel Paper (Electronic) | | X | | | | X |
| Chattel Paper (Tangible) | | X | | | X | |
| Commercial Tort Claim | | X | | | | |
| Consumer Goods | X (PMSI) | X | | | X | |
| Deposit Accounts | | | | | | X |
| Documents | | X | | | X | |
| Equipment | | X | | | X | |
| Farm Products | | X | | | X | |
| Fixtures | | X | | | | |
| General Intangibles | | X | | | | |
| Goods | | X | | | X | |
| Health care receivable | | X | | | | |
| Instruments | | X | | | X | |
| Inventory | | X | | | X | |
| Investment Property (other than certificated securities) | | X | | | | X |
| Letter of Credit Rights | | | | | | X |
| Money | | | | | X | |

Accordingly, it is important to know where to search (which state's law governs perfection) and what name to search (see discussion below). It is equally important to be able to understand the results of a search. In many states, private companies will perform searches that may be even more comprehensive than those resulting from the "official" search. However, for purposes of determining whether a creditor is perfected, only the records in the applicable state, and an official search of those records, will resolve the question. For an example of a UCC search, you may look on-line for the State of Pennsylvania at https://www.corporations.state.pa.us/ucc/soskb/SearchStandardRA9.asp. If you pick a common name, such as "John Adams" you will see a number of results. To see whether the "John Adams" you have found is the same person as the "John Adams" you were searching for, and to determine what collateral is actually encumbered, you will have to request a copy of the actual UCC-1 filed.

"Filing" is also defined by the Code. It is defined as "communication of a record to a filing office and tender of the filing fee." Article 9 sets forth reasons for which the filing office may refuse to accept a financing statement for filing, thereby rendering the filing ineffective even if it is otherwise sufficient. These reasons include communication of the financing statement by means not authorized by the filing office and failure to tender a payment at least equal to the filing fee; also included is failure to provide in the financing statement other information such as debtor's mailing address, whether debtor is an individual or an organization, etc. The reasons set forth in section 9-516(b) are the only grounds for filing office rejection. If there are such grounds for the filing office to reject the filing but the filing office nevertheless accepts the filing the filing is still effective so long as the financing statement meets the requirements for sufficiency under section 9-502.

# 4.　Financing Statements

As *Figure 7-5* illustrates, the financing statement form reflects the requirements of section 9-502. That section provides that a financing statement must (1) provide the names of the debtor and the secured party or a representative of the secured party; and (2) indicate the collateral covered by the financing statement. The financing statement is designed to give notice of a claimed security interest to anyone who properly searches the public records. Financing statements are indexed under the name of the debtor, and searches will be conducted under the name of the debtor. Searchers will pay close attention to the description of the covered collateral because that will determine whether collateral is already encumbered or whether the searcher could make a loan and be in a first lien position. Thus, it is extremely important that the debtor's name be stated properly and that the description of the collateral be sufficient to give notice to subsequent searchers of claimed liens. Although proper completion of a form UCC-1 may seem like a purely ministerial act, because of the importance of completing the financing statement correctly, it is vital that lawyers understand the requirements of section 9-502 and the different problems that have resulted in lack of perfection in a variety of cases. *Figure 7-6* summarizes the contents of a financing statement.

## Figure 7-5a:  Financing Statement Form

**UCC FINANCING STATEMENT**
FOLLOW INSTRUCTIONS

A. NAME & PHONE OF CONTACT AT FILER (optional)

B. E-MAIL CONTACT AT FILER (optional)

C. SEND ACKNOWLEDGMENT TO:   (Name and Address)

THE ABOVE SPACE IS FOR FILING OFFICE USE ONLY

1. DEBTOR'S NAME:  Provide only <u>one</u> Debtor name (1a or 1b) (use exact, full name; do not omit, modify, or abbreviate any part of the Debtor's name); if any part of the Individual Debtor's name will not fit in line 1b, leave all of item 1 blank, check here ☐ and provide the Individual Debtor information in item 10 of the Financing Statement Addendum (Form UCC1Ad)

| 1a. ORGANIZATION'S NAME | | | |
|---|---|---|---|
| OR 1b. INDIVIDUAL'S SURNAME | FIRST PERSONAL NAME | ADDITIONAL NAME(S)/INITIAL(S) | SUFFIX |
| 1c. MAILING ADDRESS | CITY | STATE | POSTAL CODE | COUNTRY |

2. DEBTOR'S NAME:  Provide only <u>one</u> Debtor name (2a or 2b) (use exact, full name; do not omit, modify, or abbreviate any part of the Debtor's name); if any part of the Individual Debtor's name will not fit in line 2b, leave all of item 2 blank, check here ☐ and provide the Individual Debtor information in item 10 of the Financing Statement Addendum (Form UCC1Ad)

| 2a. ORGANIZATION'S NAME | | | |
|---|---|---|---|
| OR 2b. INDIVIDUAL'S SURNAME | FIRST PERSONAL NAME | ADDITIONAL NAME(S)/INITIAL(S) | SUFFIX |
| 2c. MAILING ADDRESS | CITY | STATE | POSTAL CODE | COUNTRY |

3. SECURED PARTY'S NAME (or NAME of ASSIGNEE of ASSIGNOR SECURED PARTY):  Provide only <u>one</u> Secured Party name (3a or 3b)

| 3a. ORGANIZATION'S NAME | | | |
|---|---|---|---|
| OR 3b. INDIVIDUAL'S SURNAME | FIRST PERSONAL NAME | ADDITIONAL NAME(S)/INITIAL(S) | SUFFIX |
| 3c. MAILING ADDRESS | CITY | STATE | POSTAL CODE | COUNTRY |

4. COLLATERAL:  This financing statement covers the following collateral:

5. Check <u>only</u> if applicable and check <u>only</u> one box: Collateral is ☐ held in a Trust (see UCC1Ad, item 17 and Instructions)   ☐ being administered by a Decedent's Personal Representative

6a. Check <u>only</u> if applicable and check <u>only</u> one box:   ☐ Public-Finance Transaction   ☐ Manufactured-Home Transaction   ☐ A Debtor is a Transmitting Utility

6b. Check <u>only</u> if applicable and check <u>only</u> one box:   ☐ Agricultural Lien   ☐ Non-UCC Filing

7. ALTERNATIVE DESIGNATION (if applicable):   ☐ Lessee/Lessor   ☐ Consignee/Consignor   ☐ Seller/Buyer   ☐ Bailee/Bailor   ☐ Licensee/Licensor

8. OPTIONAL FILER REFERENCE DATA:

FILING OFFICE COPY — UCC FINANCING STATEMENT (Form UCC1) (Rev. 04/20/11)

## Figure 7-5b:  Financing Statement Form Instructions

### Instructions for UCC Financing Statement (Form UCC1)

Please type or laser-print this form.  Be sure it is completely legible.  Read and follow all Instructions, especially Instruction 1; use of the correct name for the Debtor is crucial.

Fill in form very carefully; mistakes may have important legal consequences.  If you have questions, consult your attorney.  The filing office cannot give legal advice.

Send completed form and any attachments to the filing office, with the required fee.

**ITEM INSTRUCTIONS**

A and B.  To assist filing offices that might wish to communicate with filer, filer may provide information in item A and item B.  These items are optional.

C.    Complete item C if filer desires an acknowledgment sent to them.  If filing in a filing office that returns an acknowledgment copy furnished by filer, present simultaneously with this form the Acknowledgment Copy or a carbon or other copy of this form for use as an acknowledgment copy.

1.    **Debtor's name.**  Carefully review applicable statutory guidance about providing the debtor's name.  Enter only one Debtor name in item 1 -- either an organization's name (1a) or an individual's name (1b).  If any part of the Individual Debtor's name will not fit in line 1b, check the box in item 1, leave all of item 1 blank, check the box in item 9 of the Financing Statement Addendum (Form UCC1Ad) and enter the Individual Debtor name in item 10 of the Financing Statement Addendum (Form UCC1Ad).  Enter Debtor's correct name.  Do not abbreviate words that are not already abbreviated in the Debtor's name.  If a portion of the Debtor's name consists of only an initial or an abbreviation rather than a full word, enter only the abbreviation or the initial.  If the collateral is held in a trust and the Debtor name is the name of the trust, enter trust name in the Organization's Name box in item 1a.

1a.   Organization Debtor Name.  "Organization Name" means the name of an entity that is not a natural person.  A sole proprietorship is **not** an organization, even if the individual proprietor does business under a trade name.  If Debtor is a registered organization (e.g., corporation, limited partnership, limited liability company), it is advisable to examine Debtor's current filed public organic records to determine Debtor's correct name.  Trade name is insufficient.  If a corporate ending (e.g., corporation, limited partnership, limited liability company) is part of the Debtor's name, it must be included.  Do not use words that are not part of the Debtor's name.

1b.   Individual Debtor Name.  "Individual Name" means the name of a natural person; this includes the name of an individual doing business as a sole proprietorship, whether or not operating under a trade name.  The term includes the name of a decedent where collateral is being administered by a personal representative of the decedent.  The term does not include the name of an entity, even if it contains, as part of the entity's name, the name of an individual.  Prefixes (e.g., Mr., Mrs., Ms.) and titles (e.g., M.D.) are generally not part of an individual name.  Indications of lineage (e.g., Jr., Sr., III) generally are not part of the individual's name, but may be entered in the Suffix box.  Enter individual Debtor's surname (family name) in Individual's Surname box, first personal name in First Personal Name box, and all additional names in Additional Name(s)/Initial(s) box.

If a Debtor's name consists of only a single word, enter that word in Individual's Surname box and leave other boxes blank.

For both organization and individual Debtors.  Do not use Debtor's trade name, DBA, AKA, FKA, division name, etc. in place of or combined with Debtor's correct name; filer may add such other names as additional Debtors if desired (but this is neither required nor recommended).

1c.   Enter a mailing address for the Debtor named in item 1a or 1b.

2.    **Additional Debtor's name.**  If an additional Debtor is included, complete item 2, determined and formatted per Instruction 1.  For additional Debtors, attach either Addendum (Form UCC1Ad) or Additional Party (Form UCC1AP) and follow Instruction 1 for determining and formatting additional names.

3.    **Secured Party's name.**  Enter name and mailing address for Secured Party or Assignee who will be the Secured Party of record.  For additional Secured Parties, attach either Addendum (Form UCC1Ad) or Additional Party (Form UCC1AP).  If there has been a full assignment of the initial Secured Party's right to be Secured Party of record before filing this form, either (1) enter Assignor Secured Party's name and mailing address in item 3 of this form and file an Amendment (Form UCC3) [see item 5 of that form]; or (2) enter Assignee's name and mailing address in item 3 of this form and, if desired, also attach Addendum (Form UCC1Ad) giving Assignor Secured Party's name and mailing address in item 11.

4.    **Collateral.**  Use item 4 to indicate the collateral covered by this financing statement.  If space in item 4 is insufficient, continue the collateral description in item 12 of the Addendum (Form UCC1Ad) or attach additional page(s) and incorporate by reference in item 12 (e.g., See Exhibit A).  Do not include social security numbers or other personally identifiable information.

Note:  If this financing statement covers timber to be cut, covers as-extracted collateral, and/or is filed as a fixture filing, attach Addendum (Form UCC1Ad) and complete the required information in items 13, 14, 15, and 16.

5.    If collateral is held in a trust or being administered by a decedent's personal representative, check the appropriate box in item 5.  If more than one Debtor has an interest in the described collateral and the check box does not apply to the interest of all Debtors, the filer should consider filing a separate Financing Statement (Form UCC1) for each Debtor.

6a.   If this financing statement relates to a Public-Finance Transaction, Manufactured-Home Transaction, or a Debtor is a Transmitting Utility, check the appropriate box in item 6a.  If a Debtor is a Transmitting Utility and the initial financing statement is filed in connection with a Public-Finance Transaction or Manufactured-Home Transaction, check only that a Debtor is a Transmitting Utility.

6b.   If this is an Agricultural Lien (as defined in applicable state's enactment of the Uniform Commercial Code) or if this is not a UCC security interest filing (e.g., a tax lien, judgment lien, etc.), check the appropriate box in item 6b and attach any other items required under other law.

7.    **Alternative Designation.**  If filer desires (at filer's option) to use the designations lessee and lessor, consignee and consignor, seller and buyer (such as in the case of the sale of a payment intangible, promissory note, account or chattel paper), bailee and bailor, or licensee and licensor instead of Debtor and Secured Party, check the appropriate box in item 7.

8.    **Optional Filer Reference Data.**  This item is optional and is for filer's use only.  For filer's convenience of reference, filer may enter in item 8 any identifying information that filer may find useful.  Do not include social security numbers or other personally identifiable information.

### Figure 7-6:  Contents of Financing Statement

| | |
|---|---|
| **Contents of Financing Statement —** In general | 9-502 |
| | (a)(1)(2)(3): name of debtor, name of secured party, indication of the collateral |
| | (b) additional information for real-estate-related interests (fixtures, as-extracted collateral, etc.) |
| | (c) Mortgage can serve as financing statement for fixtures in some circumstances |
| **Contents of Financing Statement —** Name of debtor and secured party | 9-503 |
| | Alternatives A and B for individuals |
| | Rules for: individual debtor, registered organizations, and trusts |
| **Contents of Financing Statement —** Indication of collateral | 9-504 |
| | *either* a description of collateral under Section 9-108 |
| | *or* an "all assets" or "all personal property" filing |
| **Effect of Error or Omission in Financing Statement** | 9-506 |

## 4.1  The Debtor's Name

To "sufficiently" provide the debtor's name on a financing statement has proven to be more difficult than you might expect. The 2010 amendments revised section 9-503 to offer more guidance than earlier versions of Article 9 with respect to how to set forth the debtor's name. Some of the earlier controversy with respect to determining how to reflect the name of a debtor that is a trust, or a trustee of a trust, and the name of a registered organization (in the case of differing official records) has been resolved. However, the issue of how to determine the "correct" name of an individual debtor remains controversial: as you can see, the drafters of the Code ultimately wrote two alternative provisions for determining the name of an individual debtor. Alternative A takes an "only if" approach: if the debtor has a driver's license or other specified type of state-issued identification document, the financing statement must provide the individual debtor's name as it appears on a driver's license or other specified documents. Alternative B takes a "safe harbor" approach for filers. It states that a financing statement properly sets forth the individual debtor's name if it "provides the individual name of the debtor," or the surname and first personal name of the debtor; or the name that appears on the debtor's driver's license or other identification document. As of this writing, the majority of states to adopt the 2010 revision have adopted Alternative A.

The reason for the controversy is that ascertainment of an individual debtor's name presents certain issues. What if an individual debtor commonly uses a nickname? Must a financing statement include an individual debtor's middle name or middle initial to be effective? How should common-law names, nicknames, hyphenated names, multiple middle or last names, non-Anglo naming conventions, and non-ASCII characters[5] be treated? There is no accepted national agreement on what an individual's "name" is or how it can be ascertained. The common law generally recognizes the right of a person lawfully and effectively to change his or her name at will and assume a new name — without judicial involvement — so long as it is not done for a fraudulent or illegal purpose. Indeed, it is not even clear that each individual only has one correct name.

Critics of Alternative A's "only if" approach note, among other things, that even if it were known that a debtor's name was different (as, for example, in the case of a woman who had married and changed her name but not yet changed her driver's license), the financing statement would have to be filed in the "wrong" name indicated on her driver's license. Proponents of Alternative A note that it satisfies the "certainty" and "predictability" requirements desired by many institutional lenders and that anyone can find out what name to use by reviewing the driver's license. Critics of Alternative B argue that filers will still be required to do a number of searches under different names because different names can potentially be sufficient under Alternative B.[6]

Trade names are insufficient. Whether an error in a debtor's name is seriously misleading is determined by whether a search in the relevant office under the correct name, using whatever search logic that office employs, would turn up a filing that used the erroneous name.

---

## Exercise 7-2: Debtor's Name Issues

1. Bank filed a financing statement identifying its debtor, as "EDM Corporation dba EDM Equipment." The debtor's organizational documents stated its name as "EDM Corporation." A search for EDM Corporation using the Secretary of State's standard search engine did not reveal Bank's financing statement. Was Bank perfected?

2. Secured Party filed a financing statement identifying its debtor as CW Mining Company. The company's organizational documents stated its name as C.W. Mining Company. A search for C.W. Mining Company using the Secretary of State's standard search engine did not reveal Secured Party's financing statement. Was Secured Party perfected?

3. Debtor's name is Scot Douglas. His driver's license shows his name as "Scot Douglas." It does not otherwise indicate which name is his first name and which name is his last name. How would you advise your client to complete line 1 on the UCC-1?

4. Jacob One and Mary Two are general partners in partnership known as OneTwo Partners. The General Partnership Agreement states, "The name of this partnership is OneTwo Partners, a general partnership." As required by the law of the state where they do business, they have filed a fictitious business name

---

5. E.g., the Spanish tilde ("~") over an "n," which might be reflected as "n," "n*," or "ny," or the German umlaut ("¨") over an "o," which might be reflected as "o," or "o*," or "oe".

6. Supporters of Alternative B note that even under Alternative A searchers will be forced to search under other names because of the possible existence of other types of filings, such as notices of state or federal tax liens, that are not required to be indexed by the name on the debtor's driver's license and are more likely to be filed under the name on the debtor's tax returns, which may or may not be the same as the name on the driver's license.

statement in the county where they are located, stating that the partnership OneTwo Partners is a general partnership and that its general partners are Jacob One and Mary Two. They have not filed a tax return in the partnership name. If Lender is willing to make a secured loan to OneTwo Partners, how should it complete line 1 on the UCC-1?

5. Debtor's birth certificate was issued in the name of Ben Miller, but all of his friends know him as "Bennie A. Miller." His driver's license shows his name as "Ben Miller." If a lender is willing to lend him money in exchange for a security interest in some equipment, how should it complete line 1 on the UCC-1?

## 4.2  Indication of the Collateral

Under section 9-504, a financing statement sufficiently describes the collateral if it either (1) provides a description of the collateral that would be sufficient for a security agreement under section 9-108; or (2) indicates that the financing statement covers all assets or all personal property.

### Exercise 7-3:  Description of Collateral

You will recall that a broad "all assets" or "all personal property" description of collateral is not sufficient in a security agreement. Explain why these types of collateral descriptions are permitted with respect to financing statements and not security agreements.

# 5.  Place of Filing

In almost all cases, if a financing statement must be filed to perfect a security interest, it must be filed in a central filing office in the state. If the collateral is timber to be cut, or minerals or the like, including oil or gas, in which the debtor has an interest before extraction and in which the security interest attaches to the minerals as they are extracted (or an account resulting from the sale of an interest in such minerals or the like at the wellhead or minehead),[7] the financing statement must be filed in the office where a mortgage on the related real estate would be recorded. Note that a security interest in fixtures may be perfected in the same way as is a security interest in other goods, in which case the filing is made with the appropriate central filing office.[8] Under current law, regardless of where collateral is located, the place of filing is generally in the state in which

---

7. This is "as-extracted collateral." § 9-102(a)(6).

8. A filing made in the real estate records, however, can confer priority over others claiming an interest in fixtures by reason of having a mortgage on, or ownership interest in, the underlying real property. See paragraph 6, below.

the debtor is "located," with the result that most — but not all — financing statements must be filed in the state under the laws of which a non-human debtor is organized or in the state where the debtor resides, in the case of a human debtor.

## Exercise 7-4: Debtor's Location

Complete the following table to indicate where each of the following types of debtors is "located" for filing purposes.

| Type of Debtor | Location |
| --- | --- |
| Individual | Principal residence |
| Registered Organization | State of organization |
| Non-human, non-registered Organization (other than one described in next box) | |
| Debtor whose jurisdiction of location generally does not require filings/recordings/ registrations of security interests | |
| Banks | |

## Exercise 7-5: Perfection Problems

1. Debtor executed a promissory note in favor of Creditor to evidence a loan from Creditor to Debtor. The note indicated that it was secured by an assignment of proceeds from the lawsuit filed by Debtor against the company that performed electrical work at Debtor's dairy. Shortly thereafter Debtor executed an assignment intending to secure the payment of the promissory note. What additional steps, if any, must be taken to create a perfected security interest in favor of Creditor?

2. Secured Party financed Auto Dealer's acquisition of motor vehicles, which Auto Dealer then sold to members of the public. What steps must Secured Party take to perfect a security interest in the motor vehicles?

3. Lender made a loan to Debtor, secured by a security interest in Debtor's liquor license, pursuant to a duly authenticated security agreement that described the collateral as "All of debtor's right title and interest in that certain liquor license issued in connection with Debtor's business commonly known as 'The Sup Place.'" Lender took possession of the liquor license. Does Lender have a perfected security interest in the liquor license? Why or why not?

4. Lender loaned money to Farmer, secured by a security interest in Farmer's dairy cattle, pursuant to a duly authenticated security agreement. Lender filed

a financing statement that failed to include the dairy operation's correct address. Is Lender's security interest properly perfected?

5. Lender entered into a security agreement with Debtor, a Delaware corporation, which granted Lender a security interest in essentially "all assets" of Debtor. Assume that the security agreement contained a proper description of the collateral in accordance with UCC 9-108. Debtor's principal place of business and substantially all of its assets were located in Dallas, Texas. Lender filed an "all assets" financing statement with the Texas Secretary of State. Does Lender have a perfected security interest? Why or why not?

# 6. Special Requirements for Certain Types of Collateral and Fixture Filings

There are additional requirements if the collateral is timber to be cut, minerals or the like or related accounts ("as-extracted collateral"), or if a financing statement is being filed as a fixture filing. The uniform form of financing statement contains boxes to check that will indicate the nature of the collateral or that the financing statement is being filed as a fixture filing and is to be filed in the real property records.

A fixture filing made in the county in which the related real property is located, besides perfecting a security interest in the relevant fixtures, also protects the priority of the security interest against persons claiming an interest in fixtures covered by the filing by reason of having subsequently acquired an interest in the real property to which the fixtures have become attached. (Because not all goods or other collateral associated with real property will constitute fixtures, it is always a good idea to file centrally, as well.) Note, too, that a special rule applies to fixtures owned by a transmitting utility, such as a power company (9-501(b)). A deed of trust or mortgage may be used as a fixture filing if it is duly recorded and it otherwise contains the information and statements that would be required in a financing statement covering the goods that are or are to become fixtures (except that it need not recite that it is to be filed in the real estate records).

# 7. Perfection of Security Interest in Proceeds

As you learned in Chapter 5, the attachment of a security interest in collateral also gives the secured party the right to proceeds of the collateral. If the security interest in the original collateral was perfected, the security interest in proceeds is also perfected. The security interest in proceeds will be perfected automatically for 20 days after it attaches. No additional steps and no new filing is required if the proceeds are identifiable cash proceeds,[9] or if (1) the original collateral was perfected by filing a financing statement and

---

9. The determination of whether proceeds are "identifiable" is made by applying tracing rules. See Official Comment 3 to §9-315.

(2) the proceeds were not acquired with cash proceeds and (3) the proceeds are a type of collateral which may also be perfected by filing a financing statement in the same place.

In all other cases, to remain perfected, the secured party must take the necessary steps to perfect a security interest in the proceeds by some method other than filing within 20 days of when the security interest attached to the proceeds.[10]

# 8. Change of Location, Change of Name, and "New Debtors"

When a security interest in collateral has been properly perfected, additional steps may be needed to continue perfection if (a) the debtor moves, (b) the debtor changes its name, or (c) the debtor changes its legal structure.

## 8.1 Change of Location

A distinction must be made between a change in the debtor's location and a change in the location of the collateral. Since the place of filing is generally based on the debtor's location, only when the debtor changes its location are additional steps needed to continue perfection. To permit the secured creditor time to learn of the debtor's location change, while protecting subsequent creditors who might search in the debtor's new location and find nothing on file, the Code strikes a balance by permitting perfection to continue for four months after a change of the debtor's location to another jurisdiction.[11] This time period is extended to one year if the collateral is transferred to a person that thereby becomes a debtor and is located in another jurisdiction. Of course, if perfection would have ceased at some earlier time under the law of the original jurisdiction, that earlier date will be the date that perfection ceases.

## 8.2 Change of Name

Since financing statements are indexed based on the debtor's name, it follows that if the debtor changes its name, subsequent creditors searching the UCC records under the debtor's new name would not find filings under the debtor's former name. Section 9-507 provides that in such cases (a) the filing financing statement remains effective with respect to collateral acquired by the debtor before or within four months after the financing statement becomes "seriously misleading;" and (b) the financing statement is not effective to perfect a security interest in collateral acquired more than four months after that date. As used in the Code, "seriously misleading" means the search under the debtor's correct name using the filing office's standard search logic would not disclose that financing statement.

---

10. After we have studied methods of perfection other than filing in Chapter 8, you will have an opportunity to work through some exercises regarding perfection of a security interest in proceeds.

11. §9-316.

## 8.3  Change of Legal Structure

One specific problem addressed by the Code typically arises in situations involving a change in business structure: a sole proprietor or partnership incorporates, a group of individuals form a limited liability partnership, corporations merge or one corporation acquires the assets of another. In each of these situations, the restructure of the business typically involves the acquisition of encumbered assets and assumption of liability for the existing debt. Nevertheless, the original debtor may no longer exist, and the issue arises whether the secured party retains a perfected security interest in the collateral.

The Code has adopted "new debtor" rules to address the situation. As a general rule a security interest in collateral continues notwithstanding the sale of the collateral. However, the transferee of the collateral (typically a purchaser) is usually not bound by the original security agreement that created the lien on that collateral. An exception to that general rule arises when the transferee is related to the original debtor, such as where there has been some type of restructuring, such as the incorporation of a sole proprietorship, or the merger or other business reorganization of a corporation. In such cases, section 9-102(a)(56) designates the parties involved in the transaction as the "original debtor," and the "new debtor." If the new debtor will be bound to the original debtor's security agreement (either by contract or pursuant to corporate succession law) and if it acquires substantially all of the original debtor's assets, there is no need for any additional loan agreements or formal "authentication" of any documents. The new debtor will be obligated to the creditor and the creditor's security interest will attach to the transferred assets.

A filed financing statement naming the original debtor is sufficient to continue the perfection of the security interest notwithstanding subsequent changes in the name, identity, or business structure of the debtor for a period of four months after the change, and thereafter if the financing statement has not become "seriously misleading." The financing statement is not effective to perfect a security interest in collateral acquired by the new debtor more than four months after the new debtor becomes bound. As noted above, a different rule applies if the new debtor is located in a different state than was the original debtor.

# 9.  Effectiveness of Filed Financing Statement

In most cases, a filed financing statement is effective for a period of five years after the date of filing. For the statement to remain in effect, a continuation statement must be filed within six months before the expiration of the five-year term. The Code contains detailed rules that determine (1) what constitutes filing — e.g., when a record will be treated as filed regardless of the actions of the filing office; (2) who is authorized to file financing statements; (3) how to file amendments to financing statements; (4) correction statements; and (5) termination statements. The applicable statutory provisions are relatively self-explanatory. Exercise 7-6 gives you an opportunity to sample of some of these provisions.

---

### Exercise 7-6:  Post-Filing Events

1. Lawyer assisted Client in the sale of Client's business, which included the buyer's grant of a security interest in some assets of the business to Client. Lawyer did

not advise his client of the 5-year renewal requirement of section 9-515. After the five-year period had expired, Client learned that her security interest was unperfected. Is Lawyer liable for malpractice?

2. Creditor filed a financing statement that complied with virtually all of the stated requirements, except that it failed to include the Creditor's address. Is the filed financing statement effective?

3. If the filing office noticed the omission in #2 above, could it refuse to accept the financing statement?

4. Bank Clerk filed two termination statements with respect to two financing statements representing two separate loans. At that time, only one of the loans had been paid and it was an error to file two termination statements. Is the UCC-1 representing the unpaid loan still effective, notwithstanding the mistaken filing of a termination statement?

# Additional Resources

Erwin S. Barbre, Annotation, *Sufficiency of description of crops under UCC secs. 9-203(b) and 9-402(1)*, 67 A.L.R. 3d 308 (1975).

Kristine Cordier Karnezis, Annotation, *When is filing of financing statement necessary to perfect an assignment of accounts under UCC § 9-302(1)(e)*, 85 A.L.R. 3d 1050 (1978).

Norman M. Powell, *Filings against trusts and trustees under the proposed 2010 revisions to current Article 9—Thirteen variations*, 42 UCC LJ 375 (2010).

Norman M. Powell, *Ongoing searching and filing issues under Article 9*, 37 UCC LJ 35 (2005).

Richard C. Tinney, Annotation, *Effectiveness of original financing statement under UCC Article 9 after change in debtor's name, identity, or business structure*, 99 A.L.R. 3d 1194 (1980).

Richard C. Tinney, Annotation, *Sufficiency of address of debtor in financing statement under UCC § 9-402(1)*, 99 A.L.R. 3d 807 (1980).

Richard C. Tinney, Annotation, *Sufficiency of address of secured party in financing statement under UCC § 9-402(1)*, 99 A.L.R.3d 1080.

Richard C. Tinney, Annotation, *Sufficiency of debtor's signature on security agreement or financing statement under UCC § 9-203 and 9-402*, 3 A.L.R. 4th 502 (1981).

Richard C. Tinney, Annotation, *Sufficiency of description of collateral in financing statement under UCC § 9-110 and 9-402*, 100 A.L.R. 3d 10 (1980).

Richard C. Tinney, Annotation, *Sufficiency of designation of debtor or secured party in security agreement or financing statement under UCC §§ 9-203 and 9-402*, 99 A.L.R. 3d 478 (1980).

Richard C. Tinney, Annotation, *Sufficiency of secured party's signature on security agreement or financing statement under UCC §§ 9-203 and 9-402*, 100 A.L.R. 3d 390 (1980).

# Chapter 8

# Perfection of Security Interest (Other Methods)

Figure 8-1:  Article 9 Graphic Organizer

```
                    ┌─────────────────┐
                    │    Scope of     │
                    │    Article 9    │
                    └────────┬────────┘
                             │
                             ▼
                 ┌───────────────────────────┐
                 │        Creation of        │
                 │     Security Interest     │
                 │ (Attachment and Enforceability) │
                 └─────────────┬─────────────┘
                 ┌─────────────┴─────────────┐
                 ▼                           ▼
      ┌──────────────────┐         ┌──────────────────┐
      │  Issues Arising  │         │  Issues Arising  │
      │ Out of Relationship │      │ Out of Presence of │
      │  between Debtor  │         │ Competing Claims │
      │ and Secured Party│         │ to Same Collateral │
      └────────┬─────────┘         └────────┬─────────┘
               ▼                            ▼
      ┌──────────────────┐         ┌──────────────────┐
      │     Default      │         │   Perfection     │
      └────────┬─────────┘         └────────┬─────────┘
               ▼                            ▼
      ┌──────────────────┐         ┌──────────────────┐
      │     Remedies     │         │ Priority Disputes │
      └──────────────────┘         └────────┬─────────┘
                                            ▼
                                   ┌──────────────────┐
                                   │    Bankruptcy    │
                                   │  Considerations  │
                                   └──────────────────┘
```

## Chapter Problem

---

**INTRA-OFFICE MEMORANDUM**

**Date**: November 1
**To**: Able Associate
**From**: Ima Partner
**Subject**: Octopus Owner Loan Agreement

We represent Largess Lender, who has agreed to loan money to Octopus Owner, secured by a security interest in all of Octopus's assets, now owned or hereafter acquired. I am preparing the note and loan agreement. Following is a description of Octopus's current business, which reflects its current assets. (Another associate is preparing a detailed list of assets, but this description should contain enough information to get you started.) Please write a memo, explaining in detail what Largess must do to perfect its security interest in all of Octopus's assets.

Octopus is in the business of renting trucks, trailers, portable storage boxes and self-storage spaces, and selling moving supplies, including specialty boxes for dishes, computers, and sensitive electronic equipment, as well as tapes, security locks, packing supplies, towing accessories, and propane. It also owns WEROctopus.com, an online marketplace that connects consumers to independent movers.

Its rental fleet consists of approximately 100,000 trucks, 50,000 trailers, and 25,000 towing devices, located in all fifty of the United States. It maintains its cash in various bank accounts throughout the United States. Its rentals generate a significant amount of cash and credit card receivables.

Octopus holds approximately $50 million in notes receivable from affiliates, which consist of junior unsecured notes. Octopus also owns and holds another portfolio of notes, principally collateralized by self-storage facilities and commercial properties. It receives management fees for operating various self-storage facilities, and rental income from space leased to others. Octopus has registered the trade name "OCTOPUS." It has invested in a variety of publicly-traded companies, and is a limited partner in a number of limited partnerships. As vehicles in its rental fleet age, it sells the used vehicles and purchases new ones. It maintains a number of showrooms and lots through which it sells the used vehicles.

---

## Code Sections

8-102, 9-102(b), 9-103, 9-104, 9-105, 9-106, 9-107, 9-308, 9-309, 9-310, 9-311, 9-312, 9-313, 9-314, 9-315, 9-316

# 1. Introduction

Now that you have learned about the most common method of perfection, the filing of a financing statement, this chapter studies the other methods of perfection. First,

**Figure 8-2: Methods of Perfection (Other Methods)**

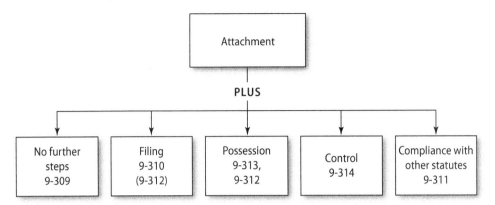

however, we introduce the purchase-money security interest, a special kind of security interest that you need to learn to identify because both the method of perfection and your analysis of priority disputes will be different when you are dealing with a purchase-money security interest.

# 2. Purchase-Money Security Interests

A purchase-money security interest is a special kind of security interest. The requirements for creation of such a security interest are the same as the requirements for the creation of any other type of security interest. Article 9 devotes an entire code section, section 9-103, to explaining how to determine when a security interest enjoys purchase-money status. A purchase-money security interest is a security interest in goods that are purchase-money collateral. Purchase-money collateral is defined as goods that secure a purchase-money obligation. A purchase-money obligation is defined as an obligation incurred as all or part of the price of collateral or for value given to enable the debtor to acquire rights in or use of the collateral if the value is in fact so used. Although these definitions may seem circular and somewhat cumbersome, recognizing a transaction that gives rise to a purchase-money security interest is relatively simple. Whenever a seller sells goods on credit and retains a security interest in the goods to secure payment of the purchase price, that is a purchase-money obligation and the seller's security interest is a purchase-money security interest. Recall that other provisions of Article 9 that you have already mastered provide that regardless of how the seller structures the credit sale, any retention or reservation by the seller of title in the goods is limited in effect to the reservation of a security interest. In addition to credit sale transactions, whenever a lender makes a loan to enable its borrower to purchase goods, and the borrower grants the lender a security interest in the goods purchased, the borrower's obligation to repay the loan is a purchase-money obligation, and the lender's security interest is a purchase-money security interest. Exercise 8-1 gives you an opportunity to be sure that you can recognize a purchase-money security interest. It also challenges you to apply some of the other provisions of section 9-103.

### Exercise 8-1:  Purchase-Money Security Interests

Which of the following transactions result in the creation of a purchase-money security interest? Explain fully.

1. Barry borrows $30,000 from Legal Loans to purchase a new car. He signs a security agreement, granting a security interest in the car to Legal Loans. Legal then remits $30,000 directly to the car dealer who is selling Barry the car.

2. Barry buys a car from Car Dealer, who has Barry sign a conditional sales contract that provides, among other things, that Car Dealer will retain title to the car until Barry has paid the purchase price of the car in full.

3. Barry buys a car from Car Dealer for $30,000, and pays for the car in cash. The next day, Barry borrows $30,000 from Loan Shark, and signs a security agreement granting Loan Shark a security interest in the car to secure repayment of the loan.

4. Barry borrows $30,000 from Legal Loans to purchase a new car. He signs a security agreement granting a security interest in the car to Legal Loans. Legal then remits $30,000 directly to the car dealer who is selling Barry the car. Approximately one month later, Barry is able to get a much better interest rate loan from Second Lender. He borrows $30,000, and signs a security agreement granting a security interest in the car to Second Lender. He uses the proceeds of the loan to pay off Legal Loans in full, and Legal Loans releases its security interest in the car.

5. Legal Loans refinances the car loan it made in 1 above, and loans Barry an additional $2,000, secured by the car.

# 3.  Perfection by Attachment; Automatic Perfection

As you learned in Chapter 7, in most cases, perfection of a security interest requires attachment plus some other step(s). However, there are some situations that do not require an additional step. In these cases, when a security interest attaches, it is automatically perfected.

First, a security interest in "related collateral" does not require additional steps for perfection. A security interest in a secured promissory note is an example of a transaction where there is "related collateral." The secured promissory note is the primary collateral. The security interest in the promissory note must be perfected in the proper manner. The security for the promissory note is "related collateral." No additional steps are needed to perfect the security interest in the related collateral once the security interest in the primary collateral (here, the promissory note) is perfected. Similarly, where the primary collateral is a securities account, the securities account is the primary collateral, and the security interest in it must be properly perfected. The security entitlements held in the securities account are related collateral. Once the security interest in the securities account is perfected, the security interest in the related collateral (the security entitlements held in the account) is also perfected.

Second, a security interest in supporting obligations does not require additional steps for perfection. Recall that "supporting obligations" are defined in UCC section 9-102(a)(78). A personal guaranty of a promissory note, for example, is a "supporting obligation" with respect to that promissory note. If the holder of the promissory note then borrows money from a second lender and grants a security interest in the note to its own creditor, that creditor must perfect its security interest in the note in the proper manner. Once that security interest is perfected, however, the creditor's security interest in the personal guaranty given in connection with that note (the supporting obligation) is automatically perfected.

Another situation that does not require additional steps for perfection is when a lender takes a purchase-money security interest in consumer goods. It has been suggested that the reasons for this exception to the general "attachment plus" approach to perfection are that (1) consumer transactions involve relatively small dollar amounts; (2) consumer transactions are high in volume, and it would be expensive for lenders to file so many financing statements, which would simply "clog up" the public records, anyway; and (3) collateral in consumer transactions rapidly depreciates in value, and it is unlikely that a subsequent creditor would advance funds in reliance on that property as collateral, making any argument about the importance of requiring public notice of a lien in these situations less than compelling.

Exercise 8-2 gives you an opportunity to read the statute and identify the situations that do not involve a purchase-money security interest in consumer goods, yet do not require additional steps for perfection.

---

## Exercise 8-2: Automatic Perfection

Compile a list of the remaining transactions that do not require any steps beyond attachment to perfect a security interest in collateral. Try to explain why you think the drafters chose to make an exception to the "attachment plus" approach for these transactions.

---

## Exercise 8-3: Perfection Problems

1. Emerald, a dedicated chef, recently purchased a home and decided she wanted new kitchen appliances. On May 2, Emerald went to Home Warehouse and purchased a refrigerator, a stove, and a microwave for her new home, using credit provided by the store. In connection with the sale, Emerald signed a contract granting Home Warehouse a security interest in the refrigerator, stove, and microwave.

   1.1 What steps must Home Warehouse take to perfect its security interest?

   1.2 Assume that Home Warehouse, in an attempt to be cautious, also listed as collateral in its contract other home furnishings already owned by Emerald. Would Home Warehouse be able to perfect a security interest in the already-owned furnishings in the same manner as in Question 1.1? If not, what steps would it have to take to perfect its security interest?

1.3 Assume Home Warehouse's security agreement included the grant of a security interest in after-acquired consumer goods. On May 15, Emerald went to American Bank for a loan — she wanted to borrow enough money to pay for a rolling antique cherry wood and marble island for her new kitchen. She signed a security agreement and granted American Bank a security interest in the rolling island. She then purchased the island from Home Warehouse, who took a security interest as outlined in 1 above. Who has a security interest in the rolling island?

2. After graduating from college and having trouble finding a job, Andy W. decided to put his award-winning art skills to use, and began to paint portraits of anyone who was interested, working out of his small studio apartment. Many of his customers did not pay in full and owed Andy money for the portraits. Within a few weeks, Andy was getting more requests, and he wanted to expand his business by renting out a studio dedicated solely to his painting. He also wanted to replenish all of his art supplies.

Andy received a loan of $15,000 from Fast Financing, secured by Andy's accounts receivable. (Note: When the text says a loan is "secured" you may assume that the requirements of section 9-203 for attachment of a security interest have been satisfied.) One of Andy's customers, Fancy, was a well-known young socialite, who was also known for not paying her debts. Andy's father, a lawyer, advised him to get someone to sign a personal guaranty of the loan, promising to pay the debt if Fancy did not.

2.1 Assume that Andy convinced Fancy that he needed a guaranty, and her parents signed one. Does Fast Financing have a security interest in the parents' guaranty? If so, what must it do to perfect its interest in the personal guaranty?

2.2 Same facts as 2.1 above. Fast Financing has asked you to assist it in preparing a UCC-1 financing statement, evidencing its interest in the accounts receivable and the personal guaranty. Complete item 4 in the form in *Figure 7-5a*.

3. Debbie Debtor owned 1,000 shares of stock in ABCD Corporation, a publicly-traded corporation, represented by certificate no. 1234. American Bank, under an authenticated security agreement, provided Debbie with a new line of credit in the amount of $3,000. The security agreement provided that the collateral was "Debtor's certificated securities" and further listed, with particularity, certificate no. 1234 representing 1,000 shares of stock in ABCD Corporation. Debbie signed the security agreement on September 2.

3.1 What steps, if any, must American Bank take to perfect the security interest in the stock? When must those steps be taken?

3.2 Assume that the stock certificate remained in her possession. On September 3, Debbie decided to sell all of the stock used as collateral in the security agreement with American Bank. If American Bank has not taken any steps to perfect its security interest in the stocks, characterize American Bank's interest in the money Debbie receives from selling the stock.

4. Trustworth Bank made a loan to Darren, which was secured by a security interest in five promissory notes. The Bank took possession of the promissory notes. On March 2, Trustworth allowed Darren to take possession of two of

the promissory notes for the purpose of presenting and collecting on the notes. On March 22, Darren returned one of the promissory notes to Trustworth. Two days later, the other promissory note in Darren's possession was accidentally destroyed.

4.1  What is the status of Trustworth's security interest with respect to the promissory notes?

4.2  What could Trustworth have done to remain perfected even while the notes were in Darren's possession?

5.  Zen Health, a small counter-service health food restaurant, received its initial start up money from Ready Money. To secure the loan, Zen Health granted Ready Money a floating lien on all of the restaurant's inventory, equipment, and fixtures. Ready Money properly perfected its security interest.

A year after opening, Zen Health decided that it should cater to the needs of customers who wanted a quick, healthy meal substitute: fresh juices. Joyful Juicers was in the business of selling juicers, both for household and restaurant purposes. On September 10, Zen Health purchased a counter-top juicing station on credit from Joyful Juicers. Two days later, the juicing station was delivered, and Zen Health immediately began selling juice to its customers.

5.1  Who has a perfected security interest in the juicing station on September 14? On October 4?

5.2  If Joyful Juicers consulted you before completing the juicer sale to Zen Health, how would you advise it to protect itself?

# 3. Perfection by Possession

Some types of collateral, such as money, can be perfected only by the secured party's taking possession of the collateral (with the exception of certain grace periods that apply under special circumstances for a short period of time). In the case of other types of collateral, such as tangible chattel paper,[1] negotiable instruments, or goods, a security interest may, but need not, be perfected by taking possession. Possession is generally effected by the secured party physically taking charge of tangible personal property. It may, however, be effected through a third party bailee.[2] The issue of who can be a third party bailee for purposes of possession depends on whether the third party is sufficiently independent of the debtor to serve as a bailee. It has been held that the issuer of a security cannot serve as a bailee, but the use of a guarantor, of an escrow agent, and even of the debtor's attorney, as a bailee has been upheld.[3]

---

1. Article 9 includes the concept of "electronic chattel paper," which is not susceptible of possession; hence the reference to "tangible chattel paper" in §9-313.

2. "Bailee" is defined in UCC §7-102(2).

3. Use of the debtor's attorney is *not* recommended, however. Can you explain why?

## Exercise 8-4: Perfection by Possession

1. Rosetta Rock wanted to help her daughter pay for college. She obtained a loan from Jolly Day Lenders in the amount of $20,000. Rosetta executed a promissory note in favor of Jolly Day and a security agreement listing her rare coin collection as the collateral for the loan. Rosetta has always kept her coin collection displayed in her home. The security agreement provided that Rosetta agreed to allow Jolly Day to file a financing statement as necessary to perfect its security interest. On the day that Rosetta went to Jolly Day's place of business and received the check for the loan proceeds, she turned over the chest containing her collection of coins.

   1.1 Must Jolly Day file a financing statement to perfect its security interest in the coins?

   1.2 Assume that Rosetta brought the chest of coins merely to confirm that she owned them, and to have Jolly Day's expert appraise their value. Upon receiving the check, Rosetta went home with her coins. Jolly Day never filed a financing statement. Can Jolly Day successfully argue that Rosetta's possession perfected its security interest in the coins?

   1.3 Why do you think the Code deems possession by the secured party to be sufficient for perfection with respect to certain types of collateral? Would that policy be served if a debtor were allowed to hold possession as the agent of the secured party?

   1.4. Now assume that Jolly Day took possession of Rosetta's coins. After being in possession of the coin collection for a few months, Jolly Day sent the coins to a coin specialist at New England Museum. The specialist was to clean and treat the coins to prevent damage. Jolly Day provided that the coins were to be cleaned for the benefit of Jolly Day, and that the coins were to be delivered to Jolly Day immediately after the process was completed. Is Jolly Day perfected while the museum is in possession of the coins?

2. Sandy Ross makes her living training neighborhood dogs. However, recently the plumbing in her old home has become troublesome, and the cost of replacing the old pipes far exceeds what she can afford. Aside from her home, the only item of value she owns is a quilt created by her ancestor, Betsy Ross, which depicts the American flag.

   Old Money Bank is willing to lend Sandy the money necessary to replace the plumbing in her home. Old Money and Sandy enter into a security agreement, using the quilt as collateral for the loan, and Old Money advances Sandy the loan funds.

   When the security interest attached, the quilt was in the possession of a group named Sea to Shining Sea, which traveled across the nation to schools, teaching American history with pieces of memorabilia such as the quilt. Sandy allowed Sea to Shining Sea to travel with her quilt, without payment.

   Old Money Bank believes that Sea to Shining Sea provides noble service to the country, and is willing to permit it to continue to travel with the quilt. What steps should Old Money Bank take to perfect its security interest, while allowing Sea to Shining Sea to continue to travel with the quilt? Does it matter whether Sea to Shining Sea is already in possession of the quilt when Old Money's security interest attaches? Does it matter whether or not Old Money files a financing statement?

3. Anachronism Furnishings specialized in repurposing antique items as functional furniture pieces. The company had exhausted its start up funds traveling and finding interesting pieces to add to its collection of materials. In need of money, Anachronism Furnishings decided to obtain funds from Furniture Financing, Inc. Furniture Financing agreed to lend Anachronism $50,000, and to establish an additional $50,000 revolving line of credit.

   We Guard Them, a company in the business of providing field warehouse services, went to Anachronism Furnishings' place of business, and placed a keypad lock on the door to the room where the collection of antique items was kept. The keypad lock was labeled "Content Controlled by WGT Field Warehouse." We Guard Them issued a negotiable warehouse receipt deliverable to Anachronism Furnishings.

   In return for the loan provided by Furniture Financing, Anachronism Furnishings provided Furniture Financings with the warehouse receipt, granting Furniture Financing a security interest in the collection of antique items and the warehouse receipt.

   3.1. What steps, if any, does Furniture Financing need to take to perfect its security interest in the collection of antique items? Would your answer change if New American Bank had previously loaned Anachronism $25,000, secured by its collection, and properly perfected that security interest?

   3.2. Assume We Guard Them paid Julian, one of Anachronism Furnishings' employees, to act as a custodian on behalf of We Guard Them. Does the fact that Julian is employed by Anachronism affect Furniture Financing's status as a perfected secured creditor when Furniture Financing is in possession of the warehouse receipt?

   3.3. Assume Furniture Financing allows Anachronism Furnishings to take possession of the warehouse receipt to take dozens of antique items from the collection for the purpose of creating furniture pieces to be sold to customers. Will Furniture Financing retain a perfected security interest in the warehouse receipt? In the antique items?

# 4. Perfection by Control

"Control" is a relatively recent concept — one that you may think of as being somewhat analogous to possession of tangibles, but involving collateral of a type that cannot be turned over to the secured party's physical possession, such as a letter of credit right or rights to a deposit account. Unlike possession, however, "control" is a creation of the Code. As the choice of the word "control" indicates, a creditor has control of collateral when it has the power to direct someone's behavior with respect to it. Hence, the specific steps that must be taken for a creditor to achieve control differ depending on the collateral involved. For example, if the collateral is a deposit account, the secured party must be able to direct the behavior of the depository bank with respect to the deposit account. Therefore, the Code provides that the creditor can achieve control in one of three ways: (a) the debtor, the secured party, and the depositary bank must have agreed in an authenticated record that the bank will comply with instructions originated by the secured party directing disposition of the funds in the deposit account without further consent by the debtor; (b) the secured party must have become the depositary bank's customer with respect to the deposit account; or (c) the secured party itself must be the depositary bank. "Control" with respect to other types of collateral is even more complex. Exercise 8-5 gives you an opportunity to read the statute and determine how a creditor achieves control in transactions involving other types of collateral.

## Exercise 8-5:  Perfection by Control

Complete the following chart, which summarizes the concept of perfection by control. Portions of the chart have been completed for you.

| Collateral | Code Sections | Method of Control |
|---|---|---|
| Deposit Accounts | 9-104 | (a) the debtor, the secured party and the depositary bank must have agreed in an authenticated record that the bank will comply with instructions originated by the secured party directing disposition of the funds in the deposit account without further consent by the debtor; (b) the secured party must have become the depositary bank's customer with respect to the deposit account; or (c) the secured party itself must be the depositary bank |
| Electronic Chattel Paper | 9-105 | |
| Investment Property | 9-106 | |
| Letter of Credit Rights | | |
| Electronic Documents | | |

## Exercise 8-6:  Control Problems

1. Ultimate Interiors, a furniture store, issued a line of credit in the amount of $2,000 to Grace, for the purchase of living room furniture for her new home. Ultimate Interiors took a security interest in all of the furniture Grace purchased. Additionally, Ultimate Interiors took a security interest in Grace's personal checking account at American Bank.

1.1. Does Article 9 apply to the purported interest in Grace's personal checking account?

1.2. Assume that the furniture Grace purchased from Ultimate Interiors was to be used to furnish the waiting room of Grace's business: Sun & Sea Spa. Would Article 9 apply to Ultimate Interior's interest in Grace's personal checking account?

1.3. Same facts as Question 1.2. Ultimate Interiors has filed a financing statement listing "Debtor's now owned or after-acquired equipment and Debtor's interest in personal checking account #123456789, held at American Bank." Has Ultimate Interiors perfected its security interest?

2. Beth and Allen are both psychologists. They have decided to merge and start a larger practice, though Beth plans to continue to spend a portion of her time at her small, separate practice. To obtain funding for the leasing of a building, furniture and other materials, Beth and Allen go to Our Money Bank. Our Money Bank provides a $250,000 loan, which is secured by the equipment and inventory to be purchased, as well as by Beth's checking account at AllAmerican Bank in which Beth deposits all money earned from her separate practice.

Allen inherited several beach homes from his parents, and though he hardly ever stayed in those homes, he has made a sizeable amount of money renting them for weekend vacations, weddings, etc. The income from the rental of Allen's beach homes is deposited in a checking account at Your Money Bank.

Additionally, Beth and Allen have had to obtain funds to be able to pay associate psychologists, clerical staff, and other services necessary to the business. Your Money Bank has loaned $800,000 to Beth and Allen, which is secured by Allen's checking account at Your Money Bank.

2.1. How can Our Money Bank perfect its security interest in Beth's checking account at AllAmerican Bank?

2.2 How can Your Money Bank perfect its security interest in Allen's checking account at Your Money Bank?

# 5. Perfection of Security Interest in Property Subject to Certain Statutes, Regulations, and Treaties

You will recall that when we first addressed the scope of Article 9, we noted that certain transactions might be subject to other state statutes, as well as federal law and regulations. These transactions are subject to some of Article 9's rules, particularly when it comes to priority disputes. However, when a transaction is subject to other state and federal laws, those laws may provide the exclusive method for perfecting the security interest. The example with which you may be most familiar is a transaction subject to another state statute, such as a statute governing liens on automobiles. Many states have statutes that require that owners hold state-issued certificates of title to motor vehicles, and further provide that to be valid, any liens on those vehicles must be noted on the certificate of title. In that situation, the only way for a secured lender to perfect its lien on a motor vehicle would be to comply with the certificate of title statute. Another common example is a lien on aircraft. Federal law provides that all interests in aircraft must be registered in a national registry, located in Oklahoma.[4] The Official Comments to section 9-311 provide other examples of statutes that you will need to consult to determine applicable perfection requirements for different types of collateral.

## Exercise 8-7:  Certificate of Title Perfection Issues

Debtor purchased a car in California, with financing from Carfunds, Inc., who duly perfected a security interest in the car by noting its lien on the California certificate of title, as required by California law. That lien interest and its effective date of December 10, Year 1, were duly noted on the certificate of title. Debtor then moved to Idaho, and on July 30, Year 2, Debtor applied for an Idaho certificate of title. Under Idaho law, the vehicle became covered in Idaho when an application and fees were tendered to the Idaho authorities. The Idaho title issued as a result of this application was dated August 6, Year 2. It shows Debtor as owner and Carfunds, Inc. as lien holder. The Idaho title shows the 'record' date for Carfunds' lien as December 10, Year 1, a date consistent with the 'issue date' on the paper California title. As of what date did Carfunds have a perfected security interest in the vehicle?

## Exercise 8-8:  Perfection of Security Interest in Proceeds

Moneybags Finance Co. lent money to BigBox Store, secured by a security interest in all of BigBox's inventory. It perfected its security interest by filing a properly completed financing statement in the proper place. Assume that BigBox sold items of inventory to a variety of customers, and received in exchange the property described below. Will Moneybags have a perfected security interest in each piece of property? Why or why not? Explain fully.

1. Cash, which BigBox deposited in its general account at URBank.

2. Checks, which BigBox also deposited in its general account at URBank.

3. Promissory notes.

4. An installment sales contract, consisting of both a promise to pay and a security agreement granting BigBox, as seller, a security interest in the item sold.

5. A used computer, which BigBox accepted as part of the purchase price for a new computer.

6. A used car. Assume that BigBox is doing business in a state that requires liens to be noted on a certificate of title to be enforceable.

---

4. 49 U.S.C. 44107-11.

# Additional Resources

Elizabeth D. Lauzon, Annotation, *Creation and Perfection of Security Interests in Insurance Proceeds Under Article 9 of Uniform Commercial Code*, 47 A.L.R. 6th 347 (2009).

Boyd J Peterson, Annotation, *Secured transactions: government agriculture program payments as "proceeds" of agriculture products under UCC § 9-306*, 79 A.L.R. 4th 903 (1990).

Gary D. Spivey, Annotation, *Perfection of Security Interests by Possession, Delivery, or Control Under Revised Article 9 of Uniform Commercial Code*, 53 A.L.R. 6th 159 (2010).

Richard C. Tinney, Annotation, *Effectiveness of original financing statement under UCC Article 9 after change in debtor's name, identity, or business structure*, 99 A.L.R. 3d 1194 (1980).

# Chapter 9

# Priority Disputes (Secured Creditors)

Figure 9-1: Article 9 Graphic Organizer

```
                    ┌─────────────────┐
                    │    Scope of     │
                    │   Article 9     │
                    └─────────────────┘
                             │
                             ▼
              ┌────────────────────────────────┐
              │          Creation of           │
              │        Security Interest       │
              │  (Attachment and Enforceability)│
              └────────────────────────────────┘
                 │                          │
        ┌────────────────┐         ┌────────────────┐
        │ Issues Arising │         │ Issues Arising │
        │ Out of         │         │ Out of Presence│
        │ Relationship   │         │ of Competing   │
        │ between Debtor │         │ Claims to Same │
        │ and Secured    │         │ Collateral     │
        │ Party          │         │                │
        └────────────────┘         └────────────────┘
                 │                          │
           ┌──────────┐              ┌──────────────┐
           │ Default  │              │  Perfection  │
           └──────────┘              └──────────────┘
                 │                          │
           ┌──────────┐              ┌──────────────┐
           │ Remedies │              │  Priority    │
           └──────────┘              │  Disputes    │
                                     └──────────────┘
                                            │
                                     ┌──────────────┐
                                     │ Bankruptcy   │
                                     │Considerations│
                                     └──────────────┘
```

## Chapter Problem

Mario Luigi ("Mario") was engaged in the manufacture and sale of ravioli products. He conducted business under the fictitious trade name of Luigi's Italian Kitchen. In Year 1, People's Bank ("People's") loaned $200,000 to Mario, pursuant to a duly authenticated loan and security agreement. He had been a customer for many years; his bank accounts were all in the name of Luigi's Italian Kitchen. When he walked into the bank, people would shout, "Luigi's Italian Kitchen is in the house!" People's filed a financing statement on August 14, Year 1. The financing statement reflected the following information:

Debtor: Luigi's Italian Kitchen

Secured Party: People's Bank.

Collateral: All of Debtor's personal property now owned and hereafter acquired.

(The actual security agreement identified the collateral as "All of debtor's inventory, accounts, equipment, fixtures, deposit accounts, and all proceeds thereof.")

Mario incorporated Luigi's Ravioli Kitchen, Inc. ("Luigi's"), on January 11, Year 3. He transferred all of the assets of Luigi's Italian Kitchen to the new corporation in exchange for stock, and the corporation assumed all of his liabilities relating to Luigi's Italian Kitchen.

On March 15, Year 3, First Bank ("First") granted Luigi's a line of credit ("LOC") with a $250,000 maximum. Luigi's signed a $250,000 promissory note and a security agreement (the "First Security Agreement") that *read in pertinent part* as follows:

---

1.   **Security Interest.** Luigi's Ravioli Kitchen, Inc. ("Debtor') hereby grants to First a security interest in all of Debtor's right, title, and interest in all of Debtor's property, whether now owned or hereafter acquired, real, personal or mixed, tangible or intangible, of every kind and description, wherever located, together with all proceeds thereof, including all accounts, chattel paper, all contracts, all deposit accounts, all equipment, all fixtures, all goods, all instruments, and all inventory of Debtor.

2.   **Obligations.** The grant of the security interest herein by the Debtor to First shall secure the payment and performance of all liabilities and obligations now or hereafter owing from Debtor to First of whatever kind or nature, whether or not currently contemplated at the time of this Agreement, whether such obligations be direct or indirect, absolute or contingent or due or to become due (the "Obligations").

---

First filed a financing statement on March 17, Year 3. The financing statement reflected the following information:

Debtor: Luigi's Ravioli Kitchen, Inc.

Secured Party: First Bank

Collateral: All of Debtor's personal property, now owned or hereafter acquired

In late March, a sharp-eyed teller at People's Bank noticed that Mario was depositing checks payable to Luigi's Ravioli Kitchen, Inc. As a result, Mario remembered to tell his loan officer about the incorporation, and on April 1, Year 3, People's filed an amendment to its initial financing statement to add, as an additional debtor, "Luigi's Ravioli Kitchen, Inc."

In January Year 4 Luigi's needed some additional working capital. It negotiated a term loan with Second Bank ("Second"), secured by a lien on all of Luigi's equipment. Second was aware of the LOC, but it was confident that there was ample value in all of Luigi's assets to satisfy the LOC. (It was unaware of the transaction with People's Bank.) Second loaned Luigi's $100,000. The parties entered into and duly authenticated a security agreement that described the collateral as "equipment." Second then filed a financing statement on January 15, Year 4, reflecting the following information:

Debtor: Luigi's Ravioli Kitchen, Inc.

Secured Party: Second Bank

Collateral: All of Debtor's equipment.

In April, Year 5, Luigi's asked Supplier if it could try out a new pizza oven sold by Supplier. Supplier agreed to allow Luigi's to use the machine for up to 30 days on a trial basis, and delivered it to Luigi's to begin the trial period on April 2. On April 25, Luigi's agreed to purchase the machine for its business. Supplier agreed to extend credit to enable Luigi's to complete the purchase, and retain title to the machine until paid in full. The parties signed a written conditional sales contract reflecting that agreement and a $10,000 purchase price. Supplier filed a properly completed financing statement on April 27, Year 5.

On July 31, Year 5, First loaned Luigi's an additional $150,000 and Luigi's signed a note in the amount of $150,000.

Luigi's has now fallen on hard times. It has defaulted on its lease and vacated the premises, leaving all of its fixtures and equipment in place. It has consulted an attorney to discuss filing for relief under the Bankruptcy Code. At that meeting, Mario tells the attorney that the approximate values of Luigi's assets are: (1) inventory: $25,000; (2) accounts receivable: $250,000; (3) equipment, excluding the oven sold by Supplier and fixtures: $50,000; (4) fixtures: $100,000; and (5) its bank account at People's Bank, with a balance of $20,000, which cannot be traced back to any of the various lenders' collateral.

Your assignment is to respond to the following specific questions. **Assume that all financing statements were filed in the proper place under section 9-501(a)(2).**

I.     Explain the respective interests of each of First Bank, Second Bank, People's Bank, and Supplier in the assets listed below.

II.    Assume that the amount owed to each creditor is as follows: First: $400,000; Second: $100,000; People's: $100,000; Supplier: $10,000. Objectively discuss the relative priority of each of First Bank, Second Bank, People's Bank and Supplier, in the assets listed below.

1. Luigi's inventory,

2. The pizza oven Luigi's acquired from Supplier,

3. Luigi's equipment (not including fixtures and the pizza oven described in #2),

4. Luigi's fixtures,

5. Luigi's accounts, and

6. The bank account at People's Bank.

---

## Code Sections

9-317, 9-322, 9-323, 9-324, 9-325, 9-326, 9-327, 9-328, 9-329

# 1. Introduction to Priority Disputes

As we discussed earlier in this book, secured creditors must consider all the things that might go wrong in the early planning stages of a transaction. We have already identified two of those things: the debtor may default, or file bankruptcy. We now consider the third major problem area: priority disputes. Someone else may claim that his or her interest in the collateral is superior to that of the secured creditor. Lawyers who practice secured transactions law speak of one interest "trumping" or "priming" another. Unless a secured creditor enters into a transaction knowing that she is taking a "second" or "junior" position, all secured creditors want to be sure that they will win any priority dispute.

Everything you have been studying up to this point of the course will now be called into play as we explore the careful priority scheme the drafters of Article 9 developed to resolve disputes between people who assert claims to the same collateral. To analyze a priority dispute, you first must determine the basis for the claim that each party is asserting. As *Figure 9-1* illustrates, when a claimant asserts a security interest, you will have to analyze whether the security interest was properly created and perfected. Next, you will have to analyze the basis for any competing claims. This chapter studies priority disputes between secured creditors and unsecured creditors, and between unperfected secured creditors and perfected secured creditors. More complex priority disputes are discussed in the next chapter. This text does not cover all such instances in detail. Students should familiarize themselves generally with all of Subpart 3 of Part 3 of Article 9, Sections 9-317 through 9-339, relating to priority.

# 2. Secured Creditors v. Unsecured Creditors

The first priority rule reflects the importance of being a secured creditor: a creditor with a properly perfected security interest will always prevail over a creditor holding an unsecured claim. Find the code section that is the authority for that rule.

# 3. Secured Creditors v. Secured Creditors

Creditors who are both secured by the same collateral may always enter into voluntary agreements, defining their respective priorities in the collateral. Such agreements are commonly referred to as "subordination agreements," or "intercreditor agreements," and the Code specifically states that parties entitled to priority may agree to subordinate their claim to that of another.[1] Barring such an agreement, to analyze a priority dispute between creditors claiming to be secured by the same collateral, you should further analyze the respective positions of the claimants.

To facilitate your analysis, you can construct a table, using the same roadmap that we have been using throughout this text, as illustrated in *Figure 9-2*. After you have mastered the task of analyzing a two-party priority dispute, you will be able to add additional parties and ultimately solve the complex chapter problem. An example of this approach to analysis follows, in Exercise 9-2.

# 3.1  Perfected Secured Creditors v. Unperfected Secured Creditors

As you learned earlier, a secured creditor must perfect its security interest to preserve its position vis-à-vis other claimants to the same collateral. Hence, a secured party who has properly perfected its security interest in collateral will prevail in a priority dispute against a secured creditor whose security interest in the same collateral is unperfected.[2] *Figure 9-2* is an example of an approach you may use to analyze such a problem, assuming two secured creditors claim a security interest in the same piece of equipment.

---

### Exercise 9-1:  Analyzing a Two-Party Priority Dispute

Bank holds a properly perfected security interest in essentially all of Producer's personal property, including equipment and fixtures. Bank properly perfected its security interest in January of Year 1 by filing a UCC-1 financing statement in the proper place.

On May 2 of Year 1, Supplier and Producer entered into a contract for Supplier to sell and install a new production system at Producer's Alabama facility. The contract provided, among other things, that: (1) Supplier would sell and install the new production system for a total price of $369,865; (2) Producer would make a 35% down-payment; and (3) Supplier would retain title to the production system pending payment in full. Producer made the agreed-upon down payment. On July 1 the majority of the system was delivered and bolted to the floor, but it was not yet fully installed and was not operational. The new system, although bolted to the floor, can be removed from Producer's facility without harming the realty. Assume that Producer is in default under its loan agreement with Bank and Bank wants to repossess the production system. In a priority dispute between Bank and Supplier, who should prevail? Why? Use the approach illustrated in *Figure 9-2* to help you answer these questions. (You should use this approach to help you analyze all of the remaining exercises in this chapter as well.)

---

1. See UCC §9-339, and Official Comment 2. A sample of such an agreement is in Appendix F.
2. See UCC §9-322(a)(1). Official Comment 11 also observes that in the unlikely case that two unperfected security interests compete for priority, the first to attach has priority.

## Figure 9-2: An Example of How to Analyze a Two-Party Priority Dispute

|  | First Party | Second Party |
|---|---|---|
| Scope | Determine whether Art. 9 applies to analyze the first party's interest in the collateral. | Determine whether Art. 9 applies to analyze the second party's interest in the collateral. |
| Characterize the Collateral | Determine what kind of property is the subject of the dispute, using the types identified in Article 9. (Here, the facts tell you that the dispute is over a piece of equipment; hence, the collateral can be properly characterized as "equipment.") | Determine what kind of property is the subject of the dispute, using the types identified in Article 9. (Here, the facts tell you that the dispute is over a piece of equipment; hence, the collateral can be properly characterized as "equipment.") |
| Creation of Security Interest | Determine whether value has been given, whether the debtor has rights in the collateral, and whether some step has been taken, such as the authentication of a security agreement that describes the collateral. (Here, the facts tell you that the first party has an unperfected security interest; therefore, you can assume that a security interest was properly created. Otherwise, you would need to analyze the facts to determine whether the security interest had attached and was enforceable.) | Determine whether value has been given, whether the debtor has rights in the collateral, and whether some step has been taken, such as the authentication of a security agreement that describes the collateral. (Here, the facts tell you that the second party has a perfected security interest; therefore, you can assume that a security interest was properly created. Otherwise, you would need to analyze the facts to determine whether the security interest had attached and was enforceable.) |
| Perfection | First, review the applicable code sections to see how to perfect a security interest in the type of collateral you have identified. Then, see if the proper steps were taken by the party. (Here, you are told that the first party is unperfected. Note that all of the problems with perfection we discussed in the previous two chapters may be involved in this part of your analysis of a priority dispute.) | First, review the applicable code sections to see how to perfect a security interest in the type of collateral you have identified. Then, see if the proper steps were taken by the party. (Here, you are told that the second party is perfected.) |
| Reach a Conclusion Regarding the Interest of Each Party | Conclusion: Unperfected Secured Creditor | Conclusion: Perfected Secured Creditor |
| Apply the Appropriate Code Section to Resolve the Priority Dispute | Section 9-322 First to file or perfect Unperfected secured creditor loses to perfected secured creditor | Section 9-322 First to file or perfect Perfected secured creditor trumps unperfected secured creditor |

## 3.2 Perfected Secured Creditors v. Perfected Secured Creditors

When both secured parties have properly perfected their security interests in the same collateral, the "first to file or perfect" will generally prevail in a priority dispute.[3]

---

### Exercise 9-2: Another Priority Dispute

Debtor, Inc., a Michigan corporation, operates a restaurant in Wisconsin. On April 1, Creditor loaned $250,000 to Debtor in exchange for a security interest in Debtor's personal property. On April 1, Debtor borrowed $130,000 from Bank, and authenticated a security agreement that granted a Bank security interest in all of Debtor's personal property as collateral for that loan. Assume that both Creditor and Bank entered into appropriate security agreements with Debtor that contain sufficient descriptions of the collateral. On April 30, Bank perfected its security interest by filing a financing statement in the proper place in Michigan. One month later, on May 30, Creditor filed a financing statement in the proper place in Michigan.

1. In a priority dispute between Creditor and Bank, who prevails?

2. If Bank had knowledge of Creditor's prior unperfected security interest, would that change the result in #1?

3. If Creditor filed a financing statement in Wisconsin before Bank filed its financing statement in Michigan, would that change the result in #1?

---

### Exercise 9-3: Priority Dispute in Deposit Accounts

Debtor and Investment Firm authenticated a loan agreement ("Loan Agreement,") pursuant to which Debtor granted a security interest to Investment Firm in all of Debtor's accounts receivable. The Loan Agreement required Debtor to direct customers with outstanding account balances to remit their payments directly to Investment Firm. Investment Firm properly filed a financing statement, identifying "accounts" as its collateral. One year later, Debtor, who maintained a commercial bank account with Bank, entered into a loan agreement with Bank. Pursuant to that loan agreement, Bank obtained a security interest in deposits maintained by Debtor at Bank and held a right of set-off against Debtor's commercial account. Customer payments generally were not deposited into Debtor's commercial deposit account. However, as the relationship between Debtor and Investment Firm slowly deteriorated, Debtor began to direct customer payments into Debtor's commercial deposit account with Bank.

---

3. See UCC § 9-322(a)(1). Never forget, however, that there are exceptions to this general rule — for example, for certain purchase-money security interests. See paragraph 3.3, *infra*. Also, the method of perfection may matter. For example, a security interest in investment property that is perfected by control will have priority over an earlier perfected security interest perfected by filing, UCC § 9-328.

In a priority dispute between Investment Firm and Bank over customer payments deposited into Debtor's commercial deposit account, who prevails? Why?

---

## 3.3  Priority Disputes Involving Purchase-Money Security Interests

Just like any other kind of security interest, the proper method of perfecting of a purchase-money security interest depends on the type of collateral involved in the transaction. There are, however, special rules that relate to the timing of perfection that you must learn to resolve priority disputes involving purchase-money security interests.

Article 9 has special priority rules that apply when one or both of the competing security interests are purchase-money security interests. The general rule is that a perfected purchase-money security interest in goods other than inventory or livestock has priority over a conflicting security interest in the same goods, if the purchase-money security interest is perfected when the debtor receives possession of the collateral or within 20 days thereafter.

If the purchase-money security interest is in inventory, the purchase-money security interest still has priority over conflicting security interests in the same inventory, provided certain requirements are met: (1) the purchase-money security interest is perfected when the debtor receives possession of the inventory; (2) the purchase-money secured creditor has also sent notification to holders of a conflicting security interest stating that (a) the person sending the notification has or expects to acquire a purchase-money security interest in the debtor's inventory and (b) describes the inventory; and (3) the holder of the conflicting security interest receives such notification within five years before the debtor receives possession of the inventory. As you will see in the following case, these notification requirements have generally been strictly construed. Questions have also been raised regarding the nature of the description required in the notice.

If the purchase-money security interest is in livestock, the purchase-money secured creditor must make a similar notification, which must be received by the holder of the conflicting security interest within six months before the debtor receives possession of livestock.

Priority disputes among multiple purchase-money-security interests in the same collateral are resolved in favor of purchase-money security interests created in favor of the seller over purchase-money security interests that secure enabling loans. The first-to-file or perfect rule of section 9-322 applies to multiple purchase-money security interests securing enabling loans.

---

### Exercise 9-4:  *In re Sports Pub., Inc.*

Read the following decision of the District Court for the Central District of Illinois, discussing the notification requirement for super-priority for purchase-money security interests. As you read the case, consider whether you agree with the decision of the court, taking into careful consideration: (1) the policies of the Code under section 1-103, (2) the purposes of the notification requirement and (3) the practical implications of a system that permits a purchase-money security interest to have "super priority" over prior existing security interests in the same collateral.

---

# In re Sports Pub., Inc.

2010 WL 75008

72 UCC Rep. Serv. 2d 383 (D.C.C.D. Ill. 2010)

## OPINION

MICHAEL P. McCUSKEY, Chief Judge.

This is an appeal from an Opinion entered by the United States Bankruptcy Court for the Central District of Illinois (Bankruptcy Case No. 08-91780) brought pursuant to 28 U.S.C. § 158(a), concerning whether a valid Purchase-Money Security Interest (PMSI) existed with regard to certain property of a debtor. In Adversary Case No. 08-09049, the Bankruptcy Court found in favor of Plaintiff-Appellee, Midland States Bank (Strategic), [At the time of the bankruptcy proceedings, the plaintiff was Strategic Capital Bank. However, in May 2009 all of Strategic's interests in various outstanding loans to Debtor Sports Publishing, LLC (Debtor) were transferred and assigned to Midland. This court has since substituted Midland for Strategic as Appellee. However, for simplicity's sake, Appellee will be referred to as "Strategic."] And against Defendant-Appellant Innerworkings, LLC/Innerworkings, Inc. (InnerWorkings). Following a thorough review of the record and relevant legal authorities, this court agrees with the decision of the Bankruptcy Court and affirms its judgment.

## BACKGROUND

The following facts are taken from the briefs of both parties filed in this court:

Debtor Sports Publishing LLC commenced the underlying bankruptcy case by filing a voluntary chapter 11 petition in the United States Bankruptcy Court for the Central District of Illinois on October 15, 2008. Strategic loaned money to Debtor, entered into a Commercial Security Agreement on July 10, 2001 with Debtor and filed Financing Statements on July 16, 2001 and February 7, 2006 (continuation filing) with the Illinois Secretary of State's Office to secure its notes and payment of the money owed by the Debtor. InnerWorkings loaned money and/or extended credit to Debtor, entered into a Commercial Security Agreement with Debtor on January 1, 2005, and filed a Financing Statement with the Illinois Secretary of State's Office on March 29, 2005, with respect to certain of Debtor's property. Subsequently, InnerWorkings entered into a series of agreements (PMSI Agreements) with Debtor and Strategic in which the parties agreed that InnerWorkings would finance certain inventory of Debtor.

On November 4, 2008, Strategic commenced the adversary proceeding from which this appeal is taken by filing its Complaint to Determine the Validity, Extent, and Priority of Lien Claims (Complaint) against InnerWorkings and other defendants. In the Complaint, Strategic requested a determination by the Bankruptcy Court as to the validity, extent, and relative priority of the lien claims of InnerWorkings and Strategic.

In its pleadings, InnerWorkings conceded that Strategic had a first priority lien on and security interest in the collateral (non-PMSI collateral) of Debtor other than the PMSI collateral and that InnerWorkings has a second priority lien on and security interest in the non-PMSI collateral. However, InnerWorkings asserted that it has a valid PMSI on certain inventory collateral (PMSI collateral), which therefore constitutes a first priority lien on and security interest in the PMSI collateral, senior to the lien and security interest of Strategic.

The PMSI Agreements in question relate to certain books InnerWorkings financed for Debtor. The language contained in the January 1, 2005, InnerWorkings Commercial Security Agreement and Uniform Commercial Code Financing Statement with Debtor stated: "Despite any other provision of this Agreement, Vendor is granted, and by virtue of the fact that it provided product to Grantor, has a purchase-money security interest in the goods that were sold to Grantor." Then in 2007 InnerWorkings and Debtor entered into the agreements in question, which established a PMSI in property of the Debtor financed by InnerWorkings.

The sole issue presented for trial was whether InnerWorkings complied with the requirements under Illinois law for the creation and enforcement of a valid PMSI on the PMSI collateral in the PMSI Agreements. As InnerWorkings was the party asserting the PSMI, it bore the burden of proof in presenting evidence that established that it has complied with the Illinois PMSI laws relating to inventory.

During the Bankruptcy Court trial on May 5, 2009, Steven Wills, the former president of Strategic, was called as an adverse witness by InnerWorkings. He was the only witness called by InnerWorkings. Wills was familiar with the lending relationship between Debtor and Strategic. He was also familiar with the relationships between InnerWorkings and Strategic and InnerWorkings and Debtor. Wills denied that he had detailed conversations with InnerWorkings's management and Strategic's management concerning InnerWorkings's attempt to sell books to Debtor, secured by a PMSI. He did admit to having "five to ten" discussions with InnerWorkings concerning Debtor's owing money to InnerWorkings. Wills again denied knowing that InnerWorkings had a PMSI with regard to certain books sold by InnerWorkings to Debtor. Wills's understanding of the book deal was that it was just a normal "client/customer relationship." Wills was then shown the agreement between Debtor and InnerWorkings for the 2007 Fall listing of books that Debtor had planned to publish. When asked by InnerWorkings's counsel if those agreements identified the books that InnerWorkings would sell to Debtor on a PMSI basis, Wills said they did not. Wills again stated the agreements to sell the books, to his knowledge, were not based on a PMSI, but rather just the normal client/customer relationship.

Although it is not explicitly stated what exact documents Wills received in his capacity as Strategic president, or what he was reviewing on the witness stand at trial, it appears the documents in question were the Commercial Security Agreement between InnerWorkings and Debtor dated January 1, 2005 (Appellate Record pp. 79-82), the UCC Financing Statement dated March 29, 2005 (Appellate Record pp. 83-84), and the Fall 2007 Agreements between Strategic, InnerWorkings, and Debtor for InnerWorkings for InnerWorkings sale of books to Debtor (Appellate Record pp. 85-93). The Commercial Security Agreement contained the line "Despite any other provisions of this Agreement, Vendor is granted, and by virtue of the fact that it provided product to Grantor, has, a purchase-money security interest in the goods that were sold to Grantor" about four or five paragraphs down on the first page entitled "Commercial Security Agreement" and not under its own separate headings. This statement is repeated in the 2005 Innerworkings-Debtor UCC Financing Statement as the very bottom paragraph, which the terms "Secured Party" and "Debtor" substituted for "Vendor" and "Grantor," respectively. Then, these documents were attached to the 2007 agreements describing InnerWorkings's interest in sales of books by Debtor.

On cross examination, Wills stated that, in the PMSI collateral agreements between InnerWorkings and Debtor, PMSI is never mentioned. It was also never mentioned in any conversation related to the agreements. Strategic did not prepare the agreements, but rather InnerWorkings prepared them. On redirect, Wills testified that he had reviewed InnerWorkings's Commercial Security Agreement and UCC Financing Statement. The first time he reviewed those documents was in April/May 2007. However, when counsel for InnerWorkings showed Wills the Commercial Security Agreement between InnerWorkings and Debtor, the document contained, on page one above the paragraph "Grantor's Representations and Warranties," that InnerWorkings maintained a PMSI in any goods sold to Debtor. However, Wills could not say that he was aware, as of April 2007, that InnerWorkings intended to sell books to Debtor on a PMSI basis.

On recross, counsel for Strategic noted that InnerWorkings Commercial Security Agreement came in a package that did not include an authenticated notice of PMSI. Neither Wills himself, nor to his knowledge anyone else at Strategic, ever received such a PMSI authenticated notice. No other evidence or witnesses were presented by either party.

The Bankruptcy Court ruled in favor of Strategic at trial, stating "[Strategic] is clearly right. The evidence is very clear. It is a slam dunk case for the plaintiff bank." In the order entered on May 6, 2009, after the conclusion of the trial, the Bankruptcy Court stated:

> "Judgment is GRANTED for Plaintiff STRATEGIC CAPITAL BANK and against Defendant INNERWORKINGS, INC. f/k/a INNERWORKINGS LLC regarding the validity of a Purchase- Money Security Interest of INNERWORKINGS for any collateral of Debtor SPORTS PUBLISHING, LLC, thus giving STRATEGIC CAPITAL BANK a first priority lien on and security interest in all the collateral of Debtor ahead of INNERWORKINGS."

InnerWorkings filed its timely notice of appeal and the case was brought before this court on appeal.

STANDARD OF REVIEW (intentionally omitted)

The Bankruptcy Court's decision will be reviewed de novo.

ANALYSIS

The issue on appeal is whether the Bankruptcy Court erred in ruling that InnerWorkings did not comply with the requirements under Illinois law for the creation and enforcement of a valid PMSI on the PMSI collateral, thus giving Strategic a first priority lien on and security interest in all of the collateral of Debtor ahead of InnerWorkings. Specifically, the parties are focused on whether InnerWorkings provided notice of the PMSI to Strategic so as to satisfy Illinois law. InnerWorkings argues that it complied with the statutory requirements for creating a PMSI.

They argue that Wills received notice of InnerWorkings's PMSI through the various discussions he had with InnerWorkings's management and through his receipt of the InnerWorkings-Debtor Commercial Security Agreement, in which "InnerWorkings's intention to sell goods to the Debtor on a 'purchase-money security' basis was disclosed in 'roughly April/May 2007.'" Further, even if Strategic had not received prior notice of InnerWorkings's intention to sell goods to the Debtor on a PMSI basis, notice was "essentially," if not "expressly," accomplished. Strategic, as a sophisticated commercial entity, should have realized that a PMSI was being created during the 2007 communications between Inner-Workings and Strategic that Wills testified to at trial.

Strategic counters that the requirements under Illinois law for the creation of a valid PMSI are strict and that InnerWorkings failed to comply with them. Strategic argues that at no time during the trial or in its pleadings has InnerWorkings presented any evidence that it sent an authenticated notification, with the required content, to Strategic. Nor did it provide evidence showing it had done so prior to Debtor receiving the alleged PMSI inventory from InnerWorkings. Strategic also argues that InnerWorkings's application of the "essentially accomplished" standard is inappropriate and misguided. Finally, Strategic posits that the InnerWorkings-Debtor Commercial Security Agreement is not the equivalent of a required authenticated PMSI notification sent to Strategic.

The parties agree that whether an interest is perfected or not as of the petition date is determined by state law, thus Illinois controls the determination in this matter. See Matter of Chaseley's Foods, Inc., 726 F.2d 303, 307 (7th Cir.1983). Under Illinois law, the requirements for perfecting a PMSI are as follows:

> "(1) the purchase-money security interest is perfected when the debtor receives possession of the inventory;
>
> (2) the purchase-money secured party sends an authenticated notification to the holder of the conflicting security interest;
>
> (3) the holder of the conflicting security interest receives the notification within five years before debtor receives possession of the inventory; and
>
> (4) the notification states that the person sending the notification has or expects to acquire a purchase-money security interest in inventory of the debtor and describes the inventory."

810 ILCS 5/9-324(b)(1-4) (West 2008).

Notification in the context of perfecting a PMSI has been addressed by a bankruptcy court in this district in In re Superior Equipment, Inc., 195 B.R. 77 (C.D.Ill.1996). In Superior Equipment, one party attempted to get priority over another when it claimed it had entered into a PMSI with the debtor over two of the debtor's trucks. One party, General Lift, had earlier leased two Mitsubishi forklift trucks to the debtor. General Lift, at a later date, filed a financing statement with the Illinois Secretary of State which contained a description of the two Mitsubishi trucks which were subject to the lease. The filing indicated on its face that it was for "information purposes" only. Debtor and General Lift then entered into a superseding lease for the two Mitsubishi forklifts. After the superseding lease, General Lift filed two new financing statements. A single Mitsubishi forklift was described in each statement, but there was no indication that the filing was for "informational purposes." General Lift did not, at any time, notify the other party who had a security interest on the debtor's property that it had or expected to acquire a PMSI in the trucks. When the debtor filed for bankruptcy, General Lift and the other party, a bank, agreed that the bankruptcy court should retain jurisdiction over the adversary proceeding to resolve the dispute as to the lien priority on the two trucks. Superior Equipment, 195 B.R. at 78.

In discussing the notice requirement for a PMSI under Illinois law, the bankruptcy court stated that " ... the provisions of § 9-312(3) [810 ILCS 5/9-312(3) is the old version of the requirements for a valid PMSI under Illinois law. It is the prior counterpart to the current 810 ILCS 5/9-324(b). The requirements are virtually identical, except § 9-312(3)(b) (the counterpart to § 9-324(b)(2)), which reads in full: "the purchase-money secured party gives notification in writing to the holder of the conflicting security interest if the holder had filed a financing statement covering the same types of inventory (i) before the date of the filing made by the purchase-money secured party, or (ii) before the beginning of the 21 day period where the purchase-money security interest is temporarily perfected without filing or possession (subsection (5) of Section 9-304)."] are an exception to the general rule of § 9-312(5) that the first to file has priority. In order to take advantage of the exception, the holder of a purchase-money security interest in inventory must jump through all the hoops set forth in § 9-312(3). [citation omitted] Complying with all the requirements of § 9-312(3) is a 'feat of some consequence,' [citation omitted] and courts have strictly construed this exception [citation omitted]. In this case, General Lift failed to give written notification of its intent to take a purchase-money security interest in the trucks, and therefore General Lift may not take advantage of § 9-312(3)." Superior Equipment, 195 B.R. at 79-80.

The court found that, among other reasons, General Lift through its failure to provide notice had failed to create a valid PMSI in the trucks. See also In re Hart, 30 B.R. 14, 16 (Bankr.C.D.Ill.1983) ("The only statutory authority available to Borg-Warner is found in 9-312(3). That section would give Borg-Warner, a holder of a perfected purchase-money security interest in inventory, priority only to the inventory and only if, inter alia, it sends notice to the bank pursuant to subparagraph (b). No notice was sent. Hence the Court cannot give Borg-Warner a priority over the bank.").

This court agrees with Strategic that, under the Illinois statute as interpreted by the Bankruptcy Courts of this district, strict compliance with the statute is required. That strict compliance is required because a PMSI is an exception to general rule of the first in time to perfect having priority. In the instant case, InnerWorkings did include the words "purchase-money security interest" in the Commercial Security Agreement. However, they appeared far down on the page for both the Commercial Security Agreement and the UCC Financing Statement. They were not under a separate heading and they would not jump out or alert a party to the presence of a possible PMSI, which would defeat the other party's first in time security interest. Further, InnerWorkings has not provided proof of an authenticated notice sent to Strategic to alert them as to the PMSI. If the court were to read the requirements of the statute strictly, InnerWorkings has not perfected a valid PMSI for its failure to properly give notice to Strategic.

InnerWorkings, however, argues that it has "essentially" accomplished notice, due to its inclusion of the purchase-money security interest language in the Commercial Security Agreement and UCC Financing Statement combined with the fact that Strategic is a sophisticated commercial entity. In support of its position InnerWorkings directs the court to In re Daniels, 35 B.R. 247 (Bankr.W.D.Okla.1983). In Daniels, the party claiming a PMSI (a bank) under Oklahoma state law had only sent out a letter to other security interest holders stating that it " 'has taken, or plans to take, a security interest' and makes no mention of a 'purchase-money security interest.' " Daniels, 35 B.R. at 248 (italics in original). While the non-PMSI party argued that the failure of the bank to state the taking of a "purchase-money security interest" in the notification was insufficient to meet the notice standards prescribed by law, the bank countered that the letter was sufficient to put the non-PMSI party on notice even though it did not contain the words "purchase-money" since there could have been no other reason for sending the notice. Daniels, 35 B.R. at 248-49.

In finding that the bank had successfully provided notice, the court reasoned that "the operation of the purchase-money interest [ ] should not be interrupted for the sake of a mere technical conformity" and that "it is generally accepted that the UCC provisions should be liberally construed in order to promote the underlying policies and purposes of the Code." Daniels, 35 B.R. at 250. The court went on to note that the reasoning behind the notice provision was for the protection of the prior secured party. The technicality of how the prior secured party was alerted to the PMSI did not matter so long as notice was achieved in some way. To support this the court looked to the definition of notice in Oklahoma law, which stated that one of the ways notice could be accomplished was when a party, "from all the facts and circumstances known to him at the time in question he has reason to know that it exist[s]" and a person notifies or gives notice or notification to another by "taking such steps as may be reasonably required to inform the other in ordinary course whether or not such other actually comes to know of it." Daniels, 35 B.R. at 250 (italics in original). The court noted that the non-PMSI secured party was a sophisticated commercial entity and the language of the notice sent out should have been enough to put it on notice of a PMSI in the listed items. The fact that a notice of any type was sent out should have put the non-PMSI party on notice, because a PMSI is the only time another creditor is required to forward any notice to the prior secured party. Daniels, 35 B.R. at 251.

Strategic distinguishes the Daniels case from the case at hand via the specific descriptions used by the Daniels bank for the items in which it was to take a PMSI. The inventory at issue was described with particularity by "listing numerous items with specific descriptions and serial numbers." Here, on the other hand, InnerWorkings failed to describe the inventory involved and also failed to send an authenticated notification to Strategic. Strategic asserts that the "essentially accomplished" standard in Daniels was used as a way to get around not specifically saying the words "purchase-money security interest" when actual or constructive notice had been achieved in every conceivable way short of the magic words, making the terms "purchase-money" de minimus. Here, however, Strategic argues that the "essentially accomplished" standard does not apply as no evidence of a PMSI authenticated notification, with similarly described inventory, was ever presented. Strategic also notes that the Daniels court concluded with "we feel that our conclusion and holding necessarily must be limited to the facts of this case." Daniels, 35 B.R. at 251.

The court agrees with Strategic that Daniels is distinguishable and does not apply to the facts at hand in the instant case. InnerWorkings argues that, as in Daniels, they have essentially accomplished a PMSI, in that all the language and context of the documents would create PMSI just short of using the words "purchase-money security interest." In the instant case, however, the documents exchanged between InnerWorkings and Strategic would not put the prior secured party on notice of a PMSI, despite the PMSI magic words being included in the Commercial Security Agreement and the UCC Financing Statement. As pointed out by Strategic, Wills testified under oath that none of the communications, whether verbal discussions or written agreements, between InnerWorkings and Strategic identified, discussed or even mentioned a PMSI or any words to that effect except the InnerWorkings-Debtor Commercial Security Agreement and InnerWorkings, as drafter of the agreement, "plugged in a single sentence (buried in the middle and not under any section header) that refers to a PMSI in 'goods' and not inventory." This is different than the separate, specific notice sent to the prior secured party in the Daniels case. The court agrees with the prior case law from this district that the PMSI notice provision of the Illinois statute should be strictly construed. See Superior Equipment, 195 B.R. at 79-80. As a result, this court sees no reason to disturb the decision of the Bankruptcy Court that InnerWorkings failed to create a valid PMSI.

IT IS THEREFORE ORDERED:

(1) The decision of the Bankruptcy Court is AFFIRMED.

(2) This case is terminated.

## Exercise 9-5:  More Priority Disputes

1. On June 2, Year 1, Debtor purchased a motorcycle, for use in his delivery business, from Dealership, pursuant to the terms and conditions of a retail installment contract. On the same day, Debtor took possession of the motorcycle, and Dealership assigned the Contract to Creditor A, who is the current holder of the Contract. On June 15, Year 1, Debtor granted a security interest in the motorcycle to Creditor B. On July 1, Year 1, Creditor B filed a financing statement covering the motorcycle in the proper place. On July 2, Year 1, a notation of Creditor A's security interest was made on the state certificate of title to the motorcycle. Assume that the state certificate of title law makes registration of liens on certificates of title mandatory. In a priority dispute between Dealership, Creditor A and Creditor B over the motorcycle, who prevails? Why?

2. Loretta Lender had a perfected purchase money security interest in all of Debby Debtor's equipment. Debby sold some of her equipment for $10,000 cash and deposited the cash in her business checking account at National Bank, which immediately before the deposit (Day 1) contained $10,000. Starting with Day 1, the bank account ledger reflects the following account activity:

| Day | Activity | Account Balance |
|-----|----------|----------------:|
| Day 1 | Starting Balance | $10,000 |
| Day 2 | Deposit from sale of equipment  $10,000 | $20,000 |
| Day 3 | Withdrawal to purchase office supplies  $1,000 | $19,000 |
| Day 4 | Withdrawal for advance on salary  $5,000 | $14,000 |
| Day 7 | Withdrawal for mortgage payment  $6,000 | $8,000 |
| Day 9 | Deposit from sales of inventory  $6,000 | $14,000 |

Assume that Debby is now "in default" under her agreement with Loretta. Can Loretta recover the $10,000 that Debby deposited in the account? Discuss fully.

3. On November 2, Barbie applies for a loan at Street Bank, to be secured by her inventory and accounts. Street immediately files a properly-completed UCC-1 in the proper place. On November 15, Street approves Barbie's loan application and Barbie executes a security agreement granting Street a security interest in "all inventory and accounts, now owned or hereafter acquired." On the same day, Barbie enters into a security agreement with Second Bank, granting Second a security interest in "all inventory and accounts, now owned or hereafter acquired." Second immediately files a properly-completed UCC-1 in the proper place. In a priority dispute between Street Bank and Second Bank who will prevail? Why?

4. Grace Jones purchased a car in Anaheim, California using funds advanced by Lender. Jones gave Lender a security interest in the car and Lender noted its security interest on the California Certificate of Title issued by the California Department of Motor Vehicles. In April of Year 1, Jones moved to Kansas. In May she obtained a "clean" certificate of title from the Kansas Department of Motor Vehicles, which did not disclose Lender's security interest. On June 1, Jones borrowed $5000 from Bank, giving Bank a security interest in the car to secure the loan. Bank took possession of the Kansas certificate of title and caused its security interest to be noted on the certificate. On June 10, Jones

sold the car to Acme Used Cars, telling Acme she, Jones, had lost the Kansas certificate. On June 15 while Jones was in default on her loan to Lender, Lender lawfully repossessed the car from Acme's lot. Lender, Bank and Acme all claim first priority to the car. Who wins?

5. Would your answer to #5 change if on June 13, before Lender could repossess the car, Acme sold the car to Carl Consumer who knew nothing about the above events? Why or why not?

# Additional Resources

Grant Gilmore, *The Purchase Money Priority*, 76 Harv. L. Rev. 1333, 1372 (1963).

Stephen L. Sepinuck, *PMSI Notification: What to Say & How to Say It*, 1 The Transactional Lawyer 1 (Gonzaga University School of Law/The Commercial Law Center, Spokane, WA), Aug. 2011, available at http://www.law.gonzaga.edu/files/Transactional-Lawyer-Aug2011.pdf.

# Chapter 10

# Priority Disputes (Secured Creditors and Others)

Figure 10-1:  Article 9 Graphic Organizer

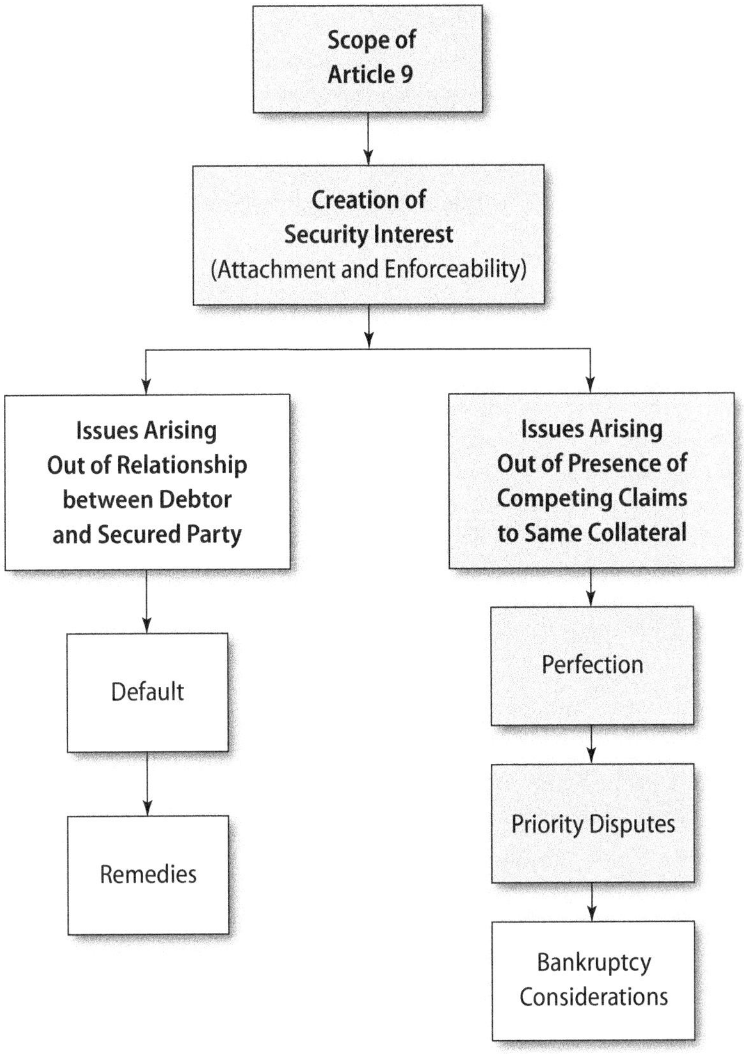

## Chapter Problem

Here is a memorandum from your supervisor. Read it carefully, and then try to predict how a court would resolve the dispute described in the memorandum, and why. By the end of this chapter, you will be able to fully analyze this problem. *For now, develop a hypothesis you will test as you work your way through the chapter. Then, as you read this chapter, keep this problem in mind and look for hints about how to go about solving it.*

---

**INTRA-OFFICE MEMORANDUM**

**Date**:    September 13
**To**:      Ann Associate
**From**:    Ima Partner
**Subject**: Barbie Borrower/Priority Disputes

Barbie Borrower is a resident of the state of Uniformity. She conducts a small business under the fictitious name of "Barbie's Bathrooms." Barbie maintains two bank accounts at Humungous National Bank ("HNB"), one for her personal use, and the other exclusively for the receipts and disbursements relating to her business.

When Barbie opened her bank accounts, she signed HNB's standard form of deposit agreement, which included the following provision:

### SECURITY INTEREST IN ACCOUNTS

You grant us a security interest in all your accounts with us, and all property in your accounts (including money, certificates of deposit, securities and other investment property, financial assets, etc.), to secure any amount you owe us or our affiliates, now or in the future. For purposes of this section, "account" includes any account you have with us or any of our affiliates (including, without limitation, agency, custody, safekeeping, securities, investment, brokerage, and revocable trust accounts) and "you" includes, without limitation, your revocable trust, any partnership in which you are a general partner, any prior or successor entity by way of an entity conversion, and any other series of your series limited liability company (as applicable).

You agree to hold us harmless from any claim arising as the result of our security interest in, or enforcement of our security interest against, your account.

On April 1, Barbie Borrower ("Borrower" or "Barbie") and Loving Lending Institution ("Lender") executed a valid security agreement, which provided in pertinent part:

To secure the repayment of any and all obligations of Borrower to Lender, Borrower hereby grants to Lender a security interest in all equipment, inventory, accounts, instruments, chattel paper, general intangibles and fixtures in which Borrower has rights at present or in the future and which are used or acquired in connection with the business she operates under the fictitious name of "Barbie's Bathrooms," together with all additions, accessions and substitutions, and all similar property hereafter acquired, and the proceeds thereof, referred to in this agreement as "collateral."

The security agreement duly authorized Lender to file a financing statement. On that same date, Lender filed a financing statement in the proper place for personal property collateral. The financing statement identified "Barbie's Bathrooms" as the debtor, Lender as secured party, and described the collateral in the same manner as it was described in the security agreement.

On April 15, Barbie needed money to pay her taxes, so she sold three promissory notes from her business, payable to "Barbie Borrower dba Barbie's Bathrooms," each in the principal sum of $5,000, to Emergitaxmoney, who gave her $10,000 for the notes and took possession of the notes.

On May 1, Lender loaned Barbie $100,000, and she signed a promissory note in that amount payable to Lender. Barbie used $65,000 to buy additional inventory and equipment for her business. She deposited $25,000 in her business account at HNB, and $10,000 in her personal account at HNB. As of May 2, Barbie's business inventory had a reasonable fair market value of $100,000 and there were outstanding accounts of $50,000.

On May 15, Vendor sold certain items of inventory to Barbie for $25,000, pursuant to a conditional sale contract that stated that Vendor retained title to the goods until receipt of payment in full. Before the goods were delivered to Barbie, Vendor sent written notice to Lender of the transaction. Vendor also filed a properly completed financing statement in the proper place.

When Lender received Vendor's notice, one of Lender's employees noticed that Vendor had used Barbie's individual name as the debtor's name on the financing statement. After consulting with legal counsel, on June 20, Lender filed a financing statement amendment form, listing Barbie Borrower as an "additional debtor."

Shortly thereafter, Barbie resold the inventory she had purchased from Vendor, and received the following: (1) $5,000 cash, which she deposited in her business account; (2) $10,000 in accounts receivable; and (3) $10,000 in chattel paper.

On July 1, Barbie bought a BMW from Dealer for $55,000, pursuant to a conditional sales contract that provided that Dealer retained title to the BMW until Dealer received payment in full. As required by state law for the registration of all liens on automobiles, Dealer completed the necessary application for a certificate of title, with its name indicated on the certificate of title as legal owner/lien holder, and forwarded it to the appropriate authority.

On July 15, Barbie's reckless driving caused severe body damage to the BMW. She took it to Robby's Repairs, who did the body work, and presented her with a bill for $10,000. Barbie refused to pay, and left the BMW with Robby.

On August 1, Barbie drew $7,500 from an unsecured line of credit she maintained at HNB.[1] She has consulted with bankruptcy counsel, and it appears that a filing is imminent.

Your assignment is to respond to the following specific questions: (I) Explain the nature and extent of the interest of each of Barbie, HNB, Lender, Emergitaxmoney, Vendor, Dealer and Robby, in each of the assets described in this memorandum; (II) Objectively discuss the relative priority of Barbie, HNB, Lender, Emergitaxmoney, Vendor, Dealer and Robby in the following assets:

---

1. If you aren't sure what this means, you may simply treat it as an unsecured loan from HNB to Barbie.

1. The inventory of Barbie's Bathrooms,

2. The three promissory notes in Emergitaxmoney's possession,

3. The BMW,

4. Barbie's personal bank account at HNB, which had a balance of $5,000 on July 15,[2]

5. Barbie's business bank account at HNB, which had a balance of $10,000 on July 15, and

6. The $10,000 in accounts receivable resulting from resale of inventory purchased from Vendor.

## Code Sections

9-317, 9-318, 9-319, 9-320, 9-321, 9-322, 9-323, 9-324, 9-325, 9-326, 9-327, 9-328, 9-329, 9-330, 9-331, 9-332, 9-333, 9-334, 9-335, 9-336, 9-337, 9-338, 9-339, 9-340, 9-341, 9-342

# 1. Secured Creditors v. Lien Creditors

Although an Article 9 secured creditor has a lien (security interest) on its collateral, when secured transactions lawyers refer to a "lien creditor" they do not mean a creditor with an Article 9 lien. Rather, the reference is to a creditor who has gained an interest in property by means of some state procedure, such as levy or attachment. If the creditor is attaching property after receiving a judgment in court, such a creditor will also be called a "judgment lien creditor." Another type of lien creditor, generally known as a "statutory lien creditor," has a lien on property because of a specific state statute. A statutory lien creditor, in contrast to a judgment lien creditor, has not sued its debtor nor even gone to court to receive a judgment. The rights of statutory lien creditors are granted by statute in service of a particular policy and usually exist only so long as the creditor remains in possession of the property on which it has a lien by virtue of the state statute. Hence, these liens are often referred to as "possessory liens." You will recall from Chapter 4 that the creation of such non-consensual liens on personal property is not governed by Article 9; however, Article 9 does contain rules establishing the priority in disputes between such lien holders and Article 9 secured creditors.

As a general rule, a personal property secured creditor who has properly perfected its security interest in collateral will defeat any subsequent lien creditor who asserts a claim to the same property. There is a narrow exception to that general rule, however, when the lien creditor is the holder of a possessory lien. A possessory lien created by statute to secure payment or performance of an obligation for services or materials furnished by a person in the ordinary course of business will have priority over an Article 9 security

---

2. Assume that so much money has flowed in and out of the two accounts at HNB that it is impossible to *trace* anything in the account to the proceeds of anyone's security interest in other collateral.

interest, even if the security interest was prior in time and properly perfected. The statute that creates the possessory lien may change this general priority rule (section 9-333).

In addition, there are special priority rules that apply to priority disputes between secured creditors and lien creditors where the secured creditor makes "future advances." As you know, under Article 9, a debtor can grant a secured creditor a lien on collateral to secure not only the obligation incurred at the time the initial advance is made but also future advances. Section 9-323(a) provides that, in such cases, for purposes of determining the priority of a perfected security interest under section 9-322(a)(1), perfection of the security interest sometimes dates from the time an advance is made. If a creditor is not obligated to make an advance (in other words, there is no contractual obligation for the lender to continue to make advances under an existing loan agreement) and nevertheless does so, the lender may lose in a priority dispute with someone who became a lien creditor more than 45 days before that advance was made. Read section 9-323, which collects all of the special rules regarding the priority of a secured party's advances when a third party acquires an interest in the collateral. You will find the examples in Official Comment 3 particularly helpful.

---

## Exercise 10-1:  Section 9-333

Write an unofficial "Official Comment" to section 9-333 that explains the policy rationale behind the stated priority rule.

---

## Exercise 10-2:  Secured Creditor v. Possessory Lien Creditor

Debtor is a corporation that operates a casino in the state of Bliss. On March 1, Debtor borrowed $80,000 from Lender. The loan agreement between the Debtor and Lender granted Lender a security interest in all of the Debtor's inventory and equipment. On March 15, countless slot machines located in Debtor's casino began to malfunction. On April 1, Debtor hired Mechanic, who worked nearby, to fix the malfunctioning slot machines. Mechanic was able to repair only a few of the slot machines on site at the casino. Many slot machines required additional work and were sent to Mechanic's shop on April 10. On April 15, Lender filed a proper financing statement in the state of Bliss, covering all Debtors' inventory and equipment. Debtor ultimately failed to pay Mechanic for repair services rendered, and defaulted on its loan with Lender. A statute in the state of Bliss provides that one who repairs slot machines has a possessory lien on the machines in its possession to assure payment of its repair fees. Lender wants to repossess Debtor's slot machines, including the machines in Mechanic's possession.

In a priority dispute between Lender and Mechanic, who would prevail? Why? Would your answer change if Lender filed its financing statement on March 30? Why or why not?

---

## Exercise 10-3:  Secured Creditor v. Lien Creditor

Loose Lender and Belle Borrower duly authenticated a security agreement that provided for the identified collateral to secure the repayment of all liabilities and obligations "now or hereafter owing from Borrower to Lender of whatever kind or nature, whether or not currently contemplated at the time of this Agreement, whether such obligations be direct or indirect, absolute or contingent or due or to become due." When the parties signed the agreement, Lender loaned Belle $100,000, and Belle signed a promissory note that provided for repayment over a five-year term. Lender had no obligation to make any additional advances to Belle. Three years later, Belle told Lender that Carey Creditor had levied on the property that was Lender's collateral. She asked Lender for another loan of $50,000, and proposed that the loan be secured by the same collateral as secured the $100,000 loan. It has now been 45 days since Carey levied on the property. If Lender agrees to loan Belle the additional $50,000:

1. Who will have priority with respect to the balance owing on the original $100,000 loan from Lender to Borrower?

2. Will Lender's $50,000 advance be secured by the collateral without the need for any additional security agreement?

3. If so, who will have priority with respect to the additional $50,000 advance by Lender?

# 2.  Priority Disputes with Buyers

Article 9 also contains rules for determining the priority between an Article 9 secured creditor and one who buys the goods that are the creditor's collateral from the creditor's debtor. These rules differ depending on whether or not the buyer is a buyer in the ordinary course, which issue depends on whether the seller is regularly engaged in selling goods of the kind.

It is very common for a retail store to finance its inventory by borrowing money, secured by a floating lien on inventory. Both the borrower and the lender understand that the inventory is held for sale. A buyer in the ordinary course would not expect to be buying property that is subject to a security interest in favor of the seller's lender. Therefore, although as a general rule, a security interest continues in collateral notwithstanding sale, where a sale is made to a buyer in the ordinary course of business, the security interest does not continue.

However, when a borrower secures a loan using collateral, such as equipment, neither the borrower nor the lender would expect that non-inventory property to be sold without the lender's permission. Hence, the general rule applies, and if, the borrower sells the property, the lender's security interest continues notwithstanding the sale.

Of course, these generalizations are also subject to special rules. Students should consult sections 9-317 and 9-320 to see if a particular fact pattern requires application of a special priority rule.

## Exercise 10-4:  Secured Creditor v. Buyer

Complete the following table, predicting the outcome of priority disputes between a secured lender and different types of buyers whose seller has encumbered the property sold to the buyer.

| Type of Buyer | Result of Priority Dispute | Code Section |
|---|---|---|
| Buyer in ordinary course of business | | 9-320 |
| Buyer of consumer goods where debtor-seller holds as "consumer goods" | | 9-320 |
| Buyer of farm products | | 9-320 OC 4 |
| Buyer of tangible chattel paper, tangible documents, goods, instruments or certificated security | | |

## Exercise 10-5:  Floor Planner v. Buyer

Top Quality Auto Sales ("Top Quality") was a used car dealership that financed the majority of its inventory through a financing agreement with ICE, an auto auction house. Pursuant to ICE's agreement with Top Quality, ICE filed a financing statement with the Indiana Secretary of State. On March 9, Top Quality purchased a used Ford truck using its financing arrangement with ICE.

On March 21, Top Quality sold the truck to Lightly Used Trucks ("Lightly"), another used car dealership, who had arranged with Buyer to purchase the truck for him. At some point, Buyer was told that Top Quality "was running on ICE money." Lightly wrote a check to Top Quality for the truck that day. Top Quality did not inform ICE of the sale or repay ICE for the truck.

On March 23, Buyer paid Lightly for the truck. Lightly tried to retrieve the title for Buyer and discovered that Top Quality had not paid ICE for the truck. ICE refuses to release the lien on the truck. In a dispute between Buyer and ICE, who should prevail? Why?

# 3. Priority Disputes over Fixtures

When a personal property secured creditor claims a security interest in goods that are or are to become fixtures, in addition to the priority disputes discussed in Chapter 9 that may arise, typical priority disputes will involve a party whose claim is based on an interest in the real property to which the fixtures have been affixed. Accordingly, a real estate owner (the landlord of the secured party's debtor) or mortgagee (the debtor's lender) is often the most likely person to dispute a personal property secured creditor's claim to fixtures. Special priority rules govern such disputes.[3]

These priority rules make sense if you consider who is most likely to have either (1) provided the funding for the acquisition of the fixtures; or (2) relied on the fixtures in underwriting its loan. As a general rule, if the fixtures were not in place at the time the real estate claimant gave value, it probably did not rely on those fixtures, and you may be able to predict that it will lose in a priority dispute with a secured creditor who provided the funds that enabled the debtor to acquire that property. Similarly, for the same reasons that purchase money security interests have priority under the Code, you may be able to predict that the party who gave value to enable the acquisition of the fixtures will trump a lien claimant who did not give such value. Of course, these generalizations are subject to particular contract provisions and Code policies.

---

### Exercise 10-6:  Article 9 Creditor v. Mortgagee

In November of Year 1, Debtor purchased a bathtub for his home from Fancy Baths, a specialty bathtub store, for $4,000. The bathtub contained many extra specialty features. Fancy Baths financed the purchase, and Debtor signed a contract granting Fancy Baths a purchase-money security interest in the bathtub. Fancy Baths took no further action. In March of Year 2, Creditor refinanced Debtor's home. The mortgage, which was duly recorded, granted Creditor a security interest in all of Debtor's personal property, including fixtures. In a priority dispute between Fancy Baths and Creditor over the bathtub, who should prevail? Why? Would your answer change if Debtor purchased the bathtub for a home that was being newly constructed and the priority dispute was with his construction lender instead of Creditor?

---

### Exercise 10-7:  Fixtures Dispute

Landlord owns a commercial building. In March of Year 1, Landlord entered into a lease agreement with X Company, leasing the premises for a term of five years. The lease included, among other things, a provision (section 9.1.12) stating that, at termination:

---

3. UCC 9-334. Secured transactions lawyers understand that to anticipate disputes over whether goods are properly classified as fixtures, a secured creditor taking a security interest in goods that are or may become fixtures should always perfect its security interest by both filing centrally and by filing a fixture filing in the real property records. See discussion of perfecting a security interest in fixtures in chapter 8, *supra*.

"all alterations, additions, floor covering and carpeting thereto and all decorations, fixtures, furnishings, partitions, heating, ventilating and cooling equipment and other equipment, which are permanently affixed to the Premises, which (if not then the property of the Landlord) shall thereupon become the property of Landlord without any payment to tenant."

In July of Year 1, X Company installed various large pieces of equipment, which it brought in piece by piece, and reassembled and welded to the premises. The equipment included silos and large extruding machines that ran from floor to ceiling, were bolted to the floor, the ceiling rafters and joists, and the walls, along with a series of pipes, tubes, and conduit carrying raw materials and electricity to the machinery. The assembly required removing some rafters in the ceiling and replacing them with new rafters.

In July of Year 3, however, X Company sold its business to Y LLC. On December 5, Year 3, X Company assigned its lease to Y LLC, and Y LLC remained in possession of the premises thereafter.

On December 15 of Year 3, Bank loaned Y LLC one million dollars. The loan was secured by a commercial security agreement between Bank and Y LLC, pursuant to which Y LLC granted a security interest in all equipment, inventory and other property of Y LLC. The security agreement and financing statement generically identified "fixtures" as security for the loan. Shortly thereafter, on December 20, Year 3, Bank filed a proper UCC financing statement in the state's central filing place.

Y LLC ceased paying rent in September of Year 6 and abandoned the leasehold in October of Year 6. In doing so, Y LLC abandoned 12 plastic extruding machines and 3 silos that were attached to the floors, ceilings and duct work, as well as heavy duty electrical systems and piping connecting the machinery.

In a priority dispute between Landlord and Bank over the plastic extruding machines and silos still in Landlord's possession, who should prevail? Why?

---

# 4. Priority Disputes Involving Dual Debtors and Transferred Collateral

As you have learned, in specified situations a "new debtor" may be bound by a security agreement between its transferor (the original debtor) and the transferor's lender. Two situations may then arise resulting in priority disputes. First, the new debtor may finance its own operations with a second lender, who may assert a lien on assets that were originally encumbered by the original debtor's lender. Second, if the transferor's lender has a floating lien on assets, that creditor's security interest will attach to any assets acquired by the new debtor that fall within the description of collateral in the original security agreement. The new debtor's lender may also be claiming a lien on those newly-acquired assets.

Because these types of factual situations often become complicated by the addition of a second lender who loans money to the new debtor secured by the new debtor's assets (which may include transferred assets), the Code has developed rules to address these priority disputes. The general rule is that the original debtor's security interest remains perfected for a period of four months after the asset transfer. Thereafter, if the new debtor's name is so different from the original debtor's name that the filed financing statement would be "seriously misleading," the original lender must file a new financing statement (or an amendment adding the new debtor's name as an additional debtor), or the floating lien will not attach and the lender will not be perfected as to assets acquired by the new debtor more than four months after the new debtor became bound to the security agreement.

---

### Exercise 10-8: New Debtor Priority Dispute

In Year 1, X Inc. granted C Bank a security interest in all of its current and future inventory and equipment to secure a series of loans. The security agreement provided that C Bank's security interest would be binding upon X Inc.'s successors and assigns. C Bank filed a proper financing statement in Year 1.

In Year 2, the principals of X Inc. organized Y Corp., and transferred a substantial amount of X Inc.'s assets to Y Corp. Y Corp. operated the same type of business as X Inc., used the same address, and had the same principals and employees. X Inc. did not inform C Bank of any of these facts. Instead, X Inc. continued to request increases in X Inc.'s line of credit, providing C Bank with false financial statements, and C Bank continued to advance funds to X Inc.

Commencing in Year 2, D Bank made a series of loans to Y Corp., and Y Corp. granted D Bank a security interest in all of its current and future inventory and equipment. D Bank filed a proper financing statement to perfect the security interest.

In a priority dispute in Year 3 between C Bank and D Bank over Y Corp.'s inventory and equipment, who should prevail?

---

# 5.  Priority Disputes Involving Goods Covered by a Certificate of Title

In Chapter 8, we discussed special perfection rules for goods covered by a certificate of title. Just as there are special perfection rules for such goods, which depend in part on the type of certificate of title statute in effect in the applicable jurisdiction, there are special priority rules when parties assert conflicting claims to the same property, and that property is covered by a certificate of title statute.

The basic priority rule states that the law of the jurisdiction that issued the most current certificate of title governs the issue of perfection; since most jurisdictions reflect only one lien holder on a certificate of title, that means that whoever has its name as lien holder on the most current certificate of title for the vehicle will win a priority dispute. The policy underlying this rule is that people should be able to rely on the information contained in a current certificate of title. Sometimes apparently harsh results will ensue, particularly when a lien holder's name is removed from a certificate of title in error and subsequent certificates are issued that fail to reflect that lien holder's interest. However, because those situations will also frequently involve a good faith purchaser for value who relied on a clean certificate of title, the priority disputes are resolved in favor of the "good faith purchaser." Remember that not only a buyer, but also a lender, may qualify as a "good faith purchaser" under the Code's definitions.

## Exercise 10-9: Transferred Collateral Scenarios

This exercise describes a variety of different scenarios that involve "new debtors," "transferred collateral," and possible priority disputes between original debtors' lenders and new debtors' lenders, or between transferors' lenders and transferees' lenders. Except where otherwise indicated, in each case, assume that the Debtor meets the requirements of a "new debtor" under 9-102(a)(56). Identify which code section will govern the analysis of a possible priority dispute between the different described lenders. Then predict who will prevail in the given dispute.

1. Debtor acquires property in a merger or reorganization, etc., subject to a security interest in favor of Original Debtor's Lender, but Debtor's name is so different from the original debtor's name that it is misleading under 9-508. Debtor acquires additional property and grants a security interest in all of its property to Second Lender.

2. Debtor acquires property in a merger or reorganization, etc., subject to a security interest in favor of Original Debtor's Lender, but Debtor is located in a jurisdiction different from that of the original debtor. Debtor acquires additional property and grants a security interest in all of its property to Second Lender.

3. Debtor purchases the assets of XYZ Corporation, subject to a security interest in favor of XYZ's lender, and finances its acquisition of the property with a loan from its own lender.

## Exercise 10-10: Priority Dispute in Goods Covered by a Certificate of Title

In Year 1, Crazy Cars financed Oliver Owner's purchase of a motor vehicle in the State of New York. As required by the New York certificate of title law, the New York certificate of title issued to Oliver reflected Crazy's security interest in the vehicle.

Oliver moved from New York to Georgia and submitted a proper application, along with the existing title and the required fee, to the county tag agent for the Georgia Department of Motor Vehicles ("DMV") to convert the existing New York certificate of title to a Georgia one. The DMV processed the application, but as a result of a clerical data entry error, the DMV issued a Georgia certificate of title that did not reflect Crazy's security interest in the vehicle.

Oliver later transferred the vehicle to Used Autos, Inc. The vehicle thereafter passed through a non-dealer owner and additional dealer owners before Octavia Owner purchased it in March Year 2. None of the subsequent Georgia certificates of title issued for the vehicle in connection with these transfers reflected Crazy's security interest.

On October 1, Year 2, Crazy located the car and repossessed it. Octavia was not aware of Crazy's lien. As a result, Octavia reported the vehicle as stolen to the police. Once she learned from the police department that her vehicle had been repossessed rather than stolen, Octavia filed suit against Crazy. What result?

# 6. Federal Tax Liens

Internal Revenue Code Section 6321 creates a lien in favor of the United States for unpaid taxes, attaching to all of the delinquent taxpayer's property. Section 6323(a) provides that, as a general rule, the lien is subordinate to perfected security interests and certain other liens that arise before notice of the Federal lien is filed in the appropriate office. A lender seeking to make a loan against equipment, for example, in addition to searching for UCC filings against the proposed borrower, can also search for existing notices of federal tax liens.

A lender providing credit to a business on a revolving basis, however—who makes future advances—has special concerns. UCC 9-323(b) grants priority to such future advances, as against a subsequent lien creditor, unless (a) the advance is made more than 45 days after the competing creditor becomes a lien creditor, and (b) the advance is made either (i) without knowledge of the lien, or (ii) pursuant to a commitment entered into without knowledge of the lien. Internal Revenue Code Section 6323(c) provides similar, but not identical, protection to future advances made under a "commercial transactions financing agreement" entered into by the debtor in the course of its business: the secured party's security interest with respect to advances made *within* 45 days after the federal tax lien is filed, but *only* if, at the time the advance is made, the secured party did not have actual notice or knowledge of the tax lien filing. Moreover, the priority apples only to "commercial financing security" (paper of a kind ordinarily arising in commercial transactions; accounts receivable; mortgages on real property; and inventory) acquired by the debtor during the 45 days after the federal tax lien is filed. Consequently, a lender seeking to protect the seniority of its security interest over federal tax liens filed against its debtor must do periodic checks for tax liens at the applicable filing office. The provisions of Section 6323, however, are highly detailed, and depend very heavily upon definitions included in the statute. You should have it in front of you whenever you need to address the subject on behalf of a client.

# Additional Resources

Alvin C. Harrel, *A Roadmap to Certificate of Title Issues in Revised UCC Article 9*, 53 Consumer Fin. L. Q. Rep. 202 (Conference on Consumer Finance Law), 1999.

Martin B. Schwam, *The Proposed UCC Article 9 Revisions: Perfection of Security Interest in Multiple State Transactions—Collateral Subject to Certificate of Title Statutes,* 51 Consumer Fin. L. Q. Rep. 385 (Conference on Consumer Finance Law), 1977.

Edwin E. Smith, *The Effect of the Uniform Certificate of Title Act on Secured Transactions*, 60 CONSUMER FIN. L. Q. REP. 366 (Conference on Consumer Finance Law), 2006.

Jane F. (Ginger) Zimmerman et al., *Lien on Me: Moving Vehicles No Longer Hidden Treasure*, AM. BANKR. INST. J., Nov. 2005, at 20.

# Chapter 11

# Bankruptcy

Figure 11-1:  Article 9 Graphic Organizer

```
          ┌─────────────────┐
          │    Scope of     │
          │    Article 9    │
          └────────┬────────┘
                   │
          ┌────────▼────────────────┐
          │     Creation of         │
          │   Security Interest     │
          │(Attachment and Enforceability)│
          └───────┬─────────────────┘
          ┌───────┴───────────────────────────┐
          │                                   │
┌─────────▼──────────┐          ┌─────────────▼──────────┐
│   Issues Arising   │          │    Issues Arising      │
│ Out of Relationship│          │  Out of Presence of    │
│  between Debtor     │          │  Competing Claims      │
│ and Secured Party  │          │  to Same Collateral    │
└─────────┬──────────┘          └─────────────┬──────────┘
          │                                   │
┌─────────▼──────────┐          ┌─────────────▼──────────┐
│                    │          │                        │
│      Default       │          │      Perfection        │
│                    │          │                        │
└─────────┬──────────┘          └─────────────┬──────────┘
          │                                   │
┌─────────▼──────────┐          ┌─────────────▼──────────┐
│                    │          │                        │
│     Remedies       │          │   Priority Disputes    │
│                    │          │                        │
└────────────────────┘          └─────────────┬──────────┘
                                               │
                                ┌──────────────▼─────────┐
                                │                        │
                                │      Bankruptcy        │
                                │    Considerations      │
                                │                        │
                                └────────────────────────┘
```

## Chapter Problem

For the past three years, your client, Fumble Finance ("FF"), has made a revolving credit facility available to specialty ladies' apparel manufacturer, wholesaler, and retailer Auntie's Scanties, Inc., a California corporation ("ASI"). The arrangement, entered into March 15, Year 1, is between ASI, and FF, and provides for a line of credit, for a term of 5 years, in a maximum amount equal to the lesser of $10,000,000 and a "Borrowing Base" equal to the sum of 85% of the total face amount of "Eligible Receivables" and 60% of "Eligible Inventory," valued at the lesser of cost and fair market value. The governing document is a duly authenticated "Loan and Security Agreement" (the "LSA"), pursuant to which ASI has granted to FF a security interest in:

> All personal property and fixtures of Auntie's Scanties, whether now existing or hereafter created or acquired, and wherever located, including, but not limited to:
>
> (a)    all accounts, chattel paper (including tangible and electronic chattel paper), commercial tort claims, deposit accounts, documents (including negotiable documents), equipment (including all accessions and additions thereto), general intangibles (including insurance policies whether or not required to be maintained pursuant to any Loan Document), payment intangibles and software), goods (including fixtures), instruments (including promissory notes), inventory (including all goods held for sale or lease or to be furnished under a contract of service, and including returns and repossessions), investment property (including securities and securities entitlements), letter of credit rights, letters of credit, and money, and all of Borrower's books and records with respect to any of the foregoing, and the computers and equipment containing said books and records; and
>
> (b)    any and all cash proceeds and/or noncash proceeds of any of the foregoing, including, without limitation, insurance proceeds, and all supporting obligations and the security therefore or for any right to payment.

The LSA provides that it is governed by California law. FF prepared a UCC-1 naming Auntie's Scanties, Inc. as debtor and itself as secured party, describing the collateral as "all assets, now owned or hereafter acquired." Counsel for FF then transmitted the UCC-1 to his secretary, instructing her to "file it."

About six months ago, ASI started to experience financial difficulties, due to declining demand for its products. It breached the earnings covenant in the LSA, and initiated discussions with FF in the hope of restructuring its loan in a way that would permit it to continue in business. Preparing for discussions between ASI and his client, counsel for FF realized that, in response to his instructions to "file" the UCC-1 he had prepared, his secretary, instead of arranging for it to be filed with the Secretary of State, had in fact merely punched holes in the documents and placed it in the law firm's file for loan to ASI. Counsel immediately arranged for it to be filed with the California Secretary of State.

The UCC-1 was filed two weeks ago. Since that time, FF has received $1,500,000 in payments under the LSA, and has made advances totaling $1,250,000. Yesterday, ASI filed for protection under the Bankruptcy Code. FF has engaged you, as a UCC specialist associated with a bankruptcy boutique firm, to help it analyze the relevant issues. Prepare a preliminary discussion outline for your first meeting with FF, outlining what you see as those facts posing the greatest risk of exposure and identifying other material questions that need to be answered before you can make an accurate assessment of that risk.

---

## Bankruptcy Code Sections

101, 361, 362, 506, 541, 544, 547, 548, 552, 558

# 1. Overview of Bankruptcy and the Secured Creditor

It has often been stated that bankruptcy is the acid test of a security interest because there are a number of special powers available in a bankruptcy proceeding that might, under proper circumstances, invalidate all or part of a secured creditor's security interest in the debtor's property. A properly perfected security interest allows a secured creditor to face the bankruptcy of its debtor and be confident that, so long as the value of the collateral is at least equal to the amount of its debt, it will ultimately be paid in full. A bankruptcy filing may delay such a creditor's ability to realize on its collateral, but will not destroy it.

Any defects in the creation or perfection of a security interest will be revealed in a bankruptcy proceeding. Indeed, even a poor job of underwriting will be revealed, because in bankruptcy there are no "secured creditors." There are only secured claims. A creditor holds a secured claim only to the extent that the collateral has value—an undersecured secured creditor will be transformed into a creditor with two claims: one secured and one unsecured.[1]

For these reasons, our study of UCC Article 9 would be incomplete without at least a glimpse at some of the provisions of bankruptcy law that may impact on the status of personal property secured creditors.[2] This chapter is designed to introduce you to these provisions.

# 2. Introduction to Bankruptcy

Bankruptcy is federal law governing insolvency proceedings for individual and organizational debtors.[3] It has been suggested that the term derives from the Latin "banca

---

1. At least, a secured creditor whose collateral is personal property is so affected. Bankruptcy Code § 1111(b) permits a lender secured by real estate, under certain circumstances, to elect to have its secured and unsecured claims treated as a single, secured claim.

2. As we suggested earlier in this text, experienced secured transactions lawyers always consider the possibility that the debtor may file bankruptcy and try to be sure that the structure and documentation of the deal will withstand bankruptcy's "acid test."

3. For more basic information about bankruptcy proceedings, see http://www.uscourts.gov/FederalCourts/Bankruptcy/BankruptcyBasics/Chapter7.aspx.

rupta," referring to the practice, in markets during the Middle Ages, of breaking the bench ("banca") from which an insolvent merchant had conducted business. The study of bankruptcy law, like the study of the UCC, involves reading and applying complex statutes. We will study only a few of them in this course.

To understand the bankruptcy rules, it is helpful to understand the policies behind the Bankruptcy Code. A bankruptcy proceeding has two major objectives: (1) To protect insolvent debtors who have become unable to repay their debts and to discharge them from most of their debts, thus giving them a chance to start over again with a relatively clean slate [this concept is generally referred to as giving the bankrupt party (the "debtor") a "fresh start"]; and (2) to provide an orderly process for collecting and paying out debtors' non-exempt assets, thus maximizing recovery to creditors and reducing the costs that creditors would otherwise face in a scramble to grab the debtor's assets (the race to the courthouse) [this concept is referred to as the principle of treating similarly situated creditors similarly]. You will see these policies reflected in the rules we study in this chapter.

A bankruptcy is initiated by the filing of a petition in federal bankruptcy court. The petition may be either voluntary (filed by the debtor) or involuntary (filed by creditors holding a certain percentage of the claims against the debtor). As we shall see, the date the petition is filed is often critical to the rights of creditors of the debtor.

In this chapter, we will focus on the Chapter 7 type of bankruptcy. In a Chapter 7, the filing of the petition creates an "estate," which is distinct from the debtor. Essentially all of the assets and debts of the debtor become assets of the estate, with the result that the debtor gets a "fresh start" free from pre-filing debts (but, subject to rules regarding exempt property, without any pre-filing assets, which will be available to pay some of the pre-filing debts). A trustee is appointed when the bankruptcy is filed. The trustee is the representative of the estate, and is charged with the duty to marshal (collect) all assets of the estate and pay the debts of the estate in accordance with the priorities of the Bankruptcy Code. Hence, a Chapter 7 is known as a "liquidation" proceeding.

Upon the filing of a bankruptcy petition, the Bankruptcy Code provides that an automatic stay goes into effect, restraining creditors from taking any action to enforce or collect a debt. For a secured creditor to foreclose on its collateral it must request relief from the stay; it can take no action without the approval of the Bankruptcy Court. At the conclusion of the case, the debtor will receive a "discharge," which essentially releases the debtor from any liability for prior debts and prevents the creditors owed those debts from taking any collection actions against the debtor. A secured creditor may, however, retain its rights against its collateral after a discharge is granted.

Regardless of the type of bankruptcy proceeding filed, the bankruptcy trustee (or debtor-in-possession in a Chapter 11) is given various powers and statuses to help collect the debtor's property and pay valid claims. These are generally referred to as the trustee's "avoiding powers," and will be of most concern to secured creditors, whose security interests may be "avoided" (set aside/invalidated) under certain circumstances.

# 3.  The Trustee's Avoiding Powers

In appropriate circumstances, the avoiding powers enable the trustee to "set aside" or "avoid" certain security interests. As a result, the secured creditor will become the holder of an unsecured claim, and the asset that was claimed as collateral will be added to the estate, resulting in more money available for distribution to all creditors. The avoiding powers are: (1) the trustee "stands in the shoes of" the debtor, and therefore may prosecute any claim of the debtor, and may assert any defense of the debtor; (2) the trustee can take the place of any actual unsecured creditor and avoid any claim that such a creditor could have avoided; (3) the trustee has the status of a hypothetical ideal judicial lien creditor with an infinite claim arising at the moment of the petition; (4) the trustee can avoid fraudulent transfers; and (5) the trustee can avoid preferential transfers. Each of these powers is explored in greater detail below, to the extent of their potential impact on a personal property secured creditor.

## 3.1  Trustee Standing in the Shoes of the Debtor

Because the Trustee essentially takes over the debtor's position, if before the bankruptcy filing the debtor had any claims or defenses to assert against a secured party, the Trustee will have the right and the power to pursue those claims or defenses.

## 3.2  Trustee Taking the Place of an Actual Unsecured Creditor

Even outside of bankruptcy, some actions of the debtor can be set aside under applicable state law. For example, under state fraudulent conveyance statutes, a creditor may bring an action to set aside certain transfers of a debtor's property if they were made with the intent to hinder, delay or defraud creditors. The granting of a security interest constitutes a "transfer" of the debtor's property within the meaning of these statutes. Accordingly, if that transfer is a fraudulent conveyance as defined in the applicable statute, the secured creditor may lose its security interest. Bankruptcy Code section 544(b) empowers the trustee to bring such state law-based actions and, if the trustee prevails, the proceeds of the transfer that has been set aside become part of the estate, to be distributed as part of the overall distribution of the estate.[4]

Even though there must be an actual unsecured creditor who could bring the state court action for the trustee to act under section 544(b), once the trustee establishes the right to bring an action, the trustee's action is not limited by the actual amount of the actual creditor's claim.[5]

## 3.3  Trustee as Hypothetical Ideal Judicial Lien Creditor

Section 544(a) is sometimes referred to as the "strong arm clause." It empowers the bankruptcy trustee to set aside any transfer that could be set aside under non-bankruptcy law (1) by a creditor (2) who extended credit and obtained a lien on the date of the filing

---

4. Another result of such an action may be to change the amount of a creditor's claim. For example, if the creditor is a transferee of a transfer that is avoided, the creditor must return the amount of the transfer to the estate; as a result, the creditor's claim against the estate will be increased.

5. This rule was established in the famous case of *Moore v. Bay*, 284 U.S. 4 (1931).

of the bankruptcy petition (3) whether or not such an actual creditor exists. (That fictitious creditor is sometimes referred to as a "hypothetical ideal judicial lien creditor.") The strong arm clause is most commonly used against a secured creditor whose security interest was unperfected as of the date of the filing of the bankruptcy petition. (With limited exceptions, under applicable state law (the UCC), a judgment lien creditor would have priority over an unperfected secured creditor; accordingly, the bankruptcy trustee can avoid the security interest, and the creditor will be the holder of an unsecured claim for purposes of sharing in the estate.)

### Exercise 11-1: Section 544(a): The Strong-Arm Clause

On June 17, Year 1, Seller entered into an agreement to sell his ski and sporting goods business (the "Business") to Buyer. Part IV of the sales agreement, entitled "Payment of Purchase Price," provided that the unpaid balance was to be represented by a note secured with the stock in trade and merchandise inventory of the Business as collateral. Although the Buyer executed and delivered a note to the Seller, the parties never executed a security agreement or other loan document in connection with the repayment of the note, nor did Seller file a UCC-1. Two years after the sale closed, because of Buyer's financial difficulties, a receiver was appointed in a state court proceeding, and took possession of all of the assets of the Business. One month later, Buyer filed a petition for relief under Chapter 7 of the Bankruptcy Code. Seller claimed that its debt was secured by all of the stock in trade and merchandise inventory of the Business. Discuss the relative priority of Seller and the Trustee in Bankruptcy with respect to Seller's claimed collateral.

### Exercise 11-2: Section 544(a)

Debtor and Creditor executed a security agreement and financing statement, both naming "Margaret Howe dba Bargain Furniture/World Finance" as the debtor. Margaret Howe is the sole shareholder of World Finance, which is a corporation whose organizational documents reflect its name as "World Financial Services Center, Inc." The corporation conducts its business under the fictitious name of "Bargain Furniture," and has now filed for bankruptcy. In bankruptcy, the trustee argues that because the security agreement does not identify the debtor as "World Financial Services Center, Inc.," Creditor does not have a security interest in property of the corporation. In the alternative, the trustee argues that even if Creditor has a valid security interest, the security interest was not properly perfected and is therefore avoidable pursuant to 11 U.S.C. section 544. Discuss the validity of the trustee's arguments.

## 3.4 Trustee's Power to Avoid Fraudulent Conveyances

Bankruptcy Code section 548 allows a trustee to set aside a fraudulent conveyance. This code section is based on the Uniform Fraudulent Transfer Act, which is also the basis of many state fraudulent conveyance statutes, discussed above. Leveraged buyouts and "upstream" and "downstream" corporate guarantees[6] are two typical transactions that may be attacked as potential fraudulent conveyances, where the question is whether the debtor received "reasonably equivalent value" for the transfer. An example of the first type of transaction is where a secured creditor finances the acquisition of a company by lending money to the acquiring party and secures the loan with assets of the target company. If the target company files for bankruptcy, its trustee may attack the secured transaction as a fraudulent conveyance because the "value" given by the secured creditor flowed to the selling shareholders and not the target company. An example of the second type of transaction is when a secured creditor takes a subsidiary corporation's guarantee (secured by that corporation's assets) as part of a transaction involving the loan of money to the parent corporation. If the subsidiary corporation subsequently files for bankruptcy, the bankruptcy trustee can attack that secured guaranty as a fraudulent conveyance, because the "value" arguably has gone to the parent and not to the subsidiary. Accordingly, the bankruptcy trustee may argue that the subsidiary did not receive "reasonably equivalent value" for its asset transfer, and set aside the secured party's security interest in the subsidiary's assets.

Since the bankruptcy trustee can sue for a fraudulent conveyance under both section 548 and 544(b) (piggybacking on state law based on the existence of an actual creditor), the decision of whether to proceed under section 548 or 544(b) will depend on (1) the actual state law provisions; and (2) the applicable statute of limitations. The bankruptcy action only reaches transfers made within two years of commencement of the bankruptcy case; applicable state law statutes of limitations will often be longer. Of course, if there is no actual creditor for the trustee to use as the basis for a state law claim, the trustee will have no choice other than to pursue the fraudulent conveyance action under the Bankruptcy Code.

---

## Exercise 11-3:  Section 548 (Fraudulent Conveyances)

Hi-Tech, a corporation, was in poor financial condition and unable to pay its debts. To enable the corporation to pay its bills, in August of Year 1, two of its shareholders, "Junior" and his wife, Lisa, loaned Hi-Tech approximately $294,355. Hi–Tech's business continued to decline throughout Year 1, and it began winding down its business operations. On September 13, Junior executed a promissory note on behalf of Hi-Tech agreeing to repay Junior and Lisa the $294,355 they had lent the company, secured by an agreement pledging Hi-Tech's fixtures and equipment as collateral. On September 20, Junior and Lisa Phillips filed a properly-completed UCC financing statement in the proper place, perfecting the security interest.

On October 7, Lisa incorporated a new corporation, HTP Floors Inc. ("HTP.") Around that time, she also began aggressive efforts to enforce her security interest in Hi-Tech's property, largely through or on behalf of HTP. Late in Year 1, she

---

6. An "upstream" guaranty is a guaranty by a subsidiary of a corporation of the obligations of its parent; a "downstream" guaranty is a guaranty by a parent corporation of the obligations of its subsidiary.

repossessed $112,500 in construction equipment, $12,635 in office equipment, and $19,400 in vehicles. That property is now in the possession of HTP.

In June of Year 2, Hi-Tech filed a petition for relief under Chapter 7 of the Bankruptcy Code. First, identify any "transfers of property of the debtor" that occurred in the 12 months before the bankruptcy filing. Next, analyze whether any of those are transfers avoidable under section 548.

---

# 3.5  Trustee's Power to Avoid Preferential Transfers

The concept of an avoidable preferential transfer is unique to bankruptcy law, and is probably the most complex of all of the Trustee's avoiding powers. The basis of a preference action is the policy underlying the Bankruptcy Code of treating similarly situated creditors similarly. Before a debtor files for bankruptcy, no law governs the debtor's choices with respect to making payments to creditors. A debtor can pay one creditor in full and refuse to pay another creditor altogether. The Bankruptcy Code changes this approach. To treat similarly-situated creditors the same, and to discourage creditors from "racing to the courthouse," certain transfers made within a relatively short time before the bankruptcy is filed may be avoided (set aside). The proceeds then become part of the estate. *Figure 11-2* sets forth the elements of a preferential transfer. We will consider each element separately in the sections that follow.

## 3.5.1  "Transfer of an interest of the debtor in property."

If you read the definition of a "transfer" under the Bankruptcy Code, you will see that the term includes "the creation of a lien," "the retention of title as a security interest" and "the foreclosure of a debtor's equity of redemption." Hence, a creditor with a security interest in a debtor's personal property may be subject to an action to avoid a preferential transfer.

## 3.5.2  "To or for the benefit of a creditor."

This element is relatively easy to establish, particularly where there is a party claiming a security interest in personal property. All that must be shown is that the party has a claim against the debtor that arose at the time of or before the filing of the bankruptcy.

## 3.5.3  "For or on account of an antecedent debt."

An antecedent debt is a debt that arose before the time of the challenged transfer. Accordingly, one must understand how the Bankruptcy Code determines the time that the transfer took place. Section 547(e)(2) defines when a transfer is made. That section is deconstructed in *Figure 11-3*, below.

A bankruptcy trustee can attack as a preferential transfer a security interest that was not perfected in a timely manner ("delayed" or "late perfection"). The Bankruptcy Code defines the time of the transfer as the time when an interest has been so far perfected that a lien creditor could not prevail in a priority dispute under state law. A lien creditor will

## Figure 11-2:  Analyzing Preferential Transfers under Bankruptcy Code § 547

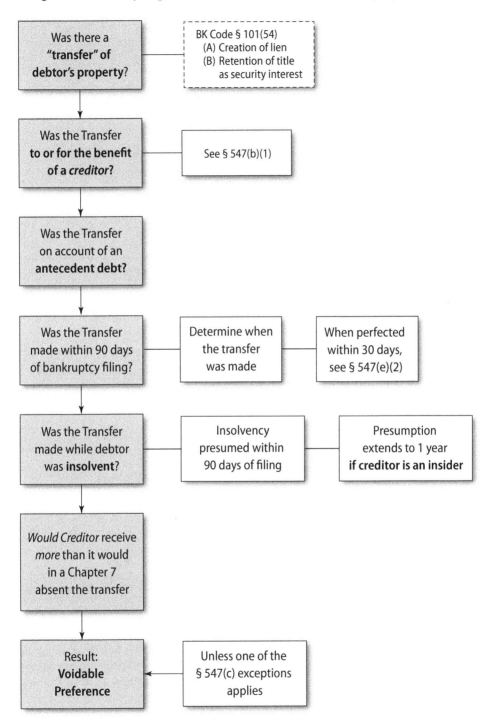

**Figure 11-3: Time of Transfer under Bankruptcy Code Section 547(e)(2)**

| Transfer is Perfected<br>A transfer of personal property is perfected when it is entitled to priority against a hypothetical subsequent judicial lien. (State law determination) | Time of Transfer under<br>Bankruptcy Code |
|---|---|
| At or within 30 days after the time when the transfer takes effect between transferor and transferee | At the time the transfer takes effect between transferor and transferee |
| More than 30 days after the time when the transfer takes effect between the transferor and transferee | At the time the transfer is perfected |
| *Not* perfected at the later of (i) commencement of case or (2) 30 days after the transfer takes effect between the transferor and transferee | Immediately before the date of the filing of the petition |

not prevail in a priority dispute if a secured creditor is perfected before the lien arises. Thus, a transfer (perfection of a security interest) is made on account of an antecedent debt if perfection occurs outside of the applicable grace period.

### 3.5.4 "Made on or within 90 days before the date of filing the petition or between 90 days and one year if the creditor was an insider."

This element is self-explanatory. The applicable time period is often referred to as "the preference period."

### 3.5.5 "Made while the debtor was insolvent."

For purposes of preference analysis, the debtor is presumed to have been insolvent on and during the 90 days immediately preceding the date of the filing of the petition.

### 3.5.6 "That enables the creditor to receive more than it otherwise would in a Chapter 7."

This element sounds more complicated than it is. To understand, it you need to know that most unsecured creditors receive very little in a Chapter 7 distribution. A fully secured creditor will eventually receive the full amount of its debt. If a secured creditor's collateral is worth more than the amount of the debt, the secured creditor will only receive the amount of its debt. If the secured creditor's collateral is worth less than the amount of its debt, the creditor will hold an "unsecured claim" for the amount of debt that is not secured by the collateral, and typically will not receive most of the amount of the unsecured claim.

Based on that information, you can now understand when it is most likely that a secured creditor would "receive more than it otherwise would in a Chapter 7." A secured creditor whose collateral is worth less than its debt may receive more than it would in a Chapter 7 if it receives a payment attributable to the debt during the preference period. If the creditor were fully secured, receipt of a payment during the preference period would not be a problem, because secured creditors generally receive 100% of the value of their collateral upon distribution in a Chapter 7 case. Thus, a fully secured creditor who receives partial payment during the preference period has not received more than what it would otherwise receive upon distribution of the estate, so there is no preferential transfer. Because the fully secured creditor has a right to its collateral or its proceeds, at most the secured creditor has received something earlier than it might have received it in a Chapter 7. If, however, the secured creditor both is undersecured and receives a payment during the preference period, that payment may result in the secured creditor receiving more than it would have received in a Chapter 7. In such case, the amount of the payment during the preference period may be set aside as a preferential transfer.

A second situation that may result in a secured creditor receiving a preferential transfer involves a secured creditor with a floating lien whose position improves during the preference period. A secured creditor who has a floating lien may be subject to a preference action if the value of the collateral for its debt increases during the preference period. For example, if the secured creditor had a valid perfected security interest in inventory worth $500,000 to secure a $1,000,000 loan ninety days before the bankruptcy was filed, and at the time of the bankruptcy filing the debtor's inventory was worth $1,000,000, the secured creditor would have improved its position by $500,000. The amount of the "improved position" may be recovered as a preferential transfer.

---

### Exercise 11-4:  Preferential Transfer (Section 547)

Same facts as in Exercise 11-1, but two years after the sale closed, because of Buyer's financial difficulties, Seller peaceably repossessed its collateral. Four days later, debtor filed a petition for relief under Chapter 7 of the Bankruptcy Code. Discuss the relative priority of Seller and the Trustee in Bankruptcy.

---

## 3.5.7  Exceptions to Preference Rules

Some transfers that initially may appear to be preferential transfers are not because of specific provisions of section 547. The exceptions that may apply to secured creditors are identified in *Figure 11-4*.

### Figure 11-4: Transfers That are Not Preferential (Bankruptcy Code § 547(c))

| Substantially contemporaneous exchange | Transfer of payment of debt in ordinary course of business | "New Value" exception | "Aggregate" exception for perfected security interest in inventory or receivables |
|---|---|---|---|

---

**Exercise 11-5:** *In re McConnell*

The following case reviews the transfer of an interest in an aircraft in satisfaction of a debtor's debt to a secured creditor, where the aircraft was the collateral for the debt. As you read the case, see if you can understand the court's application of section 547 and why it ultimately determines that the case was not appropriate for decision on a motion for summary judgment.

---

# In re McConnell
### 455 B.R. 824 (M.D. Ga. 2011)

## Opinion

*MEMORANDUM OPINION*

JAMES P. SMITH, Bankruptcy Judge.

Before the Court is Trustee's Motion For Summary Judgment. The Court, having considered the motion, the response, the affidavit of David E. Murphy and the record, now publishes this memorandum opinion.

### FACTS

Debtor Terry B. McConnell owned a 1972 Piper Cherokee (the "aircraft"). In 2003, Debtor and Defendant David E. Murphy formed a partnership wherein Defendant Murphy would help Debtor maintain and operate the aircraft. From 2006 through 2009, Defendant Murphy incurred a greater share of the expenses in the partnership than Debtor. In December 2009, Debtor voluntarily agreed to repay Defendant Murphy and, to secure the debt, Debtor signed a UCC–1 Financing Statement giving Defendant Murphy and Defendant Big Dog Aircraft, Inc. ("Big Dog") a security interest in the aircraft. The UCC–1 Financing Statement was filed with the Clerk of Houston County Superior Court, Georgia, in December 2009.

By letter dated September 15, 2010, Defendant Murphy requested that Debtor pay the debt in full, dissolve the partnership or surrender the aircraft. Debtor surrendered the aircraft in full satisfaction of his debt by signing an Aircraft Bill of Sale dated September 15, 2010, conveying the aircraft to Big Dog. The Aircraft Bill of Sale was filed with the Federal Aviation Administration (FAA) on January 11, 2011. Debtor filed his Chapter 7 bankruptcy case on March 8, 2011.

### CONCLUSIONS OF LAW

"A motion for summary judgment should be granted when 'the pleadings, depositions, answers to interrogatories, and admissions on file, together with the affidavits, if any, show that there is no genuine issue as to any material fact and that the moving party is entitled to judgment as a matter of law.' (citations omitted) On a summary judgment motion, the record and all reasonable inferences that can be drawn from it must be viewed in the light most favorable to the non-moving party. (citations omitted)

Trustee filed an adversary proceeding seeking, in part, to avoid as a preferential transfer Debtor's conveyance of the aircraft to Defendants. Section 547(b) of the Bankruptcy Code provides:

Except as provided in subsections (c) and (i) of this section, the trustee may avoid any transfer of an interest of the debtor in property—

(1) to or for the benefit of a creditor;

(2) for or on account of an antecedent debt owed by the debtor before such transfer was made;

(3) made while the debtor was insolvent;

(4) made—

(A) on or within 90 days before the date of the filing of the petition; or

(B) between ninety days and one year before the date of the filing of the petition, if such creditor at the time of such transfer was an insider; and

(5) that enables such creditor to receive more than such creditor would receive if—

(A) the case were a case under chapter 7 of this title;

(B) the transfer had not been made; and

(C) such creditor received payment of such debt to the extent provided by the provisions of this title.

Trustee has the burden of proving the avoidability of the transfer.

Defendants admitted in their answer to the complaint that the conveyance of the aircraft was a transfer of an interest in Debtor's aircraft to or for the benefit of a creditor for or on account of an antecedent debt. Defendants have presented no evidence to rebut the statutory presumption that Debtor was insolvent during the 90 days immediately preceding the bankruptcy filing. For purposes of preferential transfer actions, a transfer is deemed made at the time the transfer is perfected if the perfection occurs more than 30 days after the transfer takes effect. A transfer of personal property is perfected when it is entitled to priority against a hypothetical subsequent judicial lien. "Although state law determines priorities, all interests [in aircraft] must be federally recorded before they can obtain whatever priority to which they are entitled under state law." ...

Since the conveyance of the aircraft from Debtor to Defendants was not filed for recording with the FAA within 30 days after the Aircraft Bill of Sale was signed, the transfer is deemed to have occurred on January 11, 2011, the date the conveyance was filed for recording. Thus, the transfer is deemed to have occurred within 90 days immediately preceding the bankruptcy filing. Accordingly, Trustee has met his burden under section 547(b)(4).

Finally, under section 547(b)(5), Trustee must prove that Defendants received more than they would have received in a hypothetical Chapter 7 distribution. Defendants assert that Trustee cannot meet this burden because Defendants had a perfected lien in the aircraft as a result of their filed UCC–1 Financing Statement.

"Generally, payments to a fully secured creditor will not be considered preferential because the creditor would not receive more than in a Chapter 7 liquidation." 5 *Collier on Bankruptcy,* ¶ 547.03[7], p. 547–43 (16th ed. 2011). The affidavit of Defendant Murphy states that Defendants received from Debtor and filed with the Clerk of Superior Court of Houston County a UCC–1 Financing Statement, perfecting their lien in the aircraft which secured the debt owed by Debtor. Assuming that this lien is enforceable against Debtor and Trustee, there is no evidence in the record as to the amount of the debt owed by Debtor or the value of the aircraft at the time of the conveyance. Accordingly, there is a genuine issue of fact as to whether Defendants received, by conveyance of the aircraft, value greater than they would have received in a Chapter 7 case. Further, there is no evidence that Debtor signed a security agreement conveying to Defendants a security interest in the aircraft. In order to have an enforceable security interest, there must be a signed security agreement. The UCC–1 Financing Statement given to Defendants does not meet this requirement.

Finally, Defendants' argument also assumes that their lien is an unavoidable lien. However, if the security interest in the aircraft was not filed with the FAA then it would appear that it would be an unperfected lien which could not withstand a challenge by Trustee under 11 U.S.C. § 544(a)(1). The record is silent as to whether or not the security interest was filed with the FAA. On this point, Defendants' reliance on the case of *Southern Horizons Aviation v. Farmers & Merchants Bank of Lakeland,* 231 Ga.App. 55, 497 S.E.2d 637 (1998) is misplaced. In that case, the Georgia Court of Appeals noted that the bank's security interest which had been perfected by filing with the FAA had priority over the holder of a mechanic's lien since the holder of the mechanic's lien had never perfected that lien by filing with the FAA, holding, "A mechanic's lien which has not been recorded with the FAA is not valid." Fed.R.Civ.P. 56(g), incorporated by Bankruptcy Rule 7056, provides:

If the court does not grant all the relief requested by the motion, it may enter an order stating any material fact … that is not genuinely in dispute and treating the fact as established in the case.

Accordingly, the Court finds that Trustee has satisfied his burden and there is no genuine dispute with respect to 11 U.S.C. § 547(b)(1), (2), (3) and (4) and partial summary judgment is granted with respect thereto. However, as to 11 U.S.C. § 547(b)(5), there are material fact issues as to the existence of a security agreement, the amount of the debt, the value of the aircraft and whether the security interest in the aircraft was filed with the FAA.

*CONCLUSION*

For the reasons stated above, Trustee's Motion For Summary Judgment will be granted in part and denied in part.

---

## Exercise 11-6: Preferences

Juice Farms, Inc. ("Juice Farms") was a supplier of juice products to Debtor. By June Year 1, Debtor owed approximately $975,000 to Juice Farms. As a condition to Juice Farms continuing to supply orange juice products to Debtor, Juice Farms and Debtor entered into a Security Agreement on June 18, Year 1 ("Juice Farms Security Agreement"). Debtor granted Juice Farms a security interest in much of Debtor's personal property, including its then existing and after-acquired general intangibles and proceeds. To perfect its security interest, Juice Farms filed a "UCC–1 Financing Statement" on July 22, Year 1.

Apparently Debtor's business did not flourish. On January 20, Year 3, Debtor filed its voluntary petition under Chapter 11 of the Bankruptcy Code. The Trustee alleges that payments totaling $175,000 ("the Payments") made by Debtor to Juice Farms during the ninety days prior to the filing of Debtor's bankruptcy petition were preferential transfers avoidable under Section 547 and recoverable under Section 550 of the Bankruptcy Code.

In a separate proceeding, the Bankruptcy Judge found that as of the date of the filing of the petition, Juice Farms' claim was secured by Debtor's property to the extent of $353,000. The remainder of Juice Farms' claim, $1,109,034.93, was apparently unsecured.

Who should prevail in the trustee's avoidance action?

---

### Exercise 11-7: Section 547 (Improvement of Position)

Debtor operated an electroplating business. As such, the Debtor generated inventory and accounts receivable. During the operation of its business, Debtor had two secured creditors, both of whom had security interests in virtually all of the Debtor's assets, which included accounts receivable and inventory.

At all times during the Preference Period, the junior creditor ("Junior") was undersecured: *i.e.*, the value of its collateral, taking into account the amount of the senior secured debt, was less than the amount of its debt. During the Preference Period, some, if not all, of the accounts receivable and inventory in which it held a security interest at the beginning of the Preference Period generated cash proceeds. These proceeds were then spent in the continued operation of the business, and new inventory and accounts receivable were generated.

Pursuant to the after-acquired property clause in Junior's security agreement, Junior automatically acquired liens in the new accounts receivable and inventory generated during the Preference Period. The Trustee has presented evidence that the value of the Debtor's accounts receivable and inventory increased by $156,939 during the Preference Period.

Junior seeks summary judgment on two grounds. First, it contends that, as a matter of law, under the facts recited above, the Trustee cannot establish that the transfers of security interests in the accounts receivable and inventory acquired during the Preference Period permitted Junior to receive more than it would have received in a Chapter 7 liquidation had the transfers not occurred. 11 U.S.C. section 547(b)(5). Second, Junior contends that, even if the Trustee can establish this element of a preference claim, it is entitled to a complete defense under 11 U.S.C. section 547(c)(5). How should the court rule on Junior's motion?

---

# 4.  Other Bankruptcy Impacts on Secured Creditors

Even if a secured creditor has a properly and timely perfected security interest, the filing of a bankruptcy can have a variety of negative impacts upon a secured creditor. These include (1) the automatic stay; and (2) other restrictions in reorganization proceedings.

## 4.1  The Automatic Stay

Upon the filing of bankruptcy petition, an automatic stay or injunction issues from the federal bankruptcy court. The automatic stay bars all creditors from taking any steps to garnish, seize, sell, or otherwise collect property of the debtor. The reach of this stay is extremely broad. It not only prevents any creditor from repossessing collateral or selling repossessed collateral, it also bars filing any complaint against the debtor, proceeding with any pending litigation against the debtor (including taking discovery, etc.), or making demands for payment on the debtor.

Thus, a secured creditor may be barred from foreclosing on collateral, liquidating collateral, or taking other steps to enable it to realize upon its collateral. In addition, the secured creditor may ultimately incur higher costs in connection with necessary legal proceedings to obtain relief from the automatic stay to enable it to proceed to realize its rights against the collateral.

## 4.2  Other Restrictions in Reorganizations

Although details must await you in a bankruptcy course, you should be aware of the fact that in non-liquidation (reorganization) proceedings in bankruptcy, such as a Chapter 11, even more negative impacts await a secured creditor. By way of example, (a) another lender may be willing to finance a company (debtor-in-possession) and get a "super priority" lien over the debtor's assets;[7] (b) while the automatic stay is in effect, the debtor may be permitted to use the collateral in its possession in the ordinary course of business; and (c) the creditor's after-acquired property clause (floating lien) may be terminated.[8]

---

7. §364(d)
8. §522(a)

# Chapter 12

# Secured Transactions Problems

## Problem 12-1

Al R.E. Agent is a real estate salesperson. He works as an independent contractor affiliated with Big Broker, Inc. Al typically receives a portion of each real estate commission earned by Big on one of Al's transactions, through close of escrow. Al has heard that Big is in financial distress, and wants to be assured that he will continue to receive earned real estate commissions if Big goes bankrupt. Al knows that Big is several months behind in rent to his landlord, and is being sued by several creditors for past due debts. He is considering quitting and going to work for a more solvent broker unless there is some device to assure that he will receive the commissions to which he is entitled. Write a letter to Al explaining what steps you recommend for his protection. Your discussion should include a detailed description of what legal documents, if any, you think should be prepared and how they should be completed, as well as an explanation of why and how your recommendation will serve Al's needs. If you can't promise Al that he will be 100% protected, you should thoroughly explain any lingering risks.

## Problem 12-2

Deborah Debtor was engaged in the business of manufacturing specialty widgets. She had customers in all of the fifty states in the United States. Deborah contracted with Carriers to deliver her widgets to her customers. From August, Year 1, through January, Year 3, Carriers handled all of Deborah's shipment needs. Deborah would call Carriers when a shipment was ready, and Carriers would pick it up from Deborah's place of business and deliver the goods directly to Deborah's customer. From the time of pick up until the time of delivery, Carriers was in continuous possession of Deborah's goods. Each time Carriers picked up a shipment of goods, it would bill Deborah on its regular invoice form. During this time period, Carrier sent Deborah approximately 330 invoices with identical terms. The reverse side of the invoice contained a page of fine print entitled "Terms and Conditions." The only reference to those terms on the face of the invoice was the following:

### Terms: Net Cash

The terms and conditions under which credit is granted are stated in part in paragraphs 15 and 16 on the reverse. If you are unwilling to accept these conditions, you must pay cash upon receipt of goods or completion of service.

Paragraph 15 of the terms and conditions, which was on the reverse side of the form, stated:

15. General Lien on Property. Company [Carriers] shall have a general lien on any and all property of Customer [Deborah] in its possession, custody and control, for all claims for charges incurred by Company in connection with any shipments of Customer. If such claim remains unsatisfied for thirty (30) days after demand for its payment is made, Company may sell at public auction or private sale, upon ten (10) days written notice to Customer, the goods, wares and/or merchandise, or so much thereof as may be necessary to satisfy such liens, and apply the net proceeds of such sale to the payment of the amount due to Company. Any surplus from any such sales shall be transmitted to Customer and Customer shall be liable for any deficiency in the sale.

It is stipulated that Deborah never signed the invoices or any agreement with Carriers regarding the terms contained in the invoices.

Deborah Debtor filed a voluntary Chapter 7 petition on February 4, Year 3. At the time of the bankruptcy filing, Carriers was in possession of property of Deborah valued at $80,000. As of 90 days before the petition date, Carriers was in possession of property of Deborah valued at $60,000. Also as of the petition date, Deborah owed Carriers $40,000.

Carriers claims it is a perfected secured party. The Trustee in Bankruptcy contests that claim. Furthermore, the Trustee argues that even if Carriers had a perfected security interest, the increase in value of the property in its possession constituted a preferential transfer.

Discuss the validity, priority and extent of Carriers' lien on Deborah's property. Be sure to raise and analyze all arguments that could be made by Carriers and Trustee.

## Problem 12-3

Deborah Debtor owned three "Gifts Galore" stores, one of which was located in each of the Stargate, Solargate and Milkygate Malls. The stores sold a variety of gifts, such as tee-shirts, key chains, and books, aimed at visitors to the local area. Deborah found that her sales were excellent in the warm summer months, but dropped off during the winter, when fewer tourists were in town. She decided that she needed some financial assistance to get through the lean winter months. Accordingly, on January 5, Year 1, she borrowed money from Friendly Finance Co., who lent her $100,000. To secure the loan, Friendly had Deborah sign a security agreement, granting Friendly a security interest in "all inventory, accounts, chattel paper and promissory notes." The agreement stated, among other things, that it secured future advances. Friendly filed a UCC-1 financing statement in the proper place, identifying the debtor as "Debtor, Deborah" and describing the collateral as "all of debtor's inventory, accounts, chattel paper and promissory notes arising out of that certain business commonly known as "Gifts Galore." That summer, Deborah repaid the loan in full.

In Year 2, Deborah again borrowed $100,000 from Friendly, and signed a security agreement granting Friendly a security interest in "all inventory and accounts, now owned or hereafter acquired, and the proceeds thereof." That summer, Deborah again repaid the loan in full. Late in Year 2, Deborah incorporated each store as a separate business. The Stargate Mall store retained the name, "Gifts Galore." The Solargate store became "Great Solargate Gifts," and the Milkygate store was named "Great Milkygate Gifts."

In Year 3, Deborah again borrowed $100,000 from Friendly, based on a short telephone conversation with Friendly's president, who simply said, "Same arrangements as usual?," to which Deborah replied, "Great!"

In April, Year 3, Deborah decided that she was tired of the Stargate Mall business, and, on April 15, she sold it, in bulk, to Bill Buyer. The parties signed a simple purchase agreement, pursuant to which Bill agreed to assume all liabilities of Deborah arising out of or in any way related to the Stargate Mall business.

When Friendly learned that Deborah had sold the Stargate Mall store (Bill promptly renamed it, "I Own It!"), Friendly was furious. It immediately (May 20, Year 3) sent representatives to all three stores. When Friendly's representative showed up at the Solargate store, he gathered up as much merchandise as he could carry and walked out of the store before the astonished sales personnel could react. The merchandise had a retail value of approximately $10,000. The Milkygate store heard about what had happened at Solargate. When Friendly's representative showed up there, he was denied entry. Finally, Friendly brought an appropriate action in state court for possession of the property in the Stargate Mall store.

As you might have guessed, a good deal of litigation ensued. Please discuss the likely outcome of each of the following suits:

1. Friendly v. Deborah

2. Friendly v. Bill

3. Bill v. Deborah

## Problem 12-4

On May 17, Year 1, Richmond Fixture & Equipment Company ("Richmond") entered into a contract with and sold to Walter Chewing Restaurants, Inc. ("Chewing") certain items of restaurant furniture, fixtures and equipment (the "Property"). The Property consisted of all of the personal property and fixtures used in connection with the operation of a restaurant, including items such as moveable tables and chairs, wall coverings, light fixtures, pots and pans, dishes and silverware, stoves, refrigerators, and an elaborate built-in bar system that included pipes installed in the restaurant walls. The parties executed a written installment sales contract (the "Contract") dated May 17, Year 1. On February 20, Year 2, Richmond filed a financing statement with the office of the Secretary of State. The collateral was described as "all of debtor's personal property and fixtures used or in any way related to debtor's restaurant business, now owned or hereafter acquired, and wherever located."

The Contract provided, among other things, that Chewing would not sell the Property, or any interest in the Property, without Richmond's prior written consent. In addition to requiring Richmond's consent to such a sale, the Contract required Chewing to pay a $100 transfer fee to Richmond in the event of such a sale.

On July 23, Year 2, Chewing sold his restaurant business to Southern Properties, Inc. ("Southern"). A transfer fee was paid to Richmond. Southern and Chewing entered into an agreement pursuant to which Southern promised Chewing to assume all of Chewing's obligations to Richmond, and to indemnify and hold Chewing harmless against any and all claims that Richmond might assert under the Contract. After the sale, Southern sold most of the furniture, dishes and silverware Chewing had used in the restaurant, and totally redecorated. It bought substantially everything new, using a line of credit from Big Bank. The line of credit was evidenced by a promissory note that included, among others, a provision stating that all of the obligations under the note were secured by a security interest under Article 9 of the Uniform Commercial Code in all of Southern's owned and after acquired personal property. On July 30, Year 2, Big Bank filed a financing statement in the office of the Secretary of State. The collateral was described as "all of the debtor's furniture, fixtures and equipment, and the proceeds thereof."

On October 24, Year 2, Southern filed for relief in bankruptcy under Chapter 11 of the Bankruptcy Code. The case was converted to a Chapter 7 and a Trustee appointed.

The Trustee claims that her interest in the Property is superior to any interest Richmond may have. Who should prevail? Why?

## Problem 12-5

Faulty Finance, Inc. made a loan to Broke Borrower, LLC, a Delaware limited liability company, in August, Year 1, secured by all of Broke Borrower's assets. Faulty Finance promptly filed a properly completed financing statement with the Secretary of State of Delaware, describing the collateral as "all assets, now owned or hereafter acquired."

Several months after borrowing from Faulty Finance, Broke Borrower found itself short of operating cash, and sought to shore itself up by selling a surplus processing machine. The buyer's own lender insisted that, as a condition to making the loan to the buyer, Broke Borrower obtain an amendment to Faulty Finance's financing statement deleting the machine from the description of collateral. Faulty Finance directed an employee in its documentation department to process the amendment. Unfortunately, the employee ticked the box labeled "termination," instead of "amendment," and filed it that way.

A few months after the sale, Broke Borrower again experienced a cash crunch, and approached Faulty Finance to discuss restructuring its loan. In preparation for discussions with Broke Borrower, Faulty Finance reviewed its file, and noticed the mistaken filing. At that point, it quickly filed an "Information Statement" with the Delaware Secretary of State, explaining that the termination statement had been filed in error. It also filed a new financing statement, identical to the original one it had filed.

Unfortunately, discussions between the parties did not go well, and, less than 60 days after Faulty Finance had filed its new financing statement, Broke Borrower filed for bankruptcy. It then filed a motion seeking to avoid Faulty Finance's security interest as a preference.

You are clerking for the bankruptcy judge before whom Broke Borrower's motion will be heard. Prepare a short discussion of the issues, along with your recommendation as to whether the motion should be granted, addressed to your judge.

## Problem 12-6

Late in Year 1, Carlos Danger borrowed $3 million from Hard Money Source, Inc. Carlos Danger secured his obligations to Hard Money Source by transferring securities having a market value of $4 million into a securities account ("Collateral Account") with Busy Broker, Inc. Carlos signed a security agreement granting Hard Money Source a security interest in "securities account no. 1234444 maintained with Busy Broker, Inc." Busy Broker entered into a brokerage account agreement with Hard Money Source under which Busy Broker agreed to recognize Hard Money Source as the party entitled to exercise all rights with respect to any financial asset credited to the Collateral Account. Hard Money Source never filed a financing statement against Carlos.

In December, Year 2, Carlos filed for bankruptcy. Shortly after the commencement of the proceedings, Hard Money Source filed a motion for relief from stay, alleging that, due to market reverses, the market value of the securities credited to the Collateral Account was now less than the outstanding balance of its loan to Carlos, and seeking relief from the automatic stay, permitting it to liquidate the securities and apply them to repayment of the loan. Carlos has now filed an opposition to Hard Money Source's motion, alleging that, because Hard Money Source failed to file a financing statement against Carlos, its security interest in the Collateral Account is unperfected. Prepare a memorandum to Hard Money Source explaining whether it should be concerned.

## Problem 12-7

Clyde and his business partner, Bonnie, have developed a method for converting grass clippings into clean-burning ethanol. Together they incorporated "Grass To Gas, Inc." to exploit the technology. They bought an abandoned farm at a tax sale, and repaired the buildings to house their machinery and several grain silos to hold grass clippings awaiting processing. With money from investors and a loan from their local credit union (to which they granted a security interest in all of their assets as security for the loan), they bought the machinery they'd need and adapted it to make use of their technology. Once it was set up, they contracted with a local landscaping company, "Yardcare Experts, LLC," to buy all of the grass clippings Yardcare Experts could supply. Yardcare Experts was aware of the credit union's loan, which had been perfected by the filing of a properly-completed financing statement in the proper place, and sought to protect itself by structuring its relationship with Grass To Gas as follows:

a. Under the sales contract, Grass To Gas was obligated to buy all grass clippings Yardcare Experts could produce; title to the grass clippings being sold to Grass To Gas would not pass until Yardcare Experts received payment in full. Grass To Gas was required to pay for clippings only once title had passed to it.

b. Yardcare Experts leased two of Grass To Gas's silos for $1/year each for the storage of grass clippings pending the transfer of title to Grass To Gas. Yardcare Experts was entitled to put signs on the silos reflecting its lease to Yardcare Experts, and to hire a security guard for the silos. (In fact, Yardcare never did either, and there was no way to differentiate the silos leased to Yardcare Experts from other silos on the premises.)

c.  If Grass To Gas defaulted on any payments due to Yardcare Experts, Yardcare Experts could lock its silos and prevent Grass To Gas from accessing additional clippings.

d.  In addition, if Grass To Gas defaulted on any payments due to Yardcare Experts, Yardcare Experts could terminate the contract. In that event — in fact, in the event of any termination of the contract, for any reason whatsoever — Grass To Gas would be deemed to have purchased all unused clippings then remaining in the silos, the full purchase price of which would become immediately due and payable; Yardcare Experts would be permitted to remain in possession of the silos, and the clippings they contained, until it had been paid in full.

Ten months after entering into this arrangement, Grass To Gas failed to make a monthly payment due to Yardcare Experts. Yardcare Experts notified Grass To Gas of the default, and, when 10 days passed without Grass To Gas having paid the amount owed, Yardcare Experts declared a default under their agreement, locked its silos, and demanded payment in full. Upon learning these facts, Grass To Gas's credit union lender accelerated its loan and demanded that Yardcare Experts turn over the grass clippings in the silos, claiming a prior security interest by virtue of its filed financing statement. Yardcare Experts comes to you, and asks whether it must turn over the grass clippings to the credit union, upon pain of liability for conversion if it does not. What is your advice?

## Problem 12-8

George Jones has established a trust for the benefit of his daughter, Heidi. George is the sole trustee of the trust. The trust is established under the law of the state of Indiana, where George lived at the time he established the trust. He moved to Washington State a couple of years ago. The trust agreement states that "the name of the trust established by this Declaration of Trust is 'The Heidi Jones Loves Her Daddy Trust.'" So far, the trust has been funded with stock of the Walt Disney Company, issued to "George Jones, as trustee of The Heidi Jones Loves Her Daddy Trust." George has also contributed a contract, originally entered into between him and the record company that produced several albums for him early in his career and that still produces royalties, to the trust.

Despite having moved to Washington, George has continued to use his Indiana driver's license. It states that George's name is "George Herbert Allen Farnsworth Jones." George has never signed any contract, however, except as "George Jones."

Heidi now wants to take a trip to Europe. To finance it, George arranges for a bank to lend the trust $10,000, secured by a security interest in the royalty contract. You represent the bank. How would you fill out the UCC financing statement to perfect the bank's security interest? Where would you file it?

## Problem 12-9

You have graduated from law school and been admitted to the Bar in the jurisdiction where you reside. At your bank client's request, you have drafted a new form of security agreement for use in personal property secured-loan trans-actions. Your client has asked you to explain the meaning of the following security agreement provisions, and to explain why you have included such provisions in the security agreement.

a. "As used in this Agreement, 'Equipment' shall mean all of Debtor's equipment of whatever kind or nature, wherever located, now owned or hereafter acquired."

b. "The security interest is to secure all of Debtor's present and future debts, obligations and liabilities of whatever nature to Secured Party."

c. "Until all the Obligations are paid in full, Debtor agrees that it will preserve its corporate existence and not, in one transaction or in a series of related transactions, merge into or consolidate with any other entity, or sell all or substantially all of its assets."

d. "Until the Obligations are paid in full, Debtor agrees that it will not change the state of its incorporation."

e. "Secured Party does not authorize and Debtor agrees not to (i) make any sales or leases of any of the Collateral; (ii) license any of the Collateral; or (iii) grant any other security interest in any of the Collateral."

## Problem 12-10

Company A, a retailer of clothing, purchases piece goods and sends them or has them delivered by its seller to Company B, who manufactures the piece goods into finished items of clothing and ships the clothing back to Company A. The contract between Company A and Company B contains a clause that makes it clear that title to the piece goods remains at all times with Company A. Company B finances its operations with Last National Bank, which has a perfected security interest in Company B's presently existing and after-acquired inventory. A asks whether there is any jeopardy to its piece goods if Company B experiences financial difficulties, including (without limitation) bankruptcy. Answer A's question. Explain fully.

## Problem 12-11

On July 1, D signed a security agreement granting SP a security interest in Debtor's "inventory and accounts, existing and after-acquired." SP filed a proper financing statement in the proper place on that date. SP did not give value to D at that time. On September 15, SP loaned D $20,000 under the security agreement. On that date, the value of the collateral in which SP had a perfected SI was $15,000. On December 1, Debtor filed bankruptcy. On that date, D stipulated that on November 15, the value of the collateral was $18,000 and that D, at SP's urging, had built up the collateral by purchasing additional inventory from third parties on credit. Discuss what, if anything, the trustee can recover from SP in a preference action.

## Problem 12-12

On January 3, A and Debtor ("D") authenticated a valid security agreement. D was in the business of selling stationery and related paper products. The collateral was described as "D's inventory." A filed a properly-filled-in-financing statement with the same collateral description in the appropriate place on the same day.

B agreed to loan D $10,000. D agreed with B that D's punch press, worth $10,000, would be collateral for B's loan. On January 25, D signed and gave to B (a) a promissory note for $10,000; and (b) a security agreement granting B a security interest in the punch press. B promptly filed a financing statement, listing the punch press as collateral, in the proper place. B then gave D $10,000.

On February 18, C sold D a specialty line of paper products for D's inventory, pursuant to a conditional sale contract that stated that C retained title to the goods until C received payment in full. Before the goods were delivered to D, C sent notice to A of the transaction.

On March 3, D sold the punch press to E, a good faith purchaser who was unaware of B's security interest. In return, D received a drill worth $5,000 and a necklace worth $5,000. D promptly gave the necklace to his wife.

Within the next 2 weeks, D sold substantially all of the inventory that had been in his possession in January and February, and received the following:

a. $5,000 in checks, which were deposited in D's bank account containing funds from other sources;

b. $10,000 in accounts receivable;

c. $7,000 in negotiable promissory notes; and

d. $15,000 in cash, which D used to purchase additional inventory and equipment.

On March 20, D sold the accounts receivable to X in return for $5,000 cash, which D used for a quick trip to Las Vegas. On April 10, D filed a Chapter 7 bankruptcy petition. Discuss the relative priority of A, B, C, D, E, X, and the trustee in bankruptcy with respect to:

1. The inventory sold by D;

2. The punch press sold by D;

3. The drill worth $5,000;

4. The necklace worth $5,000;

5. The $5,000 in checks, which were deposited in D's bank account;

6. The $10,000 in accounts receivable;

7. The $7,000 in negotiable promissory notes; and

8. The inventory and equipment in D's possession at the time of the filing of the bankruptcy petition.

# Appendix A

# Secured Promissory Note

$_____$ City, State $_____$ $\_\_$, $\_\_\_\_$

FOR VALUE RECEIVED, $_____$, a $_____$ corporation ("Borrower"), hereby promises to pay to the order of $_____$, a $_____$ ("Lender"), by wire or electronic transfer to the account set forth below or to such other account as may be designated in writing from time to time by Lender, or at such other place, and in such other manner, as Lender may designate in writing from time to time, in lawful money of the United States, the principal sum of $_____$ DOLLARS ($\$_____$), together with interest thereon, as specified below. Reference is made to that certain Security Agreement executed by Borrower for the benefit of Lender of even date herewith (the "Security Agreement"). Capitalized terms not defined herein shall have the meaning ascribed to them in the Security Agreement.

1. <u>Principal Balance</u>. Borrower acknowledges the receipt, on the date of this Note, of the principal amount set forth above.

2. <u>Interest</u>. Interest on the outstanding principal balance shall accrue at the rate of \_\_\_% per annum (the "Interest Rate"). Interest not paid when due shall bear interest, at the Interest Rate, until paid. All interest shall be calculated on the basis of a year of 365 days for the actual number of days elapsed.

3. <u>Payment</u>. Subject to the terms and conditions set forth herein, the outstanding principal balance and accrued interest shall be due and payable in installments, as follows:

(a) On $_____$, $\_\_\_$: $\$_____$ in principal, together with all accrued and unpaid interest;

(b) On $_____$, $\_\_\_$: $\$_____$ in principal, together with all accrued and unpaid interest;

(c) On $_____$, $\_\_\_$: $\$_____$ in principal, together with all accrued and unpaid interest; and

(d) On $_____$, $\_\_\_$ (or such earlier date, if applicable, as specified in the Security Agreement) the remaining principal balance of this Note, together with all accrued and unpaid interest and other amounts payable to Lender under this Note or any other Related Document.

Borrower shall have no right to prepay any portion of this Note, except with Lender's prior written consent.

4. <u>Payments</u>.

(a) All payments under this Note shall be made in immediately available funds, without deduction, withholding or offset, for any reason whatsoever, before $_____$, Pacific Time, on the date that such payment is due. Any payment received after such time shall be considered for all purposes (including the calculation of interest, to the extent permitted by law) as having been made on the next business day. If the due date for any payment is not a business day, such due date shall be deemed for all purposes to fall on the next business day, and any such extension shall be included in the computation of interest payments.

(b)    Unless and until another place and/or manner of payment is designated in writing by Lender, all payments shall be made by ACH or other wire or electronic transfer to the following account:

LENDER'S BANK, N.A.

_____

_____

Bank Routing No. _____

With instructions to credit the account of

_____

Account No. _____

(c)    If any amount due hereunder is not paid when due, Borrower shall pay to Lender, upon demand, a late fee in an amount equal to ___% (_____ percent) of the overdue amount. Borrower acknowledges that late payment under this Note will cause Lender to incur costs that would be costly or inconvenient to establish. Borrower and Lender agree that it would be impractical or extremely difficult to fix Lender's actual damages if any payment is not paid when due, and the late fee provided for in this Section 4(c) represents a reasonable sum and a fair and reasonable estimate of the costs that Lender will incur by reason of late payment. Acceptance of such late fee shall not limit the right of Lender to compel performance of any obligation or exercise any other remedies under the terms of this Note or any other Related Document.

(d)    Each payment hereunder shall be applied first to the payment of fees, costs and expenses, if any, then payable to Lender, and next to accrued interest, and the balance, if any, shall be then applied to reduction of principal.

(e)    Concurrently with Borrower's execution and delivery of this Note and as a condition to Lender's obligation to fund the Loan, Borrower shall pay to Lender a loan origination fee in the amount of _____% of the original principal amount of the Loan, to be applied by Lender to the payment of Lender's costs and expenses incurred in connection with negotiating, documenting, and closing the Loan. Any excess of such loan origination fee over Lender's actual expenses so incurred shall be retained by Lender as additional consideration for Lender's agreement to make the Loan.

5.    Security Agreement. This Note is secured by the Security Agreement. The Security Agreement, among other things, contains provisions for the acceleration of the maturity of the unpaid principal amount of this Note upon the happening of certain stated events. This Note is a Related Document, and is entitled to the benefits of the Security Agreement and the other Related Documents. Without limiting the generality of the foregoing, upon the occurrence and during the continuation of any Event of Default, then: Lender may declare the whole sum of principal of the this Note, together with all accrued interest and other amounts owed in respect of this Note or under the other Related Documents, if any, immediately due and payable (or, as provided in the Security Agreement, such amounts shall automatically become due and payable), without notice or demand, whereupon such sum shall become immediately due and payable. The rights or remedies

of Lender as provided in this Note and other Related Documents are exercisable in accordance with applicable law at the sole discretion of Lender. The rights and remedies of Lender under this Note are cumulative and are not in lieu of, but are in addition to, any other rights or remedies that Lender may have under the Security Agreement or any of the other Related Documents, at law or in equity, or otherwise, and may be exercised regardless of the adequacy of security.

6. <u>Waivers</u>. No delay or omission on the part of Lender in exercising any rights under this Note, the Agreement, or any of the other Related Documents on default by Borrower shall operate as a waiver of such right or of any other right under this Note or the other Related Documents, for the same default or any other default. Borrower and all guarantors and endorsers of this Note consent, without notice, to all extensions for any period or periods of time and to the acceptance of partial payments before or after maturity, and to the acceptance, release, perfection or failure to perfect and substitution of security, all without prejudice to Lender. Lender shall similarly have the right to deal in any way, at any time, with one or more of the foregoing parties without notice to any other party, and to grant any such party any extensions of time for payment of any of the debt evidenced hereby, or to grant any other indulgences or forbearances whatsoever, without waiver of any rights and without in any way affecting the personal liability of any such party. Presentment, notice of dishonor, and protest and, to time extent permitted by applicable law, the defense of the statute of limitations, are hereby waived by all makers, guarantors and endorsers of this Note.

7. <u>Interest Rate Limitation</u>. This Note and the other Related Documents are subject to the express condition that at no time shall Borrower be obligated or required to pay interest on the debt evidenced by this Note at a rate that could subject the holder of this Note to either civil or criminal liability as a result of being in excess of the maximum interest rate that Borrower is permitted by applicable law to contract or agree to pay. If, by the terms of this Note or the other Related Documents, Borrower is at any time required or obligated to pay interest on the debt at a rate in excess of such maximum rate, the rate of interest under this Note and the other Related Documents shall be deemed to be immediately reduced to such maximum rate and the interest payable shall be computed at such maximum rate, and all prior interest payments in excess of such maximum rate shall be applied (and shall be deemed to have been payments) in reduction of the principal balance of this Note (or, to the extent in excess of the amount required to pay the principal balance of this Note in full, returned to Borrower). All sums paid or agreed to be paid to Lender for the use, forbearance, or detention of the debt evidenced by this Note shall, to the extent permitted by applicable law, be amortized, prorated, allocated, and spread throughout the full stated term of this Note until payment in full so that the rate or amount of interest on account of the debt does not exceed the maximum lawful rate of interest from time to time in effect and applicable to the debt for so long as the debt is outstanding.

8. <u>Costs of Enforcement</u>. If Lender takes any action to enforce any provision of this Note or of any Related Document, either through legal proceedings or otherwise, Borrower shall reimburse Lender upon demand for reasonable attorneys' fees and all other costs and expenses so incurred. Such costs and expenses shall include, without limitation, Lender's attorneys', expert witnesses' and consultants' fees and disbursements, including without limitation those attorneys', expert witnesses' and consultants' fees and disbursements, and other expenses, incurred by Lender in connection with any appeal, the enforcement of any judgment, or any insolvency, bankruptcy, reorganization, arrangement or other similar proceedings involving Borrower or any other obligor under

any Related Document that in any way affect the exercise by Lender of its rights and remedies hereunder.

9.    Time of Essence. Time is of the essence hereof.

10.    Successors and Assigns. Lender shall have the right to sell, assign, or otherwise transfer, either in part or in its entirety, this Note, the Security Agreement and any of the other Related Documents, without Borrower's consent. This Note shall be binding on and inure to the benefit of Borrower and Lender and their respective legal and personal representatives, parent, subsidiary and affiliate entities, devisees, successors, and assigns; provided that Borrower shall have no right to assign all or any portion of its rights or obligations hereunder or under any other Related Document except with the prior written consent of Lender.

11.    Applicable Law. This Note shall be construed according to and governed by the internal law of the State of _____, except as required by mandatory provisions of law or to the extent the perfection or priority of the security interests hereunder, or the remedies hereunder, in respect of any Collateral are governed by the law of a jurisdiction other than _____.

12.    Miscellaneous. The rules of construction set forth in the Security Agreement shall apply to the construction of this Note.

BORROWER:

_____, a _____ corporation

By: _____
Name:
Title:

# Appendix B

# Security Agreement

THIS SECURITY AGREEMENT (this "Agreement") is entered into this _____ day of _____, 2010, by and between _____, a _____ corporation ("Borrower"), and_____, a _____ ("Lender").

## RECITALS

A.  Concurrently herewith, Borrower has executed that certain Secured Promissory Note (the "Note") payable to the order of Lender in respect of a Loan, in the original principal amount of $_____, made by Lender to Borrower (the "Loan").

B.  It is a condition of the Lender's making of the Loan, among other things, that Borrower grant Lender the security interest provided for herein as security for Borrower's obligations in respect of the Loan.

1.  <u>Security Interest and Secured Obligations</u>.

(a)  Borrower hereby grants Lender a security interest in all Borrower's right, title and interest, now owned or hereafter acquired, in, to and under the property described on Exhibit A hereto (the "Collateral").

(b)  The security interest granted pursuant to this Agreement is granted to, and shall, secure the prompt and full performance and payment of all obligations, liabilities and indebtedness, whether direct or indirect, absolute or contingent, that Borrower may at any time now or hereafter owe to Lender pursuant to the Note, this Agreement, and any other document executed and delivered for the benefit of Lender in connection with the Loan (in each case, as at any time and from time to time amended, supplemented, restated or otherwise modified) (each, together with any and all guaranties executed and delivered in connection with the Loan, a "Related Document"), and including, without limitation, all amounts that Lender may now or hereafter pay or advance at any time for taxes, levies, insurance, repairs, maintenance or other protection with respect to the Collateral and all costs and expenses that Lender may incur in the administration of the Loan or in enforcing or protecting its rights with respect to the Collateral or the obligations secured by the Collateral, including reasonable attorneys' fees, all of which Borrower shall pay to Lender upon demand (all of the foregoing, whether arising before or after the filing of a petition in bankruptcy and including all interest accrued after the petition date, collectively, the "Secured Obligations").

2.  <u>Representations and Warranties</u>. Borrower represents and warrants to Lender that:

(a)  Borrower is a corporation duly existing and in good standing under the laws of its state of formation indicated in the preamble and is qualified and licensed to do business in the State of _____ and in each other state in which the conduct of its business or its ownership of property requires that it be so qualified, except where the failure to be so qualified could not reasonably be expected to have a material adverse effect.

(b)    The execution, delivery, and performance by Borrower of the Related Documents to which it is a party are within Borrower's corporate powers and have been duly authorized by all requisite corporate action. Each of the Note and this Agreement and each other Related Document, if any, to which Borrower is a party has been duly executed and delivered by Borrower and is enforceable against Borrower in accordance with its terms.

(c)    Borrower has not done business under any name other than that specified on the signature page hereof. The name specified for Borrower on the signature page hereof is Borrower's true legal name, and is the name specified for Borrower in its certificate of incorporation. Borrower is a registered organization formed under the laws of the State of _____, and has not become domesticated under the laws of any other jurisdiction. Borrower's organizational identification number issued by its state of formation is _____. The principal place of business (or, if Borrower has more than one place of business, chief executive office) of Borrower is located at the address indicated below as its address for the giving of notices. All Borrower's inventory, equipment and books are located only at such address for the giving of notices.

(d)    The patents and patent applications listed on Schedule 1 hereto constitute all material patents and patent applications in which Borrower has any interest. The trademarks listed on Schedule 2 hereto constitute all material trademarks in which Borrower has any interest. All such patents, patent applications and trademarks are owned by Borrower. Borrower owns no registered copyrights.

(e)    Borrower has the right to grant a security interest in the Collateral. Borrower's execution and delivery of this Agreement and the other Related Documents will not breach, or cause the occurrence of a default under, any other obligation of Borrower for borrowed money, any license or other agreement pursuant to which Borrower has acquired its rights with respect to any patents, trademarks or other intellectual property or any other material agreement to which Borrower is a party or by which its properties are bound.

(f)    There are no effective security interests, liens or other charges or encumbrances ("Liens") against the Collateral except in favor of Lender. Borrower has no obligation for borrowed money except to Lender.

3.    <u>Borrower's Covenants</u>. Until the Secured Obligations have been paid in full:

(a)    Borrower shall (i) keep the Collateral free from any other effective Lien; (ii) to the extent deemed prudent business conduct (to be determined by Borrower in its reasonable discretion), maintain the Collateral in good order and repair; (iii) use the Collateral in accordance with all laws, regulations and orders, and safeguard and protect all Collateral; (iv) not sell, lease, license, transfer or dispose of any of the Collateral except pursuant to sales of inventory in the ordinary course of Borrower's business and for fair market value and for licenses of intellectual property in the ordinary course of Borrower's business and on commercially reasonable terms; (v) not settle or compromise any obligation owed to Borrower in respect of any account except in the ordinary course of business and on commercially reasonable terms, consistent with past practice; (vi) promptly advise Lender of any event or circumstance that can reasonably be expected to have a material adverse effect on the Collateral or on Borrower's ability to repay the Loan in accordance with its terms or otherwise comply with the terms of the Related Documents ("Material Adverse Effect"); and (vii) to the extent not being contested in the Borrower's good faith and by appropriate proceedings, pay when due all taxes and similar obligations that might result in a Lien on the Collateral if not paid.

(b)     Borrower shall not (i) incur any indebtedness for borrowed money; (ii) issue any securities; or (iii) pay or declare any dividends or other distributions in respect of its outstanding securities.

(c)     Borrower shall give Lender prompt written notice of becoming aware of any commercial tort claim to which Borrower acquires rights, describing such commercial tort claim in reasonable detail. Such notice shall constitute a grant by Borrower to Lender of a security interest in such commercial tort claim, as security for the Secured Obligations.

(d)     Borrower shall from time to time execute and deliver to Lender, at the request of Lender, all instruments and chattel paper of Borrower, all financing statements and other documents that Lender may reasonably request, in form reasonably satisfactory to Lender, to perfect and continue the perfection of Lender's security interests in the Collateral or otherwise to protect its rights in the Collateral or in order to fully consummate all of the transactions contemplated under the Related Documents.

(e)     Without thirty (30) days prior written notification to Lender, Borrower shall not relocate its state of organization, change the type of entity it is or change its legal name.

4.     <u>Perfection and Protection of Collateral</u>. Borrower hereby authorizes Lender to file financing statements in all applicable filing offices (i) indicating the Collateral (A) as all assets of Borrower (or words of similar effect), or (B) as being of an equal or lesser scope or with greater detail, and (ii) containing any other information required by part 5 of Article 9 of the Uniform Commercial Code. Borrower shall execute, obtain, deliver and (if applicable) file or record all financing statements, correction statements and notices, and, at Lender's request, use commercially reasonable efforts to obtain consents, control agreements, landlords' waivers, acknowledgments and other documents, and take all other actions that Lender may deem necessary or advisable to perfect or protect Lender's security interest in the Collateral against the interests of third parties. Borrower agrees to pay, on demand, all of Lender's reasonable expenses (including taxes and fees) payable in connection with any such filings, recordings, notices or other actions

5.     <u>Records; Inspection</u>. Upon Lender's request, Borrower will deliver to Lender copies of financial statements and such other reports and information with respect to the Collateral as Lender may request, at Borrower's expense. Borrower shall maintain adequate books and records pertaining to the Collateral and shall permit Lender (during regular business hours, but otherwise at any time or times determined by Lender) to visit and inspect any of the Collateral and to examine Borrower's books, records and accounts with respect to the Collateral and the Secured Obligations, at Borrower's expense. Other than as expressly provided herein, all Lender's costs and expenses in connection with the foregoing shall be part of the Secured Obligations.

6.     <u>Insurance</u>.

(a)     Borrower, at its expense, shall keep the Collateral insured against loss or damage by fire, theft, explosion, sprinklers, and all other hazards and risks, and in such amounts, as are ordinarily insured against by other owners in similar businesses conducted in the locations where Borrower's business is conducted. Borrower shall also maintain insurance relating to Borrower's business, ownership and use of the Collateral in amounts and of a type that are customary to businesses similar to Borrower's.

(b)    All policies of casualty insurance shall contain a lender's loss payable endorsement, in a form satisfactory to Lender, showing Lender as an additional loss payee thereof, and all liability insurance policies shall show the Lender as an additional insured. All such policies shall specify that the insurer must give at least 20 days' notice to Lender before canceling its policy for any reason. Upon Lender's request, Borrower shall deliver or cause to be delivered to Lender certified copies of such policies of insurance and evidence of the payments of all premiums therefor. All proceeds payable under any casualty policy shall, at the option of Lender, be payable to Lender to be applied on account of the Secured Obligations.

7.    <u>Events of Default</u>. Any one or more of the following events shall constitute an Event of Default ("Event of Default"):

(a)    If Borrower fails to pay any of the Secured Obligations when due;

(b)    If an "event of default", as defined in any other Related Document, occurs;

(c)    If Borrower fails or neglects to perform or observe any term, provision, condition, covenant contained in this Agreement or any other Related Document, other than as specified in any other provision of this Section 7, and either (i) such failure or neglect to perform or observe is, by its nature, not capable of cure, or (ii) as to any such failure or neglect to perform or observe that, by its nature, can be cured, Borrower has failed to cure such default within 10 days after the earlier of (A) Borrower receiving notice thereof and (B) any officer of Borrower becoming aware thereof; provided, however, that if the failure or neglect to perform or observe cannot by its nature be cured within the 10-day period or cannot after diligent attempts by Borrower be cured within such ten 10-day period, and such default is likely to be cured within a reasonable time, then Borrower shall have an additional reasonable period to attempt to cure such default, and within such reasonable time period the failure to have cured such default shall not be deemed an Event of Default;

(d)    If any portion of the assets of Borrower or any guarantor of Borrower's obligations under the Note (a "Guarantor") is attached, seized, subjected to a writ or distress warrant, or is levied upon, or comes into the possession of any trustee, receiver or person acting in a similar capacity and such attachment, seizure, writ or distress warrant or levy has not been removed, discharged or rescinded within 10 days, or if Borrower or any Guarantor is enjoined, restrained, or in any way prevented by court order from continuing to conduct all or any material part of its business affairs, or if a judgment or other claim becomes a Lien upon any material portion of Borrower's or any Guarantor's assets, or if a notice of lien, levy, or assessment is filed of record with respect to any of Borrower's or any Guarantor's assets by the United States Government or any department, agency, or instrumentality thereof, or by any state, county, municipal, or governmental agency, and is not paid within 10 days after Borrower or such Guarantor receives notice thereof (provided that none of the foregoing shall constitute an Event of Default where such action or event is stayed or an adequate bond has been posted pending a good faith contest by Borrower or the affected Guarantor);

(e)    If Borrower or any Guarantor becomes insolvent, or if an insolvency proceeding is commenced by Borrower or any Guarantor, or if an insolvency proceeding is commenced against Borrower or any Guarantor and is not dismissed or stayed within 60 days;

(f)    If there is a default or other failure to perform under any agreement to which Borrower or any Guarantor is a party or by which it is bound resulting in a right by a third party or parties, whether or not exercised, to accelerate the maturity, or require the repurchase or redemption, of any one or more items of indebtedness aggregating in amount in excess of Fifty Thousand Dollars ($50,000), or which could have a Material Adverse Effect;

(g)    If a judgment or judgments for the payment of money in an amount, individually or in the aggregate, of at least Fifty Thousand Dollars ($50,000) is rendered against Borrower or any Guarantor and remains unsatisfied and unstayed for a period of 30 days;

(h)    Any Guarantor fails to perform or comply with any obligation under its Guaranty;

(i)    If, for any reason whatsoever, any Related Document fails to be in full force and effect, or if any Lien granted to Lender fails to be perfected with respect to any material portion of the Collateral subject thereto or to be senior to all Liens other than as expressly permitted hereunder; or any termination statement or correction statement is filed with respect to any financing statement filed in favor of Lender without Lender's prior written consent;

(j)    If any material misrepresentation or material misstatement exists now or hereafter in any warranty or representation set forth herein or in any other Related Document.

## 8.    Remedies.

(a)    Upon the occurrence of any Event of Default, and at any time thereafter, at Lender's option, the Secured Obligations shall become immediately due and payable (with interest thereon from the date of demand at the interest rate then applicable to the Loan, calculated as provided in the Loan Agreement) without pre-sentment or demand or any notice to Borrower or any other person obligated thereon, and Lender shall be entitled to exercise any or all of the rights and remedies available at law or in equity, including the rights and remedies of a secured party under the Uniform Commercial Code. These remedies include the right and power to take possession of the Collateral, wherever it may be found, and the right and power to sell, at public or private sale or sales, or otherwise collect, enforce, dispose of or use all or any portion of the Collateral in any manner authorized or permitted under the Uniform Commercial Code, in such order or manner as Lender may elect in its sole discretion. Lender shall not be required to prepare or process the Collateral before disposition, or to make any warranties of title or otherwise to any person acquiring any of the Collateral. Upon Lender's demand, Borrower agrees to assemble the Collateral at its usual place of business or at such other location as Lender may reasonably designate that is reasonably convenient to both parties, and make it available to Lender. To the extent that notice of sale is required by applicable law, Borrower agrees that notice given as provided herein, at least 10 days before the date of the proposed public sale or disposition or the date after which a private sale may be made, shall be deemed reasonable and shall fully satisfy any requirement of giving of notice. Lender may, at its option, dispose of the Collateral on credit terms, and, in such event, shall credit Borrower only with the amounts of cash proceeds actually received from time to time thereafter by Lender and applied to the Secured Obligations. Lender is hereby granted a license or other right to use during the continuance of an Event of Default, without charge, Borrower's labels, patents, copyrights, rights of use of any name, trade secrets, trade names, trademarks and advertising matter, or any tangible or intangible property or rights of a similar nature, as pertaining to the Collateral, in advertising for sale and selling any Collateral, and Borrower's rights under all licenses and all franchise agreements shall inure to Lender's benefit.

(b)   Borrower recognizes that, by reason of certain prohibitions contained in the Securities Act of 1933, as amended, and applicable state securities laws, Lender may be compelled, with respect to any sale of all or any part of the Collateral, to limit purchasers to those who will agree, among other things, to acquire the Collateral for their own account, for investment and not with a view to the distribution or resale thereof. Borrower acknowledges that any such private sales may be at prices and on terms less favorable to Borrower than those obtainable through a public sale without such restrictions, and that Lender shall have no obligation to engage in public sales and no obligation to delay the sale of any Collateral for the period of time necessary to permit the issuer thereof to register it for public sale.

(c)   Without limiting any rights or powers granted by this Agreement to Lender while no Event of Default has occurred and is continuing, Lender is hereby appointed the attorney-in-fact of Borrower for the purpose, upon the occurrence and during the continuance of any Event of Default, of carrying out the provisions of this Section 8 and taking any and all actions, and executing or otherwise authenticating any and all instruments or other records, that Lender may deem necessary or advisable to accomplish the purposes hereof, which appointment as attorney-in-fact is irrevocable and coupled with an interest. Without limiting the generality of the foregoing, so long as Lender shall be entitled under this Section 8 to make collections in respect of the Collateral, Lender shall have the right and power to receive, endorse and collect all checks made payable to the order of Borrower representing any payment or other distribution in respect of the Collateral or any part thereof and to give full discharge for the same.

9.   <u>General Authority</u>. Lender shall be under no obligation or duty to exercise any of the powers hereby conferred upon Lender, and shall have no liability for any act or failure to act in connection with any of the Collateral (including any diminution in the value of the Collateral from any cause whatsoever). Lender shall be under no duty to collect any amount that may be or become due on any of the Collateral, to redeem or realize on the Collateral, to make any presentments, demands or notices of protest in connection with any of the Collateral, to take any steps necessary to preserve rights in any instrument, contract or lease against third parties or to preserve rights against prior parties, to remove any liens or to do anything for the enforcement, collection or protection of the Collateral, except to the extent, if any, that the Uniform Commercial Code requires Lender to use reasonable care with respect to the Collateral while in its possession.

10.   <u>Borrower Waivers</u>.

(a)   Except as expressly provided herein, and to the fullest extent permitted by law, Borrower hereby waives presentment, demand and protest and notice of presentment, protest, default, non-payment, maturity, release, compromise, settlement, extension or renewal of any or all accounts, contract rights, documents, instruments, general intangibles, chattel paper and guaranties at any time held by Lender on which Borrower may in any way be liable and hereby ratifies and confirms whatever Lender may do in this regard; notice prior to taking possession or control of the Collateral or any bond or security that might be required by any court before allowing Lender to exercise any of Lender's remedies, and any right to require Lender to prepare the Collateral for sale; any marshalling of assets, or any right to compel Lender to resort first or in any particular order to any other collateral or other persons before enforcing its rights as to the Collateral or pursuing Borrower for payment of the Secured Obligations; the benefit of all valuation, appraisement and exemption laws; and any claims and defenses based on principles of suretyship or impairment of collateral.

(b)     Each of the waivers, consents and authorizations of Borrower set forth in the Guaranty shall apply to this Agreement as if set forth herein in full, *mutatis mutandis*.

11.     <u>General Provisions</u>.

(a)     <u>Notices</u>. All notices, approvals, and consents required or permitted to be given hereunder or under any other Related Document shall be in writing, and shall be deemed duly given or made (i) upon delivery or refusal of such delivery of such notice by a recognized courier service; (ii) upon personal delivery (which shall be deemed to have been given upon delivery); or (iii) upon delivery by fax machine capable of confirming receipt, and in each case addressed to the recipient at its address for notice set forth below its signature hereto (or at such other address for a party as shall be specified in a notice so given).

(b)     <u>Successors and Assigns</u>. Borrower shall not assign its rights or delegate its duties under this Agreement. Borrower's covenants and agreements herein shall bind Borrower's successors and assigns, and those who become bound to this Agreement, and shall inure to the benefit of Lender and its successors and assigns. Lender may assign the Secured Obligations to one or more assignees. As to any such assignee, Borrower waives and will not assert any claims, setoffs, recoupments or defenses that Borrower may have against Lender.

(c)     <u>Amendments and Waivers</u>. This Agreement may not be modified or amended except in writing signed by Borrower and Lender, and none of its provisions may be waived except in writing signed by Lender. No waivers shall be implied, whether from any custom or course of dealing or any delay or failure in Lender's exercise of its rights and remedies hereunder or otherwise. Any waiver granted by Lender shall not obligate Lender to grant any further, similar, or other waivers.

(d)     <u>Remedies</u>. All remedies provided to Lender herein are cumulative, in addition to all other remedies available to Lender under this Agreement or any other agreement, at law or in equity or otherwise, and the exercise or partial exercise of any such right or remedy shall not preclude the exercise of any other right or remedy.

(e)     <u>Construction</u>. Terms used in the singular shall apply to the plural, and vice versa, as the context requires; likewise, masculine, feminine and neuter genders shall be interchangeable as the context requires. Except where the context requires otherwise, the use of the disjunctive term "or" does not imply an exclusion of the conjunctive, i.e., "or" shall have the same meaning as the expression "and/or." "Including" shall not be limiting. Headings and section titles are for convenience of reference only and shall not be given effect in construing the provisions of this Agreement. References in a Related Document to a section, schedule, or exhibit, unless otherwise specified, mean a section, schedule or exhibit of or to that Related Document. Each reference to a Related Document or any other agreement or record shall mean such Related Document or other agreement or record as from time to time extended, modified, renewed, restated, reaffirmed, supplemented or amended. Unless otherwise provided, all references to statutes and related regulations shall include any amendments thereof and any successor statutes and regulations.

(**f**)  <u>Severability</u>. This Agreement is severable, and the invalidity of any provision shall not affect any other provision hereof.

(**g**)  <u>Counterparts</u>. This Agreement may be signed in counterparts, each of which shall be deemed an original, but all of which, taken together, shall constitute one and the same instrument, with the same force and effect as though each of the parties executed the same document.

(**h**)  <u>Governing Law</u>. This Agreement shall be construed according to and governed by the internal laws of the State of _____, without regard to principles of conflicts of law that would result in the application of the law of any other jurisdiction, except to the extent that any unwaivable provision of the internal laws of the State of _____ provides that the law of another jurisdiction shall apply.

(**i**)  <u>Entire Agreement</u>. This Agreement represents the entire agreement between Lender and Borrower with respect to the subject matter hereof, superseding any and all other agreements, promises or representations.

ENTERED INTO as of the date first written above.

BORROWER:                                              LENDER:

_____,      _____, a
a _____ corporation                     _____

By:                                                           By:

_____      _____

Name:                                                     Name:
Title:                                                       Title:
Address for Notices:                              Address for Notices:

_____      _____

_____      _____

_____      _____

Attn: _____                                 Attn: _____
Phone: _____                              Phone: _____
Fax: _____                                   Fax: _____
Email: _____                               Email: _____

## Exhibit A
## Collateral

All personal property and fixtures of Borrower whether now existing or hereafter created or acquired, and wherever located, including, but not limited to:

(a)    all accounts, chattel paper (including tangible and electronic chattel paper), commercial tort claims, deposit accounts, documents (including negotiable documents), equipment (including all accessions and additions thereto), general intangibles (including payment intangibles and software), goods (including fixtures), instruments (including promissory notes), inventory (including all goods held for sale or lease or to be furnished under a contract of service, and including returns and repossessions), investment property (including securities and securities entitlements), letter of credit rights, letters of credit, and money, and all of Borrower's books and records with respect to any of the foregoing, and the computers and equipment containing said books and records; and

(b)    any and all cash proceeds and/or noncash proceeds of any of the foregoing, including, without limitation, insurance proceeds, and all supporting obligations and the security therefor or for any right to payment.

All terms above have the meanings given to them in the _____ Uniform Commercial Code, as amended or supplemented from time to time.

# Appendix C

# Continuing Personal Guaranty

THIS CONTINUING PERSONAL GUARANTY ("Guaranty"), dated as of _____, is made by ("Guarantor") in favor of _____ ("Lender").

RECITALS

This Guaranty is executed in connection with that certain Revolving Loan Note ("Note") in the original principal amount of ___ and 00/100 Dollars ($ ___ 00), (the loan evidenced thereby, the "Loan") executed by _____, a _____ corporation ("Borrower"), to the order of Lender, and that certain Security Agreement ("Security Agreement") by and between Lender and Borrower, of even date herewith. The terms and provisions of the Note and Security Agreement are incorporated herein by reference.

*A.* As a condition of Lender's willingness to enter into the Security Agreement and make the Loan, Guarantor is required, and has agreed, to make this Guaranty in favor of Lender.

*B.* Guarantor expects to realize direct and indirect benefits as the result of the Loan and Security Agreement, and as a result of the execution of this Guaranty. The execution of this Guaranty is in the best interests of Guarantor.

DEFINITIONS

1. All capitalized terms not otherwise defined herein have the meanings defined for them in the Note or the Security Agreement, as the case may be.

2. "Event of Default" means any "Event of Default" under or as defined in either the Note or the Security Agreement.

3. "Guaranteed Obligations" means any and all present and future obligations of any type or nature of Borrower to Lender arising under or related to the Loan Documents, whether due or to become due, matured or unmatured, liquidated or unliquidated, or contingent or non- contingent, including obligations of performance as well as obligations of payment, including interest and other amounts that accrue after the commencement of any bankruptcy or insolvency proceeding by or against Borrower.

4. "Guaranty" means this Continuing Personal Guaranty, and any extensions, modifications, renewals, restatements, reaffirmations, supplements or amendments hereto or hereof.

5. "Loan Documents" means, individually and collectively, this Guaranty, the Note, the Security Agreement and any and all other guaranties, security agreements and other contracts, instruments, addenda and documents executed in connection with the Loan that is the subject of the Note; Security Agreement, or this Guaranty, including, without limitation, all amendments, modifications, supplements, increases, decreases, restatements, renewals or extensions of any of them, whether such amendments, modifications, supplements, restatements, renewals or extensions are evidenced by new or additional instruments, documents or agreements or change the rate of interest on any

obligation or the security therefor, if any, and whether or not such amendments, modifications, supplements, increases, decreases, restatements, renewals or extensions occur before or after any actual or purported termination, repudiation or revocation of this Guaranty by Guarantor or any of them.

AGREEMENT

NOW, THEREFORE, in order to induce Lender to make the Loan and enter into the Security Agreement, and for other good and valuable consideration, the receipt and adequacy of which hereby is acknowledged, Guarantor hereby represents, warrants, covenants, agrees and guarantees as follows:

1.    Recitals. The recitals set forth hereinabove are not merely recitals but rather form an integral part of this Guaranty, and such recitals are incorporated herein by reference.

2.    Guaranty of Guaranteed Obligations. Guarantor hereby unconditionally. Guarantees and promises to pay and perform promptly the Guaranteed Obligations. Guarantor hereby acknowledges and agrees that, if the Guaranteed Obligations are guaranteed by more than one Guarantor, Guarantor's obligations with respect to the Guaranteed Obligations shall be joint and several.

3.    Nature of Guaranty. This Guaranty is irrevocable and continuing in nature and relates to any Guaranteed Obligations now existing or hereafter arising. Guarantor expressly waives any right to terminate, repudiate, revoke or rescind this Guaranty so long as any portion of the Guaranteed Obligations remain outstanding. This Guaranty is a guaranty of prompt and punctual payment and performance and is not merely a guaranty of collection.

4.    Relationship to Other Agreements. Nothing herein shall in any way modify or limit the effect of terms or conditions set forth (a) in any other document, instrument or agreement executed by Guarantor, whether or not in connection with the Guaranteed Obligations (including, but not limited to, any other guaranty executed by Guarantor for the benefit of Lender), or (b) in any other Loan Document, but each and every term and condition hereof shall be in addition thereto. Any provision contained in any Loan Document that applies to Loan Documents generally is fully applicable to this Guaranty and is incorporated herein by this reference.

5.    Statute of Limitations and Other Laws. Until the Guaranteed Obligations shall have been irrevocably paid and performed in full, all of the rights, privileges, powers and remedies granted to Lender hereunder shall continue to exist and may be exercised by Lender at any time and from time to time, 'irrespective of the fact that any of the Guaranteed Obligations may have become barred by any statute of limitations. Guarantor expressly waives the benefit of any and all statutes of limitation, and any and all laws providing for exemption of property from execution. Guarantor agrees that the performance of any act or payment that tolls any statute of limitations applicable to the Guaranteed Obligations shall similarly operate to toll any statute of limitations applicable to Guarantor's liability hereunder.

6.    Rights Upon Default. Lender shall be entitled to payment or performance hereunder, with or without demand therefor, at any time upon the occurrence and during the continuation of an Event of Default, or an event that, with the giving of notice or the passage of time, or both, would constitute an Event of Default, at which time Lender may enforce this Guaranty independently of any other remedy or security Lender at any time may have or hold in connection with the Guaranteed Obligations, and it shall not be necessary for Lender to marshal assets in favor of Borrower, Guarantor or any other guarantor, person or entity or to proceed upon or against and/or exhaust any security or remedy before proceeding to enforce this Guaranty. If any bankruptcy or reorganization

proceeding is commenced with respect to Borrower, the entire amount of the Guaranteed Obligations shall, for purposes of this Guaranty, be deemed to have become due and payable in full. Guarantor expressly waives any right to require Lender to marshal assets in favor of Borrower, Guarantor or any other guarantor, person or entity or to proceed against Borrower or any other guarantor or any collateral provided by any person or entity, and agrees that Lender may proceed against Guarantor, any other guarantor or any collateral in such order as it shall determine in its sole and absolute discretion. Lender may file a separate action or actions against Borrower, Guarantor or any other guarantor, whether action is brought or prosecuted with respect to any security or against any other person or entity, or whether any other person or entity is joined in any such action or actions. Guarantor agrees that Lender and Borrower may deal with each other in connection with the Guaranteed Obligations or otherwise, or alter any contracts or agreements now or hereafter existing between them, in any manner whatsoever, without notice to Guarantor, all without in any way altering or affecting the continuing efficacy and security of this Guaranty. Lender's rights hereunder shall be reinstated and revived, and the enforceability of this Guaranty shall continue, with respect to any amount at any time paid on account of the Guaranteed Obligations which thereafter shall be required to be restored or returned by Lender upon the bankruptcy, insolvency or reorganization of Borrower, Guarantor or any other person or entity, all as though such amount had not been paid. The rights of Lender created or granted herein and the enforceability of this Guaranty at all times shall remain effective to guarantee the full amount of all the Guaranteed Obligations even though the Guaranteed Obligations, including any part thereof or any other security or guaranty therefor, may be or hereafter may become invalid or otherwise unenforceable as against Borrower or Guarantor and whether or not Borrower or Guarantor shall have any personal liability with respect thereto. Guarantor hereby expressly acknowledges that the Guaranteed Obligations arise under a Security, and further understands and acknowledges that the obligations under the Note and Security Agreement may reoccur as a result of Borrower making partial or complete repayments and re-borrowing against the line of credit limit as set forth in the Note and Security Agreement.

7. <u>Waivers and Consents.</u> (a) Guarantor acknowledges that the obligations of Guarantor undertaken herein involve the guarantee of obligations of persons and/or entities other than Guarantor: and, in full recognition of that fact, Guarantor consents and agrees that Lender may, at any time and from time to time, without notice or demand (except as otherwise herein provided), whether before or after any actual or purported termination, repudiation or revocation of this Guaranty by Guarantor, and without affecting the enforceability or continuing effectiveness hereof as to Guarantor: (i) supplement, restate, modify, amend, increase, decrease, extend, renew, accelerate or otherwise change the time for payment or the terms of the Guaranteed Obligations or any part thereof including any increase or decrease of the rate(s) of interest thereon; (ii) supplement, restate, modify, amend, increase, decrease, or waive, or enter into or give any agreement, approval or consent with respect to, the Guaranteed Obligations or any part thereof, or any additional security or guaranties, or any condition, covenant, default, remedy, right, representation or term thereof or thereunder; (iii) accept new or additional instruments, documents or agreements in exchange for or relative to any of the Loan Documents or the Guaranteed Obligations or any part thereof; (iv) accept partial payments on the Guaranteed Obligations; (v) receive and hold additional security or guaranties for the Guaranteed Obligations or any part thereof; (vi) release, reconvey, terminate, waive, abandon, fail to perfect, subordinate, exchange, substitute, transfer and/or enforce any security or guaranties, in whole or in part, and apply any security and direct the order or manner of sale thereof as

Lender in its sole and absolute discretion may determine; (vii) release any other person or entity from any personal liability with respect to the Guaranteed Obligations or any part thereof; (viii) settle, release on terms satisfactory to Lender or by operation of applicable laws or otherwise liquidate or enforce any Guaranteed Obligations and any security or guaranty in any manner, consent to the transfer of any security and bid and purchase at any sale; and/or (ix) consent to the merger, change or any other restructuring or termination of the corporate or partnership existence of Borrower or Guarantor or any other guarantor, person or entity, and correspondingly restructure the Guaranteed Obligations, and any such merger, change, restructuring or termination shall not affect the liability of Guarantor or the continuing effectiveness hereof, or the enforceability hereof with respect to all or any part of the Guaranteed Obligations. (b) Guarantor expressly waives any and all defenses now or hereafter arising or asserted by reason of (i) any disability or other defense of Borrower or any other person or entity with respect to the Guaranteed Obligations or the application by Borrower of the proceeds of the Loan for purposes other than the purposes represented by Borrower to Lender or intended or understood by Lender or Guarantor; (ii) the unenforceability or invalidity of any security or guaranty for the Guaranteed Obligations or the lack of perfection or continuing perfection or failure of priority of any security for the Guaranteed Obligations; (iii) the cessation for any cause whatsoever of the liability of Borrower or any other person or entity (other than by reason of the full payment and performance of all Guaranteed Obligations); (iv) any failure of Lender to marshal assets in favor of Guarantor or any other person or entity; (v) any failure of Lender to give notice of sale or other disposition of collateral to Guarantor or any other person or entity, or any defect in any notice that may be given in connection with any such sale or disposition; (vi) any failure of Lender to comply with applicable laws in connection with the sale or other disposition of any collateral or other security for any Guaranteed Obligation; (vii) any act or omission of Lender or others that directly or indirectly results in or aids the discharge or release of any of Borrower, Guarantor or any other person or entity or the Guaranteed Obligations or any other security or guaranty therefor; by operation of law or otherwise; (viii) any law which provides that the obligation of a surety or guarantor must neither be larger in amount nor in other respects more burdensome than that of the principal or which reduces a surety's or guarantor's 'obligation in proportion to the principal obligation; (ix) any failure of Lender to file or enforce a claim in any bankruptcy or other proceeding with respect to any person or entity; (x) the election by Lender, in any bankruptcy proceeding of any person or entity, of the application or non-application of Section 1111(b)(2) of the United States Bankruptcy Code; (xi) any extension of credit or the grant of any lien under Section 364 of the United States Bankruptcy Code; (xii) any use of cash collateral under Section 363 of the United States Bankruptcy Code; (xiii) any agreement or stipulation with respect to the provision of adequate protection in any bankruptcy proceeding of any person or entity; (xiv) the avoidance of any lien in favor of Lender for any reason; or (xv) any bankruptcy, insolvency, reorganization, arrangement, readjustment of debt, liquidation or dissolution proceeding commenced by or against any person or entity, including any discharge of, or bar or stay against collecting, all or any of the Guaranteed Obligations (or any interest thereon) in or as a result of any such proceeding. Until no part of any commitment to lend remains outstanding and all of the Guaranteed Obligations have been paid and performed in full, Guarantor shall have no right of subrogation, contribution, reimbursement or indemnity, and Guarantor expressly waives any right to enforce any remedy that Lender now has or hereafter may have against any other person or entity and waives the benefit of, or any right to participate in, any other security now or hereafter held by Lender. Guarantor expressly waives all setoffs and counterclaims and all presentments, demands for payment or performance, notices of nonpayment or nonperformance, protests, notices of protest, notices of dishonor and all other 'notices or demands of any kind or nature whatsoever with respect to the Guaranteed Obligations, and all notices of acceptance of this Guaranty or of the existence, creation or incurring of new or additional Guaranteed Obligations.

8. <u>Additional Waivers of Rights and Defenses.</u> Without limiting the generality of the immediately preceding paragraph 7:

(a) Guarantor hereby expressly, unconditionally and irrevocably waives, subject only to the provisions of the preceding paragraph 7(b) with respect to Guarantor's rights of subrogation, contribution, reimbursement and indemnity, any and all rights and defenses that are or may become available to Guarantor by reason of Sections 2787 to 2855, inclusive, 2899 or 3433 of the California Civil Code.

(b) Guarantor hereby expressly, unconditionally and irrevocably waives (i) any and all rights and defenses that are or may become available to Guarantor by reason of any election of remedies by Lender, and (ii) any and all rights or defenses that are or may become available to Guarantor because all or any portion of the Guaranteed Obligations now, or at any time hereafter, are secured by real property or an estate for years, including, without limitation, rights or defenses based upon, directly or indirectly, the application of Section 580a, 580b, 580d or 726 of the California Code of Civil Procedure. This means, among other things, that (1) Lender may collect from Guarantor without first foreclosing on any real or personal property pledged by Borrower or any other person or entity, and (2) if Lender forecloses on any real property collateral pledged by Borrower or any other person or entity: (A) the amount of the Guaranteed Obligations may be reduced only by the price for which the collateral is sold at the foreclosure sale, even if the collateral is worth more than the sale price; and (B) Lender may collect from Guarantor even if. Lender, by foreclosing on the real property collateral, has destroyed any right Guarantor may have to collect from Borrower or any other person or entity.

9. <u>Condition of Borrower.</u> Guarantor represents and warrants to Lender that Guarantor has established adequate means of obtaining from Borrower, on a continuing basis, financial and other information pertaining to the businesses, operations and condition (financial and otherwise) of Borrower and its assets, and Guarantor now is and hereafter will be completely familiar with the businesses, operations and condition (financial and otherwise) of Borrower and its assets. Guarantor hereby expressly waives and relinquishes any duty on the part of Lender (should any such duty exist) to disclose to Guarantor any matter, fact or thing related to the businesses, operations or condition (financial or otherwise) of Borrower or its assets, whether now known or hereafter known by Lender during the life of this Guaranty. With respect to any of the Guaranteed Obligations, Lender need not inquire into the powers of Borrower, Guarantor or the officers or employees acting or purporting to act on their respective behalf, and all Guaranteed Obligations made or created in good faith reliance upon any such professed exercise of such powers shall be guaranteed hereby.

10. <u>Additional Covenants of Guarantor.</u>

(a) Guarantor shall at all times [remain the sole shareholder in Borrower][maintain the interest in Borrower reflected on Schedule T to the Line of Credit Agreement].

(b) Guarantor shall not sell, lease, assign, encumber, hypothecate, transfer or otherwise dispose of all or substantially all of Guarantor's assets, or agree to do so, except with Lender's prior written consent.

11. <u>Subordination.</u>

(a)    (i)    All existing or future obligations owed to Guarantor by Borrower or any other person or entity liable in respect of all or any portion of the Guaranteed Obligations (collectively, whether for principal, interest, fees or any other amount, "Subordinated Indebtedness"), and any security interest, lien or other encumbrance, of any nature whatsoever, securing all or any portion of such Subordinated Indebtedness, are hereby subordinated, respectively, to all Guaranteed Obligations and to the obligations of such other person or entity under any Loan Document ("Third Party Obligations") and to the security interests and liens in favor of Lender. Until all commitments of Lender to extend credit under the Loan Documents have been terminated and all Guaranteed Obligations have been paid in full in cash, except with Lender's prior written consent: (A) no payment in respect of any Subordinated Indebtedness shall be demanded, created or accepted by or for the benefit of Guarantor; and (B) no security interest, lien or other encumbrance securing the payment or performance of any Subordinated Indebtedness shall be demanded, created or accepted by or for the benefit of Guarantor. If any amount is received by Guarantor in respect of any Subordinated Indebtedness in violation of the foregoing prohibition, Guarantor shall receive such amount as the property of, and as trustee for, Lender, and shall pay such amount over to Lender on account of the Guaranteed Obligations (or Third Party Obligations, as the case may be) in exactly the form received, together with any required endorsement or assignment of Guarantor, but without reducing or affecting in any manner the liability of Guarantor under the other provisions of this Guaranty.

(ii)    In the event of any insolvency of Borrower or any other person or entity liable in respect of all or any portion of the Guaranteed Obligations, or of any distribution, division or application, whether partial or complete, voluntary or involuntary, by operation of law or otherwise, of all or any part of the assets (or proceeds of assets) of any person or entity obligated in respect of Subordinated Indebtedness, the Guaranteed Obligations and Third Party Obligations shall be paid in full, in cash, before any payment is made on such Subordinated Indebtedness, and all dividends, payments and other distributions of any nature whatsoever, whether in cash or in other property, that would otherwise be payable or deliverable upon or in respect of the Subordinated Indebtedness shall be paid over or delivered directly to Lender, for application to the Guaranteed Obligations and Third Party Obligations, until they have been paid in full.

(b)    The subordination provided for herein shall apply to all Subordinated Indebtedness and to all Guaranteed Obligations and Third Party Obligations, in each case, whether in respect of principal, interest, fees, charges, indemnity obligations or constituting a payment obligation of any other nature whatsoever, and whether accrued before or after the commencement of any bankruptcy, insolvency or reorganization proceeding in respect of Borrower or any other person or entity obligated in respect of any Subordinated Indebtedness.

(c)    All existing or future Subordinated Indebtedness owed to Guarantor is hereby assigned to Lender by Guarantor as security for the Guaranteed Obligations and Third Party Obligations, and, if requested by Lender during the continuance of any Event of Default, shall be collected and received by Guarantor as trustee for

Lender and paid over to Lender, on account of the Guaranteed Obligations or Third Party Obligations, as Lender may elect, but without reducing or affecting in any manner the liability of Guarantor under the other provisions of this Guaranty. All notes now or hereafter evidencing Subordinated Indebtedness shall be marked with a legend that they are subject to the security interest created by, and the other provisions of, this Guaranty and, if Lender so requests, shall be delivered to Lender, endorsed in blank. In addition, Guarantor shall, upon request, provide Lender with access to and copies of Guarantor's records that pertain to the Subordinated Indebtedness and shall execute such instruments as may be required by Lender to enable it to enforce all claims of Guarantor in respect of such Subordinated Indebtedness and to collect all dividends, payments or other disbursements that may be made on account thereof. For such purposes, Guarantor hereby irrevocably authorizes Lender, in its discretion, to make and present for or on behalf of Guarantor such proofs of claim on account of Subordinated Indebtedness as Lender may deem expedient or proper, to vote such claims in any bankruptcy, insolvency or reorganization proceeding, to receive and collect any and all dividends, payments or other disbursements made thereon, in whatever form, and to apply such dividends, payments or other disbursements to the Obligations or Third Party Obligations, as Lender may elect.

(d) Guarantor hereby acknowledges and agrees that, until all commitments of Lender to extend credit under the Loan Documents have been terminated and all Guaranteed Obligations have been paid in full in cash, under no circumstances shall it be entitled to be subrogated to any rights of Lender in respect of the Guaranteed Obligations performed by it hereunder or otherwise, and Guarantor hereby expressly and irrevocably waives, until all commitments of Lender to extend credit under the Loan Documents have been terminated and all Guaranteed Obligations have been paid in full in cash, each and every such right of subrogation and any claims, reimbursements, right or right of action relating thereto (whether arising by contract or operation of law or otherwise by reason of Guarantor's execution, delivery or performance of this Guaranty).

12. <u>Guaranty Enforceable; Other Representations.</u>

(a) This Guaranty is a legally valid and binding obligation of Guarantor, enforceable in accordance with its terms. The execution and delivery of this Guaranty by Guarantor and the performance by Guarantor of its obligations hereunder have not and will not constitute a default or breach under any agreement, court order, judgment or law by or under which Guarantor is bound or may be affected.

(b) Guarantor's personal financial statements that have been delivered to Lender fairly and accurately reflect Guarantor's financial condition as of the date of their submission to Lender, and, since the most recently submitted financial statements, there has been no material adverse change in Guarantor's financial condition or business. Except for such defaults as have been waived pursuant to waivers that are in full force and effect, Guarantor is not in default under the terms of any contract or agreement to which Guarantor is a party relating to any loan, borrowing or other indebtedness or any other contract or agreement to which Guarantor is a party, the result of which could reasonably be expected to have a material adverse effect on the financial condition or business of Guarantor, or upon Guarantor's ability to perform any of its obligations under this Guaranty or any other Loan Document to which Guarantor is a party.

(c)   Guarantor is solvent, and will not be rendered insolvent by Guarantor's incurrence of Guarantor's obligations hereunder.

(d)   Guarantor has not heretofore sold, leased, assigned, encumbered, hypothecated, transferred or otherwise disposed of all or substantially all of Guarantor's assets.

13.   <u>Setoff.</u> In addition to any rights now or hereafter granted under applicable law and not by way of limitation of any such rights, Lender is hereby authorized by Guarantor at any time and from time to time, upon the occurrence of an uncured Event of Default and during. the continuation of such uncured Event of Default, without notice to Guarantor or to any other person or entity, any such notice being hereby expressly waived to the extent it may lawfully be so waived, to set off or to apply any and all indebtedness at any time owing by Lender to or for the credit or the account of Guarantor or Borrower, against and on account of the Guaranteed Obligations, irrespective of whether Lender shall have made any demand under this Guaranty. No lien or right of setoff shall be deemed to have been waived by any act or conduct on the part of Lender, or by any neglect to exercise such right of setoff or to enforce any lien created by such right of setoff, or by any delay in so doing, and every right of setoff and lien shall continue in full force and effect until such right of setoff or lien is specifically waived or released by an instrument in writing executed by Lender.

14.   <u>Understandings With Respect to Rights upon Default; Waivers and Consents.</u> Guarantor warrants and agrees that each of the waivers and consents set forth herein is made after opportunity for consultation with independent legal counsel selected by Guarantor and with full knowledge of its significance and consequences, with the understanding that events giving rise to any defense or right waived may diminish, destroy or otherwise adversely affect rights that Guarantor otherwise may have against Borrower, Lender or others, or against or with respect to any collateral or security. If any of the waivers or consents herein are determined to be contrary to any applicable law or public policy, such waivers and consents shall be effective to the maximum extent permitted by law.

15.   <u>Release of Guarantor.</u> Except as otherwise provided below, this Guaranty and all obligations of Guarantor hereunder shall be released when all obligations of Borrower and Guarantor under each Loan Document have been paid in full in cash or otherwise performed in full, and when no portion of any commitment of Lender to Borrower under any Loan Document remains outstanding. Upon such release of Guarantor's obligations hereunder, and except as otherwise provided below, Lender shall endorse, execute, deliver, record and file all instruments and documents, and do all other acts and things, reasonably required to evidence or document the release of Lender's rights arising under this Guaranty, all as reasonably requested by, and at the sole expense of, Guarantor. Notwithstanding anything to the contrary in this paragraph, the rights of Guarantor provided for herein are subject to the revival and reinstatement provisions set forth herein, and Lender shall not be required to cancel or surrender this Guaranty until all applicable periods of limitation have expired for the avoidance of any transfers to Lender under any of the Loan Documents.

16.   <u>Construction of this Guaranty.</u> This Guaranty is intended to give rise to absolute and unconditional obligations of Guarantor; hence, in any construction hereof, notwithstanding any provision of any Loan Document to the contrary, this Guaranty shall be construed strictly in favor of Lender in order to accomplish its stated purpose.

17.   <u>Cumulative Remedies; No Waiver.</u> The rights, powers, privileges and remedies of Lender provided herein or in any other Loan Document are cumulative and not exclusive

of any right, power, privilege or remedy provided by law or equity. No failure or delay on the part of Lender in exercising any right, power, privilege or remedy may be, or may be deemed to be, a waiver thereof, nor may any single or partial exercise of any right, power, privilege or remedy preclude any other or further exercise of the same or any other right, power, privilege or remedy.

18.    Assignments; Secondary Market Transactions. This Guaranty shall be binding upon and inure to the benefit of Guarantor and Lender and their respective successors and assigns; provided, however, that Guarantor may not assign or transfer Guarantor's rights or obligations hereunder except with Lender's prior written consent. Lender reserves the right to sell, assign, transfer, negotiate or grant participations in all or any part of, or any interest in, Lender's rights and obligations under the Security Agreement, the Note and/or any other Loan Document (including, in connection with any such transaction involving the Guaranteed Obligations, all or any part of, or any interest in, this Guaranty as it relates to the Guaranteed Obligations subject to such transaction). In that connection, Lender may disclose all documents and information that Lender may now or hereafter have relating to the Guaranteed Obligations, this Guaranty or Guarantor.

Without limiting the generality of the foregoing, Guarantor acknowledges that Lender and its successors and assigns may enter into one or more Secondary Market Transactions, as contemplated by the Security Agreement. Guarantor shall, at Lender's expense, cooperate in good faith with Lender in effecting any such Secondary Market Transaction and shall cooperate in good faith to implement all requirements reasonably imposed by the participants involved in any Secondary. Market Transaction (including, without limitation, a rating agency and/or an institutional purchaser, participant or investor), to the same extent as provided in the Security Agreement with respect to Borrower.

19.    Governing Law; Jurisdiction and Venue; Arbitration. This Guaranty shall be deemed to be executed and delivered in the State of California. Each of Guarantor and Lender (i) agrees that this Guaranty shall be construed according to and governed by the laws of the State of California, without regard to principles of conflicts of law other than California Civil Code Section 1646.5, (ii) consents to personal jurisdiction in the State of California, and (iii) consents to venue in Los Angeles County, California, for all actions and proceedings with respect to this Guaranty and the Loan Documents, and waives any right it may have to assert the doctrine of forum non convenience or to object to venue to the extent any proceeding is brought in accordance with this, paragraph 19.

20.    WAIVER OF RIGHT TO TRIAL BY JURY. GUARANTOR AND Lender HEREBY WAIVE THE RIGHT TO TRIAL BY JURY IN ANY ACTION, PROCEEDING OR COUNTERCLAIM, WHETHER IN CONTRACT, TORT OR OTHERWISE, RELATING DIRECTLY OR INDIRECTLY TO THIS GUARANTY OR ANY OTHER LOAN DOCUMENT OR ANY ACTS OR OMISSIONS OF Lender OR GUARANTOR OR THEIR RESPECTIVE OFFICERS, DIRECTORS, EMPLOYEES, AGENTS, PARENTS SUBSIDIARIES OR AFFILIATES.

21.    Severability of Provisions. Any provision in this Guaranty that is held to be inoperative; unenforceable or invalid as to any party or in any jurisdiction shall, as to that party or jurisdiction, be inoperative, unenforceable or invalid without affecting the remaining provisions or the operation, enforceability or validity of that provision as to any other party or in any other jurisdiction, and to this end the provisions of this Guaranty are declared to be severable and shall be enforced to the fullest extent permitted by applicable law.

22.     Use of Terms; Headings. Terms used in the singular shall apply to the plural, and vice versa, as the context requires; likewise masculine, feminine and neuter genders shall be interchangeable as the context requires. The use of the disjunctive term "or" does not imply an exclusion of the conjunctive, i.e., "or" shall have the same meaning as the expression "and/or." "Including" shall not be limiting. Headings and section titles are for convenience of reference only and are not substantive parts of this Guaranty, and shall not be given effect in construing the provisions of this Guaranty. Each reference to a Loan Document shall mean such Loan Document as from time to time extended, modified, renewed, restated, reaffirmed, supplemented or amended.

23.     Time of the Essence. Time is of the essence of the obligations and agreements of Guarantor set forth herein.

24.     Costs and Expenses. Guarantor agrees to pay to Lender immediately upon demand all costs and expenses (including, without limitation, attorneys' fees and disbursements) incurred by Lender in connection with or incidental to the workout, enforcement or attempted enforcement of this Guaranty or the protection of Lender's interests hereunder, whether or not an action is filed in connection therewith, and in connection with or incidental to the workout, enforcement or attempted enforcement, of any waiver or amendment of any term or provision hereof. All advances, charges, costs and expenses, including attorneys', expert witnesses' and consultants' fees and disbursements, incurred or paid by Lender in exercising any right, privilege, power or remedy conferred by, or in protecting Lender's interests under, this Guaranty, in the amendment (including any waiver of or consent to any departure from, any provision hereof), workout, enforcement or attempted enforcement thereof (including the enforcement of any judgment and all costs of appeal), or if Borrower or any other party purporting to hold an interest in the property securing all or any portion of the Guaranteed Obligations, or Guarantor or any other guarantor of all or any portion of the Guaranteed Obligations, becomes subject to a proceeding under the provisions of the United States Bankruptcy Code or the California Probate Code or any law having similar effect, shall be subject hereto, shall become a part of the Guaranteed Obligations and shall be paid to Lender by Guarantor, immediately upon demand, together with interest thereon from the date of demand until paid at the Default Interest Rate provided for under the Line of Credit Agreement and Note.

> Telephone: (  ) _____
> Facsimile: (  ) _____

> Any notice, request, demand, direction or other communication to Lender shall be sent to Lender at:

> Telephone: ( ) _____
> Facsimile: ( ) _____

IN WITNESS WHEREOF, Guarantor, as a continuing guarantor, has executed this Guaranty as of the date first, written above.

> "GUARANTOR"

> _____

> Printed Name:

# Appendix D

# Lock Box Agreement

This Agreement ("Agreement") is executed as of _____ [*Date*], between _____, a _____ corporation ("Lender"), _____, a _____ limited partnership ("Borrower"), and _____, a _____ (*"Manager"*), with reference to the following facts:

A. Lender has made a loan to Borrower evidenced by that certain Note (the "Note") dated as of _____ in the principal amount of secured by a Security Agreement dated _____[*Date*] (the "Security Agreement"), executed by the Borrower, as debtor to Lender as secured party, encumbering certain accounts and other personal property (collectively, the "Collateral.")

B. The parties now wish to enter into this agreement to set forth certain agreements of the parties regarding the collection and use of revenues received with respect to the Collateral.

In consideration of the foregoing and for other good and valuable consideration, the receipt and sufficiency of which is acknowledged here, the parties here agree as follows:

1. All proceeds received with respect to the Collateral ("Receipts") shall be collected by Borrower and Borrower shall immediately deposit all Receipts in the Account, as defined below.

2. Assignment. Borrower, to secure its obligations under the Note and Security Agreement (collectively, the "Secured Obligations"), does grant to Lender a security interest in, and assign and transfer to and pledge with Lender all right, title, and interest (whether legal, equitable or beneficial) of Borrower in and to the security described below (collectively, the "Account Collateral"):

Account No. _____ (*the "Account"*) with or payable by _____ Bank (the "Bank") at its office at _____, in the name of Borrower, including all sums now or at any time hereafter on deposit in the Account and all sums due or to become due on the Account (including interest), and any proceeds of and replacements of the Account.

3. Withdrawals.

(a). Before Default. Before the occurrence of an Event of Default (as defined in the Security Agreement, withdrawals or disbursements of funds in the Account shall only be used as follows: (i) Borrower shall on the first day of each month pay to the Lender on the first of each month an amount equal to payments due under the Note; (ii) the remainder, less an appropriate reserve approved by Lender, shall on the first day of each calendar quarter be paid to Borrower.

(b). After Default. Upon the occurrence of an Event of Default, Lender may give notice of the Event of Default to Bank and thereafter withdrawals or disbursements from the account may be made only by Lender.

4. Financial Reporting. (intentionally omitted)

5. Power of Attorney. Borrower constitutes and irrevocably appoints Lender the true and lawful attorney of Borrower, with full power of substitution, to ask, demand, collect, receive, or receipt for any and all amounts which may be or become due and payable under the Account, to execute any and all checks, drafts, withdrawal statements, receipts, or other orders for the payment of money drawn on the Account, and to endorse the name of Borrower on all commercial paper given in payment or in part payment, and in its discretion to file any claim or take any other action or proceeding, either in its own name or in the name of Borrower or otherwise, which Lender may deem necessary or appropriate to protect and preserve the security interest of Lender under this Agreement.

6. Remedies. Upon the occurrence of an Event of Default, Lender may at any time and from time to time and without demand or notice, withdraw and receive the Account Collateral up to the outstanding amount of the Secured Obligations, and apply the proceeds (including any interest) to the Secured Obligations. If there is a deficiency, Borrower covenants and agrees promptly to pay the same to Lender. Borrower acknowledges that the Account is a deposit account denominated in dollars and that a sale of it is unnecessary to establish or realize upon the value of it. Borrower agrees that the disposition of the Account Collateral as set forth above is a commercially reasonable disposition of the Account Collateral and waives any rights it may have to receive notice of any such withdrawals or disbursements or to require a sale of the Account at a public or private sale.

7. Waivers. Borrower waives any right to require Lender to (a) make or give any presentment, demands for performances, notices of nonperformance, protests, notices of protest, or notices of dishonor in connection with the Secured Obligations or the withdrawal of the Account Collateral, (b) proceed against or exhaust any other collateral, or (c) pursue any other remedy in Lender's power.

8. Termination. This Agreement shall remain in full force and effect until all Secured Obligations are indefeasibly satisfied in full.

9. Representation and Covenants. Borrower represents, warrants, and covenants that ownership of the Account Collateral is free and clear of all liens and encumbrances of any nature whatsoever and shall remain so during the term of this Agreement. Borrower will not attempt to withdraw the Account Collateral and will not attempt to amend or supplement the instructions to the Bank set forth in this Agreement and in the Notice of Security Interest without the prior written consent of Lender.

10. Further Assurances. Borrower shall execute and deliver such further assignments, notices, and other documents as Lender may reasonably require from time to time to better assure, assign, and transfer to Lender the rights now or hereafter intended to be granted to Lender under this Agreement for carrying out the intention of facilitating the performance of the terms of this Assignment.

11. Costs and Expenses. All costs and expenses, including reasonable attorneys' fees, incurred or paid by Lender in exercising any right, power, or remedy conferred by this Agreement or in the enforcement thereof, shall become a part of the Secured Obligations, shall be secured by the Account Collateral, and shall be paid to Lender by Borrower immediately upon demand.

12. Miscellaneous. The rights, powers, and remedies of Lender under this Agreement shall be in addition to all rights, powers, and remedies of Lender at law or under the Security Agreement or any other agreement or instrument. Any forbearance or failure or delay by Lender in exercising any right, power, or remedy under this Agreement shall not be deemed to be a waiver of such right, power, or remedy, and any single or partial exercise of any right, power, or remedy under this Agreement shall not preclude the further exercise

of it. This Agreement and all representations and warranties, powers, and rights it contains are binding upon and shall inure to the benefit of the parties here and their respective successors and assigns.

13. Governing Law. This Agreement shall be governed by and construed in accordance with the laws of the State of _____.

14. Counterparts. This Agreement may be executed in one or more counterparts, each of which shall be deemed an original, but all of which together shall constitute one and the same instrument.

In witness, the parties have executed this Agreement as of the date first set forth above.

[Signatures]

# Appendix E

# Glossary of Terms[1]

## Introduction

As the text indicates, part of the beauty of Article 9 is the introduction of the unitary security device, in place of the wide range of independent security devices that existed in the past. Although Article 9 has now been in effect for well over fifty years, some lawyers and businesspeople continue to refer to the former security devices, at least by name. Therefore, it is helpful for students to have some understanding of the common terms. The following descriptions do not convey the intricate details of each different device, which varied in terms of the type of collateral that could be encumbered and the procedure that had to be followed to protect the lender's interest.

## Bailment Lease

Typically a device permitted in some jurisdictions that did not recognize conditional sales, the bailment lease permitted the lessor (owner, otherwise "seller") to retain title and retake property if the lessee (buyer) failed to make payments (called "rent.")

## Chattel Mortgage

One of the earliest of the independent security devices that preceded the UCC security interest, the chattel mortgage was a statutory device roughly analogous to a mortgage on real property. This device made possible a loan secured by personal property without the necessity of a change in the possession of the property, yet insulated the transaction from attack as a fraudulent conveyance. As with real property mortgages, the statutes generally imposed some type of recording requirement (indexed under the name of the debtor) so that third parties would have notice of the lien on the personal property.

## Conditional Sale

Conceptually the conditional sale was, in contrast to a "sale absolute," a sale on condition. In other words, the sale is made only on a condition that the buyer pays the price. If the condition fails, the seller has a right under the contract to get the goods back. (In a sale absolute the seller has no rights to the goods after the buyer takes possession; the seller's only recourse is to sue the buyer for the unpaid price.) This device was used only in financing sales transactions. It could not be used in any situation where a loan was to be secured by property owned by the borrower at the time the loan was made.

## Consignment

An owner of goods delivers them to a consignee for sale. If the consignee sells them, he must account to the owner-consignor for the proceeds of sale less his commission. If he does not sell the goods, he must return them to the owner. The consignee is never re-

---

1. These definitions are taken from the discussion in Grant Gilmore, SECURITY INTERESTS IN PERSONAL PROPERTY, Volume 1, Part 1 (1965).

sponsible for the price of the goods if they are not sold. Title to the goods remains in the consignor during the consignment and passes to the buyer upon sale—it never vests in the consignee. (A "true consignment" is not in fact a security device since its purpose is to sell goods rather than to secure repayment of an obligation.)

## Pledge

Historically, the simplest of the security devices, the pledge is a security arrangement under which the secured creditor takes possession of the collateral until the loan is paid in full.

## Factor's Lien

Grant Gilmore defined a twentieth-century "factor" as a person who lends money on the security of merchandise inventory or accounts receivable or both, but who is not in any way connected with their sale.[2] Factor's Lien Acts were widely enacted statutes that dealt with inventory and accounts receivable financing. Under such acts a financing factor could have a lien on merchandise not physically in his possession by posting a sign on the borrower's premises and filing a notice of lien in the appropriate place.

## Field Warehousing

In the standard field warehousing arrangement there are three parties: borrower lender and warehouseman. In such an arrangement, the property that is the lender's collateral is enclosed or sealed so that only the warehouseman has access. Signs are posted to notify creditors of the warehousing arrangement. The conditions on which goods are released from the warehouse are spelled out to permit payments to the lender as goods are released.

## Trust Receipt

Another statutory security device, the trust receipt was typically used to finance inventory. In a trust receipt transaction, title to the goods is held by the lender, but the borrower retains possession of and the right to sell the goods (and the sales proceeds are to be used to repay the loan).

---

2. *Id.* at 128.

# Appendix F

# Intercreditor and Subordination Agreement

This INTERCREDITOR AGREEMENT, dated as of _____, _____, is between _____ ("Creditor"), and _____ ("Lender").

## RECITALS

A. _____ ("Borrower") has or may hereafter become obligated with respect to certain credit accommodations from Lender (the "Lender Obligations"), which are or may be from time to time secured by certain assets and property of Borrower, including accounts, including health care receivables, chattel paper, inventory, general intangibles, equipment, deposit accounts, investment property, documents, instruments, including promissory notes, letter of credit rights, any commercial tort claim of Borrower which is now or hereafter identified by Borrower or Lender, and other property, whether now existing or hereafter acquired or created (the "Lender Collateral").

B. Borrower has or may hereafter become obligated with respect to certain credit accommodations from Creditor (the "Creditor Obligations"), which are or may be from time to time secured by certain assets and property of Borrower (the "Creditor Collateral").

C. The Lender Collateral and Creditor Collateral each include a security interest in inventory of Borrower and in the proceeds of any insurance in respect thereof (the "Excluded Collateral," and the Lender Collateral other than the Excluded Collateral, the "Lender First-Lien Collateral"), except that the Excluded Collateral shall in no case include any of Borrower's accounts, chattel paper, or (except to the extent of insurance proceeds constituting Excluded Collateral) general intangibles constituting accounts receivable or any books or records relating to the foregoing (including records maintained on any computer or other electronic media) or any proceeds of such accounts, chattel paper, or general intangibles.

D. In order to induce Lender to extend credit to Borrower and, at any time or from time to time, at Lender's option, to make such further loans, extensions of credit, or other accommodations to or for the account of Borrower, or to extend credit upon any instrument or writing in respect of which Borrower may be liable in any capacity, or to grant such renewals or extension of any such loan, extension of credit, or other accommodation as Lender may deem advisable, Creditor is willing to subordinate Creditor's security interests, if any, in the Lender First-Lien Collateral upon the terms and conditions herein provided.

NOW, THEREFORE, THE PARTIES AGREE AS FOLLOWS:

1. Creditor subordinates to Lender any security interest or lien that Creditor may have in any Lender First-Lien Collateral, and Lender subordinates to Creditor any security interest or lien that Lender may have in any Excluded Collateral. Notwithstanding the respective dates of attachment or perfection of the security interest of Creditor and the

security interest of Lender, (a) the security interest of Lender in the Lender First-Lien Collateral shall at all times be prior to the security interest of Creditor, and (b) the security interest of Creditor in the Excluded Collateral shall at all times be prior to the security interest of Lender.

2.    Notwithstanding anything to the contrary herein contained, (a) Creditor hereby consents to and authorizes the sale (with or without recourse) to Lender of, or the grant of a security interest to Lender in, Borrower's accounts, chattel paper, or general intangibles constituting accounts receivable to Lender and agrees that, in the case of any sale of any such accounts, chattel paper, or general intangibles (whether to Lender or by way of foreclosure), such sale shall be free of all liens, security interests or encumbrances held by Creditor, and (b) Lender hereby consents to and authorizes the sale (whether in the ordinary course of Borrower's business or otherwise, and including, without limitation, any disposition by way of foreclosure or in lieu of foreclosure), or the grant of a security interest in, the Excluded Collateral and agrees that any such sale shall be free of all liens, security interests or encumbrances held by Lender.

3.    Creditor agrees that it will not enforce or apply its security interests or in any manner interfere with Lender's security interests in the Lender First-Lien Collateral unless and until Lender has notified Creditor that Borrower has satisfied, in full, the Lender Obligations. Without limiting the generality of the foregoing, Creditor agrees that it will not seek to notify account debtors or other obligors of its subordinated security interest in the Lender First-Lien Collateral, nor will Creditor collect any amounts owed by such account debtors or other obligors constituting Lender First-Lien Collateral, unless and until Lender has notified Creditor that Borrower has satisfied, in full, the Lender Obligations. Lender agrees that it will not enforce or apply its security interests or in any manner interfere with Creditor's security interests in the Excluded Collateral, until 180 days after Lender has notified Creditor that an event of default has occurred with respect to the Lender Obligations, and then only if Creditor has not commenced enforcement of Creditor's own remedies against the Excluded Collateral.

4.    (a)    All Creditor Obligations are subordinated in right of payment to all Lender Obligations to the extent provided in this Section 4. Except for (i) regularly scheduled payments of principal and interest paid prior to Lender's delivery of notice to Creditor of the existence of an Event of Default in respect of the Lender Obligations (as defined in the governing documentation for the Lender Obligations); and (ii) for enforcement of Creditor's rights and remedies in respect of the Excluded Collateral, Creditor will not demand or receive from Borrower (and Borrower will not pay to Creditor) all or any part of the Creditor Obligations, by way of payment, prepayment, setoff, lawsuit or otherwise, nor will Creditor commence, or cause to commence, prosecute or participate in any administrative, legal or equitable action against Borrower, for so long as any portion of the Lender Obligations remain outstanding. In the event of Borrower's insolvency, re-organization, or any case or proceeding under any bankruptcy or insolvency law or laws relating to the relief of debtors, these provisions shall remain in full force and effect, and Lender's claims against Borrower and the estate of Borrower (other than the Excluded Collateral) shall be paid in full before any payment is made to Creditor. Creditor shall promptly deliver to Lender in the form received (except for endorsement or assignment by Creditor where required by Lender), for application to the Lender Obligations, any payment, distribution, security or proceeds received by Creditor with respect to the Creditor Obligations other than as permitted by this Section 4. No amendment of the documents evidencing or relating to the Creditor Obligations shall directly or indirectly modify the provisions of the Creditor Obligations in any manner which might impair the provisions of this Agreement. By way of example (but not limitation), such documents

shall not be amended to (1) change the manner or terms of payment of the Creditor Obligations in a manner intended to circumvent the restrictions of this Section 4. Neither Creditor nor Lender shall amend the documents evidencing or relating to the Creditor Obligations or the Lender Obligations, respectively, to (i) increase the rate of interest with respect thereto, or (2) accelerate the payment of the principal or interest or any other portion thereof.

(b)     Subject to the limitations of Section 4(a), at any time and from time to time, without notice to Creditor, Lender may take such actions with respect to the Lender Obligations as Lender, in its sole discretion, may deem appropriate, including, without limitation, terminating advances to Borrower, increasing the principal amount, extending the time of payment, renewing, compromising or otherwise amending the terms of any documents affecting the Lender Obligations and any Lender Collateral, and enforcing or failing to enforce any rights against Borrower or any other person. No such action or inaction shall impair or otherwise affect Lender's rights hereunder. Creditor waives, to the extent otherwise available to Creditor, any and all rights, benefits and defenses of a guarantor or surety under applicable law.

5.     This Agreement shall remain effective for so long as Borrower owes any amounts with respect to the Lender Obligations. If, at any time after payment in full of the Lender Obligations, any payments of the Lender Obligations must be disgorged by Lender for any reason (including, without limitation, the bankruptcy of Borrower), this Agreement and the relative rights and priorities set forth herein shall be reinstated as to all such disgorged payments as though such payments had not been made.

6.     Each party to this Agreement hereby waives, subject to Section 4, any right to require the other party to marshal any security or collateral or otherwise to compel the other party to seek recourse against or satisfaction of the indebtedness owed to it from one source before seeking recourse or satisfaction from another source.

7.     Subject to the shared priority and respective rights of the parties contained in the Agreement, each party to this Agreement shall be entitled to be designated mortgagee/secured party and to obtain loss payee endorsements (with Creditor named as the first loss payee with respect to the Excluded Collateral and Lender so named with respect to the Lender First-Lien Collateral) and additional insured status with respect to any and all policies of insurance now or hereafter obtained by the Borrower during against casualty or other loss to any property of the Borrower in which either party hereto may have a security interest or mortgage lien, and, in connection therewith, may file claims, settle disputes, make adjustments and take any and all other action otherwise then permitted to each party hereto with regard thereto which it may deem advisable with respect to any assets of the Borrower. The provisions of this Agreement shall govern the respective rights of the parties hereto to insurance proceeds despite any inconsistent provisions or any inconsistent designation of rights or priorities among secured creditors in any insurance policy.

8.     This Agreement is entered into solely for the purposes set forth in the Recitals above, and, except as is expressly provided otherwise herein, neither party to this Agreement assumes any responsibility to the other party to advise such other party of information known to such party regarding the financial condition of the Borrower or regarding any collateral of the Borrower or of any other circumstances bearing upon the risk of nonpayment of the obligations of the Borrower to the parties hereto. Each party shall be responsible for managing its relation with the Borrower and neither party shall be deemed the agent of the other party for any purpose. Each of the parties hereto may alter, amend,

supplement, release, discharge or otherwise modify any terms of the documents evidencing and embodying their respective loans without notice to or consent of the other.

9.    Any notice required or permitted in connection with this Agreement shall be in writing and shall be made by hand delivery, by overnight delivery service, or by certified mail, return receipt requested, postage prepaid, addressed to the applicable party at the appropriate address set forth below its signature hereon or to such other address as may be hereafter specified by written notice by such party to the other party and shall be considered given as of the date when actually received.

10.    This Agreement shall bind, and inure to the benefit of, the successors and assignees of the parties. This Agreement is solely for the benefit of Creditor and Lender and not for the benefit of Borrower or any other party. Creditor further agrees that if Borrower is in the process of refinancing a portion of the Lender Obligations with a new lender, and if Lender makes a request of Creditor, Creditor shall enter into a new intercreditor agreement with the new lender on substantially the terms and conditions of this Agreement.

11.    This Agreement may be executed in two or more counterparts, each of which shall be deemed an original and all of which together shall constitute one instrument.

12.    This Agreement shall be governed by and construed in accordance with the laws of the State of California, without giving effect to conflicts of law principles.

13.    This Agreement represents the entire agreement between the parties with respect to the subject matter hereof, and supersedes all prior negotiations, agreements and commitments. Neither Creditor nor Lender is relying on any representations by the other party, or by Borrower, in entering into this Agreement, and each of Creditor and Lender has kept and will continue to keep itself fully apprised of the financial and other condition of Borrower. This Agreement may be amended only by written instrument signed by Creditor and Lender.

14.    In the event of any legal action to enforce the rights of a party under this Agreement, the party prevailing in such action shall be entitled, in addition to such other relief as may be granted, all reasonable costs and expenses, including reasonable attorneys' fees, incurred in such action.

IN WITNESS WHEREOF, the undersigned have executed this Agreement as of the date first above written.


**CREDITOR:**

[CREDITOR NAME]

By: _____

Name: _____

Title: _____


Address for Notices:

_____

_____

_____

**LENDER:**

[LENDER NAME]

By: _____

Name: _____

Title: _____


Address for Notices:

_____

_____

_____


The undersigned approves the terms of this Agreement.

**BORROWER:**

By: _____

Name: _____

Title: _____

# Appendix G

# LLC Security Agreement

LLC SECURITY AGREEMENT (this "*Agreement*") dated as of _____, is entered into by PENNY RIOS ("*Debtor*"), an individual resident in the State of California, and MERTZ'S MEZZANINE LOANS, LLC, a Delaware limited liability company ("*Secured Party*").

## RECITALS

A.     Debtor has requested that Secured Party make a loan to Debtor in the principal amount of $_____ (the "*Loan*"), as evidenced by Debtor's promissory note of even date herewith, executed by Debtor and payable to the order of Secured Party (the "*Note*").

B.     Secured Party is willing to make the Loan on the condition, among other things, the Debtor grant to Secured Party a security interest in Debtor's interest in Century Ventures, LLC, a Delaware limited liability company (the "**Company**").

## AGREEMENT

NOW, THEREFORE, Debtor and Secured Party agree as follows:

12.    Definitions. Terms defined in the Note are used herein as defined therein. In addition, as used herein:

"*Collateral*" has the meaning given to it in Section 2.1.

"*Obligations*" has the meaning given to it in Section 2.2.

"*Company*" means Century Ventures, LLC, a Delaware limited liability company.

"*Event of Default*" means any "Event of Default" under, and as defined in, the Note.

"*Operating Agreement*" means the Operating Agreement of the Company, as in effect from time to time.

"*Relevant Documents*" means the Operating Agreement and all other organizational documents of the Company, in each case, as amended, restated, replaced, supplemented or otherwise modified from time to time.

"*Uniform Commercial Code*" shall mean the Uniform Commercial Code as in effect from time to time in the state of California.

13.    Pledge of Collateral; Obligations.

(a)    The Pledge. As continuing collateral security for the prompt payment and performance, in full when due (whether at stated maturity, by acceleration or otherwise) of the Obligations, Debtor grants to Secured Party a security interest in the following property, whether now owned by Debtor or hereafter acquired and whether now existing or hereafter coming into existence (all being collectively referred to herein as "*Collateral*"):

      i.     All of Debtor's limited liability company interest in the Company.

      ii.    All proceeds of Debtor's limited liability company interest in the Company.

     **(b)**   <u>Obligations</u>. This Agreement secures the payment (of the principal of, interest on, and all other amounts and payments due pursuant to or evidenced by) and performance of all other obligations of Debtor under or in respect of the following (collectively, the "Obligations"):

      i.     the Note;

      ii.    any and all future loans or amounts advanced by Secured Party to Debtor when evidenced by a written instrument or document that specifically provides for the obligations evidenced thereby to be secured by this Agreement;

      iii.   this Agreement;

      iv.   any rearrangement, amendment, modification, extension, renewal, restatement, substitution or replacement of the Note or this Agreement or any other instrument or document evidencing an obligation secured by this Agreement; and

      v.    the expenses and costs incurred or paid by Secured Party in the maintenance and preservation of the Collateral and the enforcement of the rights of Secured Party and the duties and obligations of Debtor as stated in the Note, this Agreement or any other instrument or document evidencing an obligation secured hereby, including, but not limited to, funds paid or advanced to protect the security or priority of this Agreement, attorney's fees, court costs, foreclosure expenses, and witness fees.

     **(c)**   <u>Delivery of the Collateral</u>. All certificates or instruments, if any, representing or evidencing the Collateral shall be delivered to and held by or on behalf of Secured Party pursuant hereto and shall be in suitable form for transfer by delivery, or shall be accompanied by duly executed instruments of transfer endorsed by Debtor in blank, or assignments in blank, all in form and substance satisfactory to Secured Party. Upon the occurrence and during the continuance of an Event of Default, Secured Party shall have the right, at any time, in its discretion, to transfer to or to register in the name of Secured Party or its nominee any or all of the Collateral.

     **14.**   <u>Representations and Warranties and Related Covenants</u>. Debtor represents to Secured Party as of the date hereof, and warrants and covenants for the benefit of Secured Party that until the Obligations have been paid in full:

     **(a)**   Debtor is and will be the sole owner of the Collateral. Debtor's limited liability company interest represents 33.33% of the outstanding equity interests in the Company.

     **(b)**   This Agreement is effective to create a security interest in the Collateral in favor of Secured Party. The Collateral is and will be free and clear of any adverse claims and any liens, encumbrances or security interests other than the security interest of Secured Party therein under this Agreement.

     **(c)**   Each of the Note and this Agreement has been duly executed and delivered by Debtor and constitutes the legal, valid and binding obligation of Debtor, enforceable against Debtor in accordance with its terms.

     **(d)**   Debtor is, and has been for at least the five-year period preceding the date hereof, a resident of the State of California. Debtor has a mailing address at the address set forth in <u>Section 5.3</u> below as Debtor's address for notice. Debtor's correct name is, and for at least the five-year period preceding the date hereof, has been, Penelope Rios. Debtor will immediately notify Secured Party in writing of any change in Debtor's address or change in Debtor's name, and Debtor will, upon request of Secured Party, execute or authenticate any additional financing statements or other certificates or records necessary to reflect the change in Debtor's address or name.

(e)     Debtor's limited liability company interest in the Company is neither (i) a security governed by Article 8 of the Uniform Commercial Code, nor (ii) evidenced by any certificate, and Debtor shall not cause or permit it to become a security or to be evidenced by any certificate;

(f)     Debtor is the record and beneficial owner of the Collateral;

(g)     Debtor has delivered to Secured Party a true and correct copy of the Operating Agreement, as in full force and effect on the date hereof. Except with Secured Party's prior written consent, Debtor shall not agree to, or permit, any amendment of any provision of, or modify or waive any right or rights of Debtor, or allow the dilution of Debtor's interest under, the Operating Agreement (including, without limitation, any right to receive distributions or other payments constituting, or in respect of, the Collateral).

15.     Further Assurances; Remedies. In furtherance of the grant of the pledge and security interest pursuant to Section 2 hereof, Debtor hereby agrees with Secured Party as follows:

(a)     Delivery and Other Perfection.

i.     Debtor hereby represents and warrants that as of the date hereof the Collateral not represented by any instruments or certificates. If at any time after the date hereof any Collateral shall be evidenced by an instrument or a certificate, Debtor shall, or shall cause the Company to, promptly deliver any such instrument or certificate, duly endorsed or subscribed by Debtor or accompanied by appropriate instruments of transfer or assignment duly executed in blank by Debtor, to Secured Party as additional Collateral. Any such instruments or certificates received by Debtor shall be held by Debtor in trust, as agent for Secured Party.

ii.     Debtor shall give, execute, deliver, file and/or record any financing statement, notice, instrument, document, agreement or other papers that may be necessary (in the reasonable judgment of Secured Party) to create, preserve or perfect the security interest granted pursuant hereto or, after the occurrence and during the continuance of an Event of Default, to enable Secured Party to exercise and enforce its rights hereunder with respect to such pledge and security interest.

iii.     Debtor shall permit representatives of Secured Party, upon reasonable notice, at any time during normal business hours to inspect and make abstracts from its books and records pertaining to the Collateral, and permit representatives of Secured Party to be present at Debtor's place of business to receive copies of all communications and remittances relating to the Collateral, and forward copies of any notices or communications received by Debtor with respect to the Collateral, all in such manner as Secured Party may reasonably require.

iv.     Debtor shall not permit the Company, without Secured Party's prior written consent, (i) to create, assume, incur, guarantee, permit to exist or otherwise be or become or be liable with respect to any indebtedness except for indebtedness in existence on the date hereof; (ii) to sell or otherwise transfer all or any material portion of the Company's interest in its assets; or (iii) to issue any additional interests or otherwise dilute Debtor's interest in the Company.

(b)     Preservation of Rights. Except in accordance with applicable law, Secured Party shall not be required to take steps necessary to preserve any rights against prior parties to any of the Collateral.

(c)     Pledged Collateral; Distributions.

i.      So long as no Event of Default shall have occurred and be continuing, Debtor shall have the right to exercise all of Debtor's rights in respect of the Collateral under the Relevant Documents for all purposes not inconsistent with the terms of this Agreement or the Note or any other instrument or agreement referred to herein or therein, including the right to exercise any and all voting rights, the right to receive distributions on the Collateral, and other rights relating to the Collateral, *except that* that Debtor shall cause any and all distributions in respect of the Collateral, to the extent required to pay the Obligations in full, to be paid directly to Secured Party to be so applied, and, in the event that Debtor receives any such distribution, Debtor shall segregate such distribution from other funds of Debtor and shall forthwith turn it over to Secured Party in the same form as so received (with any necessary endorsement) for application to the Obligations. Secured Party shall execute and deliver to Debtor, or cause to be executed and delivered to Debtor, all such powers of attorney, distribution and other orders, and all such instruments, without recourse, as Debtor may reasonably request for the purpose of enabling Debtor to exercise the rights and powers which Debtor is entitled to exercise pursuant to this Section 4.3(a).

ii.     Without limiting in any manner Debtor's obligations, or Secured Party's rights, in respect of distributions pursuant to Section 4.3(a): if any Event of Default shall have occurred, then so long as such Event of Default shall continue, and whether or not Secured Party exercises any available right to declare any of the Obligations due and payable or seeks or pursues any other relief or remedy available to it under applicable law or under this Agreement or any other Loan Document, (i) all distributions in respect of the Collateral shall be paid directly to Secured Party for application to the Obligations pursuant to the terms hereof and the Note, (ii) if Secured Party shall so request in writing, Debtor agrees to execute and deliver to Secured Party appropriate distribution and other orders and documents to that end and (iii) Debtor hereby irrevocably authorizes and directs the Company, after an Event of Default and for so long as such Event of Default is continuing, to pay all such distributions in respect of the Collateral directly to Secured Party for application to the Obligations in the order, priority and manner set forth herein and in the Note. The foregoing authorization and instructions are irrevocable, may be relied upon by the Company and may not be modified in any manner other than by Secured Party sending to the Company a notice terminating such authorization and direction.

iii.    Anything to the contrary notwithstanding, (i) Debtor shall remain liable under the Relevant Documents to perform all of its duties and obligations thereunder to the same extent as if this Agreement had not been executed, (ii) the exercise by Secured Party of any of its rights hereunder shall not release Debtor from any of its duties or obligations under the Relevant Documents and (iii) Secured Party shall have no obligation or liability under the Relevant Documents by reason of this Agreement, nor shall Secured Party be obligated to perform any of the obligations or duties of Debtor thereunder or to take any action to collect or enforce any claim for payment assigned hereunder, except as provided by applicable law.

(d)     Events of Default; Remedies, etc. During the period during which an Event of Default shall have occurred and be continuing, without limitation of any other rights and remedies that Secured Party may have under the Note, under any other agreement, or under applicable law:

i.      Secured Party shall have all of the rights and remedies with respect to the Collateral of a secured party under the Uniform Commercial Code (whether or not said Code is in effect in the jurisdiction where the rights and remedies are asserted) and such additional rights and remedies to which a secured party is entitled under the laws in effect in any jurisdiction where any rights and remedies hereunder may be asserted;

ii.      Secured Party in its discretion may, in its name or in the name of Debtor or otherwise, demand, sue for, collect or receive any money or property at any time payable or receivable on account of or in exchange for any of the Collateral, but shall be under no obligation to do so;

iii.      Secured Party may, upon 10 days' prior written notice to Debtor of the time and place, with respect to the Collateral or any part thereof which shall then be or shall thereafter come into the possession, custody or control of Secured Party or any of its agents, sell, assign or otherwise dispose of all or any part of such Collateral, at such place or places as Secured Party deems best, and for cash or on credit or for future delivery (without thereby assuming any credit risk), at public or private sale, without demand of performance or notice of intention to effect any such disposition or of time or place thereof (except such notice as is required above or by applicable statute and cannot be waived) and Secured Party or anyone else may be the purchaser, assignee or recipient of any or all of the Collateral so disposed of at any public sale (or, to the extent permitted by law, at any private sale), and thereafter hold the same absolutely, free from any claim or right of whatsoever kind, including any right or equity of redemption (statutory or otherwise), of Debtor, any such demand, notice or right and equity being hereby expressly waived and released. Unless prohibited by applicable law, Secured Party may, without notice or publication, adjourn any public or private sale or cause the same to be adjourned from time to time by announcement at the time and place fixed for the sale, and such sale may be made at any time or place to which the same may be so adjourned; and

iv.      all payments received by Debtor under or in connection with the Relevant Documents or otherwise in respect of the Collateral during the continuance of such Event of Default shall be received in trust for the benefit of Secured Party, shall be segregated from other funds of Debtor and shall be forthwith paid over to Secured Party in the same form as so received (with any necessary endorsement).

The proceeds of each collection, sale or other disposition under this Section 4.4 shall be applied by Secured Party to the Obligations pursuant to Section 4.6 hereof.

Debtor recognizes that, by reason of certain prohibitions contained in the Securities Act of 1933, as amended, and applicable state securities laws, Secured Party may be compelled, with respect to any sale of all or any part of the Collateral, to limit purchasers to those who will agree, among other things, to acquire the Collateral for their own account, for investment and not with a view to the distribution or resale thereof. Debtor acknowledges that any such private sales may be at prices and on terms less favorable to Secured Party than those obtainable through a public sale without such restrictions, and that Secured Party shall have no obligation to engage in public sales and no obligation to delay the sale of any Collateral for the period of time necessary to permit the issuer thereof to register it for public sale.

(e)      Private Sale. Secured Party shall not incur any liability as a result of the sale of the Collateral, or any part thereof, at any private sale pursuant to Section 4.4 hereof conducted in a commercially reasonable manner. Debtor hereby waives any claims, excepting only those arising under Section 9-615(f) of the Uniform Commercial Code, against Secured Party arising by reason of the fact that the price at which the Collateral may have been sold at such a private sale was less than the price which might have been obtained at a public sale or was less than the aggregate amount of the Obligations, even if Secured Party accepts the first offer received and does not offer the Collateral to more than one offeree.

(f)  Application of Proceeds. Except as otherwise herein expressly provided, the proceeds of any collection, sale or other realization of all or any part of the Collateral pursuant hereto, and any other cash at the time held by Secured Party under this Section 4, shall be applied by Secured Party:

*First*, to the payment of the costs and expenses of such collection, sale or other realization, including reasonable out-of-pocket costs and expenses of Secured Party and the fees and expenses of their respective agents and counsel, and all expenses, and advances made or incurred by Secured Party in connection therewith, pro rata between Waugh and Meyer in accordance with the respective amounts owed to them, or as otherwise agreed between them;

*Next*, to the payment in full of the Obligations, in such order as Secured Party may elect, in its sole discretion, but, in respect of principal of and interest on the Note, pro rata between Waugh and Meyer in accordance with the respective amounts owed to them, or as otherwise agreed between them; and

*Finally*, to the payment to Debtor, or its successors or assigns or as a court of competent jurisdiction may direct, of any surplus then remaining.

Debtor shall be liable for any deficiency in respect of the Obligations.

(g)  Attorney-in-Fact. Without limiting any rights or powers granted by this Agreement to Secured Party while no Event of Default has occurred and is continuing, Secured Party is hereby appointed the attorney-in-fact of Debtor for the purpose, upon the occurrence and during the continuance of any Event of Default, of carrying out the provisions of this Section 4 and taking any action and executing any instruments which Secured Party may deem necessary or advisable to accomplish the purposes hereof, which appointment as attorney-in-fact is irrevocable and coupled with an interest. Without limiting the generality of the foregoing, so long as Secured Party shall be entitled under this Section 4 to make collections in respect of the Collateral, Secured Party shall have the right and power to receive, endorse and collect all checks made payable to the order of Debtor representing any payment or other distribution in respect of the Collateral or any part thereof and to give full discharge for the same.

(h)  Termination. When all Obligations shall have been paid in full, Secured Party shall forthwith cause to be assigned, transferred and delivered, against receipt but without any recourse, warranty or representation whatsoever (except that Secured Party has not sold, created or suffered to exist thereon any lien, security interest or encumbrance in favor of any third party) any remaining Collateral and money received in respect thereof, to or on the order of Debtor.

(i)  Further Assurances. Debtor agrees that, from time to time upon the written request of Secured Party, Debtor will execute and deliver such further documents and do such other acts and things as Secured Party may reasonably request in order fully to effect the purposes of this Agreement.

16.  Miscellaneous.

(a)  No Waiver. No failure on the part of Secured Party or any of its agents to exercise, and no course of dealing with respect to, and no delay in exercising, any right, power or remedy hereunder shall operate as a waiver thereof; nor shall any single or partial exercise by Secured Party or any of its agents of any right, power or remedy hereunder preclude any other or further exercise thereof or the exercise of any other right, power or remedy. The remedies provided herein are cumulative and are not exclusive of any remedies provided by law.

(b)    Governing Law. THIS AGREEMENT AND THE OBLIGATIONS ARISING HEREUNDER SHALL BE GOVERNED BY, AND CONSTRUED IN ACCORDANCE WITH, THE LAWS OF THE STATE OF CALIFORNIA APPLICABLE TO CONTRACTS MADE AND PERFORMED IN SUCH STATE AND ANY APPLICABLE LAW OF THE UNITED STATES OF AMERICA.

(c)    Notices. All notices and other communications required or permitted to be given hereunder or otherwise relating to the subject matter of this Agreement or the Note shall be in writing and shall be sent by: (a) certified or registered mail, postage prepaid, return receipt requested, (b) personal delivery, or (c) a recognized overnight carrier that provides proof of delivery, and shall be addressed as follows:

If to Debtor:

Penny Rios
123 Main Street
Coaling, CA

If to Secured Party:

Mertz's Mezzanine Loans, LLC
456 Broadway
Coaling, CA

Notices shall be deemed effective upon receipt or rejection only.

(d)    Waivers, etc. The terms of this Agreement may be waived, altered or amended only by an instrument in writing duly executed by Debtor and Secured Party. Any such amendment or waiver shall be binding upon Secured Party and Debtor.

(e)    Successors and Assigns. This Agreement shall be binding upon the successors and assigns of Debtor and inure to the benefit of the successors and assigns of Secured Party (provided, however, that Debtor shall not assign or transfer its rights hereunder without the prior written consent of Secured Party, and any assignment or transfer without such consent shall be void and of no effect.).

(f)    Indemnification. Debtor hereby agrees to indemnify Secured Party and its directors, officers, employees and agents from, and hold each of them harmless against, any and all losses, liabilities, claims, damages or expenses incurred by any of them arising out of or by reason of any claim of any person (1) relating to or arising out of the acts or omissions of Debtor under this Agreement or the Relevant Documents (but excluding any such losses, liabilities, claims, damages or expenses incurred by reason of the gross negligence or willful misconduct of the person to be indemnified), or (2) resulting from the ownership of or lien on any Collateral, including, without limitation, the reasonable fees and disbursements of counsel incurred in connection with any such investigation or litigation or other proceedings (but excluding any such losses, liabilities, claims, damages or expenses incurred by reason of the gross negligence or willful misconduct of the person to be indemnified).

(g)    Severability. If any provision hereof is invalid and unenforceable in any jurisdiction, then, to the fullest extent permitted by law, (i) the other provisions hereof shall remain in full force and effect in such jurisdiction and shall be liberally construed in favor of Secured Party in order to carry out the intentions of the parties hereto as nearly as may be possible and (ii) the invalidity or unenforceability of any provision hereof in any jurisdiction shall not affect the validity or enforceability of such provision in any other jurisdiction.

[SIGNATURE PAGES ATTACHED]

IN WITNESS WHEREOF, Debtor and Secured Party have caused this Agreement to be duly executed as of the day and year first above written.

"DEBTOR"

_____

PENNY RIOS

"SECURED PARTY"

MERTZ'S MEZZANINE LOANS, LLC

By: _____

Name:

Title:

# Appendix H

# Retail Installment Contract and Disclosure Statement

See form on following page.

_____

Seller

## Retail Installment Contract and Disclosure Statement
## (Simple Interest)

_____                    _____

(BUYER)                                                              (DATE)

_____

(ADDRESS)

### DISCLOSURES REQUIRED BY LAW

| ANNUAL PERCENTAGE RATE | FINANCE CHARGE | AMOUNT FINANCED | TOTAL OF PAYMENTS | TOTAL SALES PRICE |
|---|---|---|---|---|
| The cost of your credit as a yearly rate. | The dollar amount the credit will cost you. | The amount of credit provided to you or on your behalf. | The amount you will have paid after you have made all payments as scheduled. | The total cost of your purchase on credit, including your downpayment of $ _____. |
| % | $ | $ | $ | $ |

Your payment schedule will be:

| Number of Payments | Amount of Payments | When Payments are Due |
|---|---|---|
|  |  |  |
|  |  |  |

Security:  You are giving a security interest in:
     The goods or property being purchased: _____
See your contract terms for any additional information about nonpayment, default, and required repayment in full before the scheduled date and prepayment refunds.

### ITEMIZATION OF AMOUNT FINANCED

| | | | |
|---|---|---|---|
| Cash Price (Including Sales Tax) | $ _____ | Unpaid Balance of Cash Price | $ _____ |
| Down Payment | | *Amounts Paid to Others on Your Behalf | |
|   Cash | $ _____ |   Filing Fees or Title Fees | $ _____ |
|   Trade in (Net of any Loan Balance) | $ _____ |   Credit Life and or Disability Insurance | $ _____ |
| Trade In Description: Year _____ Make _____ | | Vendors Single Interest Insurance | $ _____ |
| Serial Number _____ | | Other _____ | $ _____ |
| Total Down Payment | $ _____ | Amount Financed | $ _____ |
| | | *Dealer or Lender may be retaining a portion of these fees | |

### SIMPLE INTEREST CONTRACT TERMS

1.   Seller agrees to sell and Buyer agrees to buy the following described property in which Seller retains a security interest to secure payment of all obligations under this contract: _____

2.   Buyer agrees to pay the amount financed plus interest at the rate of _____ % according to the payment schedule set forth above.

3.   There is no penalty for prepayment in full, but Seller may retain a minimum charge of $5.00 if the Amount Financed is $75.00 or less and $7.50 if the Amount Financed exceeds $75.00.  If the amount financed is $250.00 or more, Buyer agrees to pay a minimum charge of $25.00.

4.   Buyer agrees to insure the vehicle.  Insurance may be obtained from a person of Buyer's choice.

5.   The following events shall constitute a default: a) If the Buyer fails to make a payment as required by this contract; or b) If the prospect of payment, performance, or realization of collateral is significantly impaired.  The following without limitation shall constitute a significant impairment of the prospect of payment, performance or realization of collateral:

    A.    Death, insolvency, assignment for the benefit of creditors, or the commencement of any proceeding under any bankruptcy or insolvency laws by or against debtors;

    B.    Loss, theft, substantial damage to or destruction of the collateral not covered by insurance;

    C.    Sale or prior encumbrance of the collateral;

    D.    Failure  by the borrower to renew insurance on the collateral; or termination of insurance on the collateral when substitute  insurance is not obtained before the insurance coverage terminates; or

    E.    Discovery by the seller of a misstatement of a material fact in any document signed by the buyer which forms part of the basis for extending   credit.

6.   In the event of default, Seller may demand the remaining payments or repossess the collateral.  In the event of default due to nonpayment, Buyer is entitled to receive one notice of right to cure default in any 12-month period, providing 14 days to pay all amounts then due.

**NOTICE**

_____
Signature of Seller

_____
Signature of Buyer

_____
Signature of Co-Buyer

**NOTICE TO BUYER:**
**1. DO NOT  SIGN THIS  AGREEMENT BEFORE YOU  READ IT.**
**2. YOU  ARE  ENTITLED TO A  COPY OF  THIS AGREEMENT.**
**BUYER ACKNOWLEDGES THAT  HE  HAS  READ  AND RECEIVED  A  TRUE COPY OF  THIS  CONTRACT IN  ITS COMPLETED FORM.**

**NOTICE TO CO-SIGNERS**

BY SIGNING THIS CONTRACT BETWEEN _____ AND _____ (BUYERS), DATED _____, _____, YOU OBLIGATE YOURSELF TO PAY THE TOTAL OF PAYMENTS OF $_____, PLUS COSTS OF REPOSSESSION THAT MAY BE ASSESSED. EVEN THOUGH YOU MAY RECEIVE NO PERSONAL BENEFIT FROM THIS TRANSACTION, AND YOU CAN BE SUED TO ENFORCE THAT OBLIGATION. YOU HAVE A RIGHT TO RECEIVE A COPY OF THIS AGREEMENT.

# Appendix I

# An Abbreviated Road Map to Article Nine

| | Primary | Secondary |
|---|---|---|
| SCOPE | 9-109<br>1-201(a)35 Security<br>Interest | 1-203 Lease v. security interest<br>1-201(a)(5) Agricultural Lien<br>1-201(a)(11) Chattel paper<br>1-201(a)(20) Consignment<br>1-201(a)(61) Payment intangibles<br>1-201(a)(65) Promissory note |
| DEFINITIONS | 9-102 | 1-201<br>1-202 Notice<br>1-205 Reasonable time<br>9-103 Purchase-money security<br>interest |
| CREATION OF<br>SECURITY<br>INTEREST;<br>ATTACHMENT | 9-108 Description<br>9-201<br>9-203 | 1-204 Value<br>9-102(a)(7) Authenticate<br>9-102(a)(12) Collateral<br>9-102(a)(28) Debtor<br>9-102 (a)(56) New debtor<br>9-102(a)(59) Obligor<br>9-102(a)(60) Original debtor<br>9-102(a)(64) Proceeds<br>9-102(a)(72) Secondary Obligor<br>9-102(a)(73) Secured Party<br>9-102(74) Security agreement<br>9-102(a)(78) Supporting<br>Obligation<br>9-204 After acquired property |
| LAW GOVERNING<br>PERFECTION<br>AND PRIORITY | 9-301 | 9-302<br>9-303<br>9-304<br>9-305<br>9-306 |

|  | Primary | Secondary |
|---|---|---|
| **PERFECTION OF SECURITY INTEREST** | 9-308<br>9-309<br>9-310<br>9-311<br>9-312<br>9-313<br>9-314<br>9-315<br>9-316 | 9-104 Control of deposit account<br>9-105 Control of elec. chattel paper<br>9-105 Control of investment property<br>9-107 Control of letter of credit rights<br>9-307 Location of debtor<br>9-501<br>9-502<br>9-503<br>9-504<br>9-505<br>9-506<br>9-507<br>9-508<br>9-509<br>9-510<br>9-511<br>9-512<br>9-513<br>9-514<br>9-515<br>9-517<br>9-518<br>9-519<br>9-520<br>9-521<br>9-522<br>9-523<br>9-524<br>9-525<br>9-526<br>9-527 |
| **PRIORITY DISPUTES** | 9-317<br>9-320 (Buyers)<br>9-322<br>9-323<br>9-324<br>9-325<br>9-326<br>9-333<br>9-334<br>9-337<br>9-338 | 9-318<br>9-319<br>9-321<br>9-327<br>9-328<br>9-329<br>9-330<br>9-331<br>9-332<br>9-335<br>9-336<br>9-339 |

| | Primary | Secondary |
|---|---|---|
| | | 9-340 |
| | | 9-341 |
| | | 9-342 |
| DEFAULT and REMEDIES | 9-601 | 1-103(b) |
| | 9-602 | 9-207 |
| | 9-603 | 9-208 |
| | 9-610 | 9-209 |
| | | 9-604 |
| | | 9-605 |
| | | 9-606 |
| | | 9-607 |
| | | 9-608 |
| | | 9-609 |
| | | 9-611 |
| | | 9-612 |
| | | 9-613 |
| | | 9-614 |
| | | 9-615 |
| | | 9-616 |
| | | 9-617 |
| | | 9-618 |
| | | 9-619 |
| | | 9-620 |
| | | 9-621 |
| | | 9-622 |
| | | 9-623 |
| | | 9-624 |
| | | 9-625 |
| | | 9-626 |
| | | 9-627 |
| | | 9-628 |

# Index

*Page numbers in italics indicate figures.*